A DISCONTENTED DIASPORA

A Discontented Diaspora

Japanese Brazilians and the Meanings of

Ethnic Militancy, 1960–1980

———••———

Jeffrey Lesser

Duke University Press • Durham and London 2007

© 2007 Duke University Press

All rights reserved

Printed in the United States

of America on acid-free paper ∞

Designed by Katy Clove

Typeset in Quadraat by Keystone Typesetting, Inc.

Library of Congress Cataloging-in-

Publication Data appear on the last

printed page of this book.

Dedicated to the memories of my father,

William Morris Lesser, זײל

my sogro,

Michael Shavitt, זײל

and my mentor,

Warren Dean

Contents

Illustrations and Tables

Preface and Acknowledgments

People respond to my research on Japanese-Brazilians in numerous ways. Academics from the United States are usually aware of concepts like *ethnicity* and *diaspora*, but they are often surprised that the United States is not the only multicultural country in the Americas and that São Paulo has the largest population of Japanese descent of any city in the world outside Japan. Brazilians, be they academics or not, are often puzzled that a researcher (me), born outside of Brazil (in the United States) and belonging to a non-Asian ethnic group (Jewish) would be interested in Brazilian Nikkei.

As I conducted the research for this book, many people I met asked, "I know someone who is Japanese-Brazilian; would you like to meet her (or him)?" This did not come as a surprise: São Paulo is filled with Japanese-Brazilians. Evangelicals or atheists, auto mechanics or economists, old or young, male or female, gay or straight, they all have what Daphne Patai termed "Minority Status and the Stigma of 'Surplus Visibility.'"[1] Although Japanese-Brazilians are a minority both numerically and conceptually, members of the majority often extrapolate individual experiences with Nikkei to the whole group. This book, then, is about how ethnicity operates in a city where Japanese-Brazilians are the most visible ethnic minority of all.

The inspiration for A *Discontented Diaspora* came from my undergraduate mentor, Anani Dzidzienyo, and my graduate mentor, the late Warren Dean. It was Professor Dzidizienyo who led me, and an entire generation of Brown University students, to study Brazil. His classes were always passionate and political, much like the subjects of this book. For Professor Dzidzienyo, actions spoke louder than words. Professor Dean was equally passionate and political, demanding that his students look for the agency among historical actors. Both Professor Dzidzienyo and Professor Dean insisted that I spend as much time as possible in Brazil, not only reading documents but listening to people. I hope that their influence is apparent in this book's theme and in its style.

•••

This book could not have been written without the generosity of many people. Patrick Allitt, Roney Cytrynowicz, Jerry Dávila, Lane Ryo Hirabayashi, Koichi Mori, and Thomas Skidmore read the entire manuscript (some of them more than once!), and their comments always pushed me to rethink my ideas. Stephanie Dennison, Sandra McGee Deutsch, James Green, Shuhei Hosokawa, Victoria Langland, Kenneth Serbin, Kerry Smith, Tzvi Tal, and Barbara Weinstein all read chapters, and all helped to improve the manuscript.

Many colleagues at Emory University commented on parts of the manuscript, including Matthew Bernstein, Tom Burns, Clifton Crais, Ivan Karp, Corinne Kratz, Cristine Levundiski, Bianca Premo, Mark Ravina, Philippe Rosenberg, and Susan Socolow. Rafael Ioris, Ryan Lynch, William Martins, and Phil Misevich provided research assistance. Ligia Kiss transcribed most of the interviews, and my conversations with her about these texts were invaluable. Fabrício Prado was a wonderful interlocutor and deserves all the credit for the maps, tables, and images in this book. Marcos Toffoli was involved with this project since its inception, and I could not have completed it without his help and friendship.

I particularly appreciated those colleagues who remembered this project as they conducted their own research and generously shared information with me: Célia Abe Oi, Matthew Bernstein, Jerry Dávila, Stephanie Dennison, Carlos Fico, Alessandra Gasparotto, James Green, Victoria Langland, Robert Lee, Joseph Love, Marcos Chor Maio, Chico Mattos, Jeffrey D. Needell, Anthony Pereira, Charles Perone, Evan Ross, Kenneth Serbin, Harold D. Sims, and Sílvio Tendler. I want to give special thanks to Marco Aurélio Vannucchi and Walter Swensson for their invaluable help.

Many of my ideas were refined or modified after seminar presentations. My deep appreciation goes to the faculty and students at the following institutions: the University of Florida, Emory University, Brown University, the Brazilian Center for Analysis and Planning (Centro Brasileiro de Análise e Planejamento, CEBRAP), the State University of Campinas (Universidade Estadual de Campinas, UNICAMP), the Casa de Oswaldo Cruz, the University of Vale do Rio dos Sinos (Universidade do Vale do Rio dos Sinos, UNI-

SINOS), the Federal University of Rio Grande do Sul (Universidade Federal do Rio Grande do Sul, UFRGS), the São Paulo State University (Universidade Estadual Paulista, UNESP)–Marília, the Institute of Philosophy and Social Science (Instituto de Filosofia e Ciências Sociais, IFCS)–Rio de Janeiro, Michigan State University, the Southern Japan Seminar at Florida International University, the German Association of Latin American Studies (ADLAF), and the Federal University of Santa Maria (Universidade Federal de Santa Maria, UFSM). Special thanks go to my students at Emory University, who have never failed to ask the hard questions that constantly inspire me.

A number of foundations were extraordinarily generous in funding my research and writing over the past few years: the American Council of Learned Societies, the Ford Foundation Program in Human Rights and Society, the J. William Fulbright Commission, the Fulbright-Hays Commission, the International Nikkei Research Project, and the Lucius N. Littauer Foundation. Emory University aided the project with both funds and time, and I want to particularly thank Walter Adamson, Cristine Levenduski, James Melton, Robert Paul, and Steven Sanderson for their support. Sussumu Miyao and Kazunori Wakisaka invited me to spend a year as a fellow of the Centro de Estudos Nipo-Brasileiros, and Marco Antônio Rocha and Eva Reichman from the Brazilian Fulbright Commission were always helpful and kind as I did my research.

The staffs of the many archives and libraries mentioned in the text and notes deserve special mention. They were unfailingly helpful and good natured, often digging out items that had been forgotten for years. Other friends and colleagues who supported my research include, in Brazil: Bela Bianco, Sidney Chalhoub, Elcio Cornelson, Alberto Dines, Liana Dines, Carlos Alberto Diniz, Martin Dreher, Alessandro Gamo, René E. Gertz, Mônica Grin, Flávio Heniz, André Joanilho, Margareth Rago, Benito Schmidt, Karl Erik Schoelhammer, José Carlos Sebe, Sílvio Tendler, Tullo Vigevani, Tizuka Yamasaki, and Paulo Yokota. The students in my class at the Universidade de São Paulo were always fun, stimulating, and helpful. In Japan my work was aided by Mark Caprio, Alexis Dudden, Shuhei Hosokawa, Fuminao Okumura and his family, and Shigeru Suzuki. In Israel, I wish to thank the faculty and students at the Institute for Latin American and Iberian Studies and the S. Daniel Abraham Center for International Studies, both at Tel Aviv University.

This work could not have been developed without friends and family. I particularly want to thank (of those not already mentioned) Eduardo Barcellos, Ronald and Heather Florence, Samy Katz, Roberto Lang, Alina Skonieczny and Nando Duarte, Harold Solomon, and Celso Zilbovicius.

For the past decade Valerie Millholland at Duke University Press has been a wonderful editor to me and to an entire generation of Latin Americanists. She, Assistant Editor Miriam Angress, Assistant Managing Editor Mark Mastromarino, and copyeditor Alex Martin have been critical in bringing this book to completion.

The final editing of this book was done as I taught a graduate seminar on Diasporas in Latin America with the support of a Fulbright Fellowship at the S. Daniel Abraham Center for International and Regional Studies at Tel Aviv University. The wonderful students in that seminar read the final draft of the manuscript, and their intellectual and cultural challenges to my work were a constant inspiration. My dear friends in Tel Aviv, Raanan, Esti, Omer, and Noa Rein, as well as Rosalie and David Sitman, helped make my family's stay a pleasure.

To the Lesser and Shavitt families goes my great love. Finally, and most important, I want to thank my wife, Eliana Shavitt Lesser, and our twin sons, Gabriel Zev and Aron Yosef, for their love, sense of adventure, and good nature.

Abbreviations

ACENB	Arquivo do Centro de Estudos Nipo-Brasileiros (Archive of the Center for Japanese-Brazilian Studies, São Paulo)
AEL	Arquivo Edgard Leuenroth, Instituto de Filosofia e Ciências Humanas da Unicamp
AERP	Assessoria Especial de Relações Públicas (Special Advisory Body for Public Relations)
AESP	Arquivo do Estado de São Paulo (São Paulo State Archive)
AHI-R	Arquivo Histórico Itamaraty, Brasília (Archive of the Brazilian Foreign Ministry)
ALN	Ação Libertadora Nacional (National Liberation Action)
AN	Arquivo Nacional, Rio de Janeiro (Brazilian National Archive)
APERJ	Arquivo Público do Estado do Rio de Janeiro (Public Archive of the State of Rio de Janeiro)
APP, SJ	Arquivos das Polícias Politícas, Setor Japonês (Archives of the Political Police, Japanese Section)
ARP	Assessoria de Relações Públicas (Advisory Body for Public Relations)
BJKS	Biblioteca Jenny Klabin Segall of the Museu Lasar Segall, São Paulo
BN	Biblioteca Nacional, Rio de Janeiro
CEAGESP	Companhia de Entrepostos e Armazéns Gerais de São Paulo (Warehouse and General Grocery Stores Company of São Paulo)
CEDEM	Centro de Documentação e Memória, São Paulo

CENB	Centro de Estudos Nipo-Brasileiros (Center for Japanese-Brazilian Studies)
CENIMAR	Centro de Informações da Marinha (Naval Intelligence Center)
CIE	Centro de Informações do Exército (Army Information Center)
COLINA	Comando de Libertação Nacional (National Liberation Command)
CPDOC	Centro de Pesquisa e Documentação de História Contemporânea do Brasil, Fundação Getúlio Vargas, Rio de Janeiro (Center for Research and Documentation on the Contemporary History of Brazil)
DEDOC	Departamento de Documentação da Editora Abril (Department of Documentation of the Abril publishing house)
DEOPS	Departamento Estadual de Ordem Política e Social de São Paulo (São Paulo State Department of Political and Social Order)
DOI-CODI	Destacamento de Operações de Informações—Centro de Operações de Defesa Interna (Department of Operations Information—Center of Internal Defense Operations)
ECA	Escola de Comunicações e Artes (School of Communications and Arts, University of São Paulo)
FAL	Fuzil Automático Leve (Light Automatic Rifle, a Belgian-made light machine gun)
FCB	Fundação Cinemateca Brasileira, São Paulo
GV	Getúlio Vargas
IBGE	Instituto Brasileiro de Geografia e Estatística (Brazilian Institute of Geography and Statistics)
IHGB	Instituto Histórico e Geográfico Brasileiro (Brazilian Historical and Geographic Institute)
INA	Indústria Nacional de Armas (a Brazilian-made .45 caliber machine gun)
INC	Instituto Nacional do Cinema (National Cinema Institute)
INCRA	Instituto Nacional de Colonização e Reforma Agrária (National Institute for Colonization and Agrarian Reform
ISI	import-substitution industrialization
ITA	Instituto Tecnológico de Aeronáutica (Aeronautics Technological Institute)
JAL	Japan Airlines
MASP	Museu de Arte de São Paulo (São Paulo Museum of Art)

MOLIPO	Movimento de Libertação Popular (Movement for Popular Liberation)
MR-8	Movimento Revolucionário 8 de Outubro (8 October Revolutionary Movement)
NARC	National Archives and Record Center, Washington, D.C.
OBAN	Operação Bandeirante
PC do B	Partido Comunista do Brasil (Communist Party of Brazil)
PCB	Partido Comunista Brasileiro (Brazilian Communist Party)
POLOP	Política Operária (Workers' Politics, Marxist Revolution Organization)
PRO	Public Records Office, London
PT	Partido dos Trabalhadores (Workers Party)
SABESP	Companhia de Saneamento Básico do Estado de São Paulo (Basic Sanitation Company of the State of São Paulo)
SNI	Serviço Nacional de Informações (National Intelligence Service)
UNESCO	United Nations Educational, Scientific and Cultural Organization
USP	Universidade de São Paulo (University of São Paulo)
VAR-Palmares	Vanguarda Armada Revolucionária–Palmares (Armed Revolutionary Vanguard–Palmares)
VPR	Vanguarda Popular Revolucionária (Popular Revolutionary Vanguard)

FIGURE I. Semp Toshiba advertisement,
"Our Japanese are more creative than everyone else's Japanese"

Prologue

THE LIMITS OF FLEXIBILITY

———•———

This catchphrase shown in figure 1, an advertisement created by the Talent agency in 1992 for the Brazilian consumer electronics firm Semp Toshiba, was "one of the most talked about . . . in Brazilian advertising."[1] It reflected a complex relationship between Brazil and Japan that was linked to the national identities of Brazil's one million citizens of Japanese descent. Connecting Brazil to Japan was not simply a marketing strategy: in popular language Nikkei (the term many Japanese-Brazilians use for themselves) are known simply as "japonês," because no linguistic distinction exists between Brazilians of Japanese descent and inhabitants of Japan itself.[2] Rachel de Queiroz's short story "Nacionalidade" illustrates the point. Its young protagonist is called "japonês" by his friends, even though he constantly reminds them that he and his parents were born in Brazil. One child insists that "I never saw a person who was Brazilian and had a Japanese face. I thought that all Brazilians were the same."[3] In the story race is a powerful metaphor for national identity and social hierarchy for Nikkei and for all Brazilians who are not "the same."

Relating ideas about Brazil and Japan to people of Japanese descent has a long history. It began in 1908, when the first of some 250,000 Japanese immigrants arrived. By 1960 Brazil had the largest Nikkei population in the world. São Paulo was the world's largest "Japanese" city outside of Japan.

Over the course of the twentieth century, ties between Brazil and Japan included interactions at all political, economic, cultural, and social levels.[4] Ideas about Japan flowed constantly into Brazil, via images, products, and people. Brazil and Japan were deeply enmeshed in popular culture: Brazilian parents told their children that if they dug deep enough they would arrive in Japan, while Japanese parents told their children that if they kept digging they would pop out in Brazil.[5] Some people considered this tale in more "adult" ways. A 1969 cartoon in a Brazilian men's magazine showed a man leering through the earth at a woman (i.e., from below) and explaining happily, "If the world was transparent I would live in Japan."[6]

This unusual bond between Brazil, Japan, and Japanese-Brazilians was apparent in the Semp Toshiba advertisement. "Our Japanese are more creative than everyone else's Japanese" was a nationalistic slogan, but it suggested ambivalence since national pride might be expected to result in a phrase like "Our Brazilians." Yet for many in São Paulo "our Japanese" was a code for a superior kind of Brazilian, and elites in the nation's most populous, economically powerful, and politically dominant city spread ideas about race and national identity to all Brazilians through the media, educational materials, and government policies.[7] "Our Japanese are more creative than everyone else's Japanese" implied that São Paulo was better than the rest of Brazil, but this hierarchy was not the advertising agency's invention. Throughout the twentieth century, São Paulo's elite often looked to Japanese international power as a goal and to Japanese industry and society as models.[8] Political and economic leaders saw the city's "Japanese" residents as important actors in making São Paulo better than the rest of Brazil. In the 1970s the São Paulo–based Bamerindus bank insisted in its advertising that "[we] need more Brazilians like the Japanese."[9]

This book triangulates one city (São Paulo), one country (Japan), and one ethnic group (Japanese-Brazilians) and asks what the relationship between the three in the sixties and seventies teaches us about ethnicity and national identity. My approach thus presumes that identity (ethnic, national, regional) is multifaceted and simultaneously global and local. My arguments are based on the word *and* rather than *or*, but this is not a linguistic trick. Rather it allows what might appear as contradictory phenomena to be analyzed as part of the regular lived experiences of identity.[10] While the subjects of this book made "either/or"-type choices in their *presentation* of identity, they were also comfortable holding multiple identities that might seem superficially contradictory.

●●●

On the first day of each semester my students and I examine the book titles on our syllabus. My goal is to convince them that the titles were carefully chosen and, when analyzed, will tell a great deal about an author's approach and content. The title of this book, A Discontented Diaspora: Japanese-Brazilians and the Meanings of Ethnic Militancy, 1960–1980, is not simply a collection of buzzwords. The questions I have asked myself are: "Do Japanese-Brazilians have a sense of diasporic identity?" "Were Brazilian Nikkei discontented?" "If so, what made this diaspora more or less discontented than any other?" and finally "Why did Japanese-Brazilians become a focus of cultural comment in São Paulo, and by extension Brazil?"

"A discontented diaspora" suggests that many people in Brazil erroneously assume that Nikkei feel "Japanese" and thus have an emotional attachment to Japan as an irrefutable homeland. While Japanese-Brazilians rarely see themselves as diasporic in this classic sense, the strong imprint from the majority has had an impact on their identity construction. The Nikkei subjects of this book always asserted their claims of Brazilianness and the presumed diaspora, which was so vibrantly imagined in São Paulo by non-Nikkei society and by their Japanese immigrant parents, created an oppressive ethnic community and an oppressive majority society. It produced discontent by making questions about the location of home, and thus Japanese-Brazilian loyalty, ever present.

"Ethnic militancy" also demands attention. U.S. readers may imagine the term to mean an openly asserted ethnicity where people join political movements or demand to be denominated in certain ways. In the United States "ethnic militancy" brings to mind African-American, Latino, Asian-American, and Jewish-American mobilization both separately and in coalition. In Brazil this kind of militancy occasionally took place in Afro-Brazilian political and cultural movements, but it was rarely seen among other ethnic groups.[11]

So why use "ethnic militancy" in the title? Because in the absence of formally constituted Nikkei rights movements, ethnic militancy took other forms. In the United States in the sixties and seventies this often included carving out "ethnic spaces" in the national arena, but in Brazil the majority presumed that minority groups wanted to live entirely in "ethnic spaces." For Japanese-Brazilians militancy meant escaping the ethnic boxes of majority society and of their immigrant parents' generation in an emphatic way. Whether joining banned political movements, training as guerrilla fighters, or acting in erotic films, the subjects of this book militantly asserted their

Brazilianness and in doing so, much to their surprise, reinforced their minority status.

In putting together ideas of diaspora, discontent, ethnicity, and militancy, I take seriously the "nation" and "national identity." While the latter is a heuristic device that the state attempts to create and control, it is constantly modified through lived experience. This line of analysis is useful because the heavy presence of Japanese and Japanese-Brazilian images and products in São Paulo is contextualized by a population of Japanese descent numbering 750,000. São Paulo is different from other cities in the Americas where images of Japan may be strong but where the Japanese descent population is small and the personification of images only occasional.

Nikkei are engaging subjects for several reasons. The long-standing and deep Brazilian adherence to the cultural ideology of modernization linked Japanese-Brazilians with Japan, one of the world's strongest and fastest-growing economic powers. In contrast, Portugal, Brazil's "mother country," figured unfavorably on the world stage through most of the twentieth century as a place of repression and economic and cultural stagnation. Since at least 1920, many in the Brazilian elite saw Japan, not Portugal, as a national model where traditional and economic modernization created international power. Nikkei appeared to many of their fellow Brazilian citizens as hard working, enterprising, and successful, just like Japan itself. When the magazine *Realidade* asked in 1966, "Is it worth being Brazilian?" one positive answer came from the naturalized farmer Hiroshi Saito (born in Nagasaki), who made Brazil better by planting "foreign" agricultural products.[12] The way for Brazil to move forward was to import a foreign population with foreign products, foreign technologies, and a foreign work ethic.

Analyzing Nikkei identity makes clear some of the ways Brazil differs from other American republics with significant populations of Japanese descent. In Peru, many citizens of Japanese descent are configured as Chinese, creating a complex Asianness that competes with the identity of the indigenous majority.[13] In the United States, most Japanese immigration was prohibited in 1907 (just when it began in Brazil), and the state unjustly interned U.S. citizens of Japanese descent during World War II.[14] By the sixties and seventies ambivalence in the United States was related to a fear of Japanese efficiency and economic growth, which reminded many Americans of the values of individuality that they imagined most Japanese lacked. Brazil also stands out from the United States because ethnic, physical, or gendered attributes are discussed explicitly, although not necessarily comfortably, in the former. People call each other *gordinho* (fatty), *gostoso* (hot), *careca* (baldy), or *japonês* (Japanese). The Nikkei experience in Brazil thus reveals what is often hidden in the United States, where, starting in the 1960s, cultural pressure often muted public expressions of stereotypes.

In Brazil upward social mobility often brought a change in ethnic and racial categorization, and Japanese-Brazilians generally have been economically successful. By the 1930s Nikkei were often moved from the "yellow" (the term used in the Brazilian census) into the "white" category: when a federal deputy said before the Brazilian House in 1935 that "Japanese colonists . . . are even whiter than Portuguese (ones)," there was little disagreement.[15] These racial shifts were not unique to Nikkei. The anthropologist Darcy Ribeiro tells of a cocktail party conversation between the famous painter Santa Rosa and a young Afro-Brazilian complaining about racial barriers to his ascent in the diplomatic service: "I understand your case perfectly, my dear boy," Santa Rosa supposedly replied. "I was black once, too."[16]

The belief that race could be subsumed by class, and was thus inconsequential, made Brazil a racial showcase by the second half of the twentieth century. A post–World War II UNESCO study suggested that Brazil was a location of positive race relations *and* an example of the permanence of racial inequality without legal segregation.[17] This research reformulated intolerance as primarily a class issue and suggested that socially ascendant individuals and groups could not be victims of racism. With class as the critical marker, many "ethnic" Brazilians became part of a vague whiteness. The association of affluence with entry into the common Brazilian "race" means that studying Japanese-Brazilian ethnicity, while commonsensical in the United States, seems odd in Brazil, where presumed prosperity often makes Nikkei seem at times nonethnic and at others non-Brazilian. The hundreds of thousands of Japanese-Brazilians in São Paulo in the 1960s and 1970s were simultaneously exotic and commonplace.

For this study, I have not chosen to analyze typical experiences. Rather, my focus is on two potent topics that emerged in the 1960s, sexuality in cinema and political militancy. I have chosen these two themes because they highlight how Japanese-Brazilians imagined themselves to be Brazilian. Nikkei were sure that their participation in these two realms would be recognized for its Brazilianness, and they were constantly faced with the reality that they were incorrect. Nikkei saw themselves as ethnic militants for their rejection of ideas about "Japanese" ethnicity, but what they learned was that marking themselves as Brazilians only brought their Japaneseness to the fore. Nikkei were trapped in a framework of normalcy and convention, and swerving from the well-traveled path did not lead the subjects of this study to unusual ethnic experiences. On the contrary, it underscored the cultural artifacts of Brazilianness so integral to ethnicity. While this book's Japanese-Brazilian subjects were not normative, their ethnic experiences were.

• • •

Brazil is a huge country and São Paulo is its largest city. Between 1960 and 1980 São Paulo grew from 4.7 million (out of a national population of 70 million) to 12.5 million people (out of a population of 119 million) (see table 1). During these decades, ideas about Japan and Japaneseness influenced most major events in the city and images of Japan and Japanese-Brazilians became common throughout Brazil. In Belém do Pará (at the mouth of the Amazon), Campo Grande (in far Western Brazil), and in cities large and small throughout the states of Paraná and São Paulo, one might see São Paulo–like Nikkei ethnicity in its broadest sense. Studying São Paulo, then, is similar to studying New York City: both ethnic centers have a widely diffused national resonance.

In São Paulo, where residents believed their regional identity should also be the national one, the relationship between Brazilianness and Japaneseness was the subject of constant discussion. For many of the city's residents, contacts with images of Japan and with real Nikkei were as daily a reality between 1960 and 1980 as they are today. Residents of the city bought their *pasteis* (fried filled dough) from "Japanese" street vendors, they brought their clothes to "Japanese" dry cleaners, and they purchased their fruits and vegetables from "Japanese" stands in open markets around the city. Students met Nikkei in their classes and city dwellers had Nikkei neighbors. In the popular imagination, the neighborhood of Liberdade, São Paulo's centrally located "Japantown," represented an ideal of social ascent to petit-bourgeois status.[18] In the sixties and seventies a trip to that "exotic" district gave Brazilians the impression that visiting a foreign country was only a bus or car ride away.

The belief that Japan was in São Paulo, however, was not limited to a single neighborhood. Japanese gardens were a rage among the elite in the fifties and sixties, as were Japanese industrial and managerial models in the sixties and seventies. In the sixties "Japanese" decoration and fake characters became familiar in the city, frequently without any Japanese or Nikkei context. The advertising campaign for Brazil's most famous "Japanese"

TABLE 1. Population, São Paulo (state and city) and Brazil, 1960 and 1980, with percentage increase

Year	State of São Paulo	City of São Paulo	Brazil
1960	12,809,231	4,791,245	70,070,457
1980	25,040,698 (+95%)	12,588,725 (+162%)	119,002,706 (+70%)

Source: Instituto Brasileiro de Geografia e Estatística, Evolução da População Residente: Brasil, Estado de São Paulo, Grande São Paulo, 1960, 1980.

film, Tizuka Yamasaki's Gaijin: Os Caminhos da Liberdade (Gaijin: The Roads to Freedom), framed Japan as critical to its central message of mestiçagem (racial and ethnic mixing) and Brazilian national identity (figure 2). The names of cast members prominently (and perhaps unintentionally) represented all of São Paulo's major immigrant groups (Portuguese, Italian, and Japanese), whose arrival in the late nineteenth and twentieth centuries created uncertainty about the authenticity of Brazilianness. In Gaijin, as in São Paulo, Nikkei became a focal point for national identity anxiety; as the newspaper advertisement suggested, Japanese immigration and its aftermath were unique spaces for characterizing broad Brazilian experiences of ethnicity.

The Gaijin advertisement invites readers to think of this book with another title (that is now the title of chap. 1), "The Pacific Rim in the Atlantic World." In the introduction to that book I might have argued that the image makes clear a problem with using oceans to discuss national and regional space. The advertisement's reproduction of Japan in Brazil and its linkage to Nikkei shows the ease with which transnational imagery flows without direct oceanic contact.[19] Japanese-Brazilians seem the embodiment of how global and local relate in a transnational and a transoceanic world.

Real and imagined geography is critical to the construction of ethnic identity. For many paulistanos (residents of the city of São Paulo), Japan served as a backdrop to explore their own national pathos, be it in politics, culture, or economic development. They imagined a powerful relationship between Nikkei and Japan because they rejected in Nikkei what many scholars have pointed to as a dominant feature of Brazilian culture: ethnic mutability. Nikkei in São Paulo, more than any other ethnic group in the sixties, seventies, and eighties, were essentialized by the majority and they essentialized themselves.

FIGURE 2. Newspaper advertisement for the film *Gaijin* (1980)

There was a twist, however: the same people who believed Nikkei to be ethnically rigid and impenetrable (and thus not truly Brazilian) often took the position that the Brazilian nation would improve by becoming "more Japanese." Nikkei by and large accepted an identity where they *were not* Brazilians of the present but *were* Brazilians of future.[20] It was precisely the "foreignness" of Japanese immigrants and their children that made them so Paulistano.

What differentiated Japanese-Brazilians from other ethnic groups in São Paulo was the heavy presence in the city of Japan and Japaneseness, in advertising, in food, in products, in retail and commercial relationships, in politics, and in the media. Nikkei were the most visible immigrant-originated ethnic minority in São Paulo, in contrast with those of Italian, Spanish, or Portuguese descent, whose Southern European background provided Catholicism and whiteness as advantages and a lack of industrial modernity as a demerit, at least when compared to Northern Europeans. Jews and Syrian-Lebanese (the term typically used to describe Brazilians of Middle Eastern descent) were also constructed as different from Nikkei. Brazilians often believed that they possessed the natural "gift" of commerce but their visibility was limited by an ability to change names, religions, and cultural practices without notice.[21] While individuals from most ethnic groups could choose to downplay (or even deny) their ethnicity in public since they did not differ physically from the majority of Brazilians, this was not the case for Nikkei. Japanese-Brazilians were physiognomic outsiders whose economic and political culture was highly desirable. They represented both hypertradition and hypermodernity. For Nikkei, Brazilianness was not simply contested. It was a constantly shifting set of positive and negative characteristics which, over time, created oppositions as the rule rather than the exception.

While many Brazilians believed that they were part of an ethnically flexible national culture, some groups had less room to maneuver than others. The Talent Agency's 2004 commercials for Semp Toshiba drive home the point (figs. 3, 4, 5). On the surface, the advertisements suggest that any Brazilian can "turn Japanese." "Pretending to be Japanese is easy" contrasted the implied falsity of the images with the essentialized notion that Semp Toshiba products are "truly" Japanese. These commercials, then, faithfully represented what residents of São Paulo believe, that Japanese-Brazilians are the last ethnically immutable group in a nation that exalts the flexibility of ethnic and racial categories. In São Paulo, Japan was an ethnic commodity and Nikkei were as well.

The regularity of conscious and unconscious images was not just about Japan as "over there." Rather Paulistanos constantly had their notions reinforced and challenged by real Nikkei who became the signifiers of a special bond with Japan. In fact, many among São Paulo's elite had an unusually deep ideological connection to Japan, even though few had ever been there.[22] In the sixties, São Paulo was the economic locomotive of Brazil, and Japan, Inc., as it was known, played the same role on the international stage. Japan in the sixties and seventies was what São Paulo's elites hoped for their own future. As in all fantasies, reality helped to create possibilities and a cultural ideology developed that suggested that São Paulo should not be like Japan, it should *become* Japan.

Japanese-Brazilians became the vehicle for this transformation. As Nikkei moved from the agricultural countryside of their immigrant parents into various urban professions, they became the "best Brazilians" in terms of their ability to modernize the country and the "worst Brazilians" because they were believed unlikely to fulfill the cultural dream of whitening. Majority essentialist presumptions about Japanese-Brazilian identity were mimicked in the discourses of the Nikkei minority. As a result, in-group and out-group stereotypes of Nikkei frequently coincided. Japanese-Brazilians were portrayed by the majority, and they portrayed themselves, as uniquely productive, whether as farmers, fruit and vegetable venders, or dry cleaners in

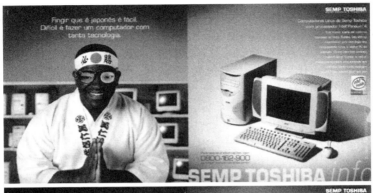

FIGURES 3, 4, 5. The advertisements read,
"Pretending to be Japanese is easy.
Making a computer with so much technology is difficult."
From Semp Toshiba Web site (www.semptoshiba.com.br/fr—institucional.htm)

the forties and fifties, as technological innovators or political activists in the sixties and seventies, or as liberal professionals in the eighties and nineties.

Nikkei both resisted and conformed to the idea of themselves as a "model minority." Some Japanese-Brazilians eagerly participated in formal community institutions both broad and narrow. Others rejected such participation and its implications. For many Nikkei, endogamy was crucial, but for an equally large group exogamy was the norm. Non-Nikkei, likewise, held multiple views of Japanese-Brazilians. Some of them viewed Nikkei as inassimilable aliens, even after generations of Brazilian citizenship. Others in the majority saw them as model citizens, a Brazilianized version of the U.S. "model minority" construct with all of its associated stereotypes and precariousness.[23] Most held both views simultaneously and applied them situationally. In this regard my research on Brazil supports Colleen Lye's contention that "yellow peril and model minority are best understood as two aspects of the same, long running, racial form."[24]

While Lye sees "economic efficiency" as the dominant model in the United States, the Brazilian case includes a sense of cultural efficiency as well. Even those Japanese-Brazilians who did not follow the paths set out by their parents, and expected by the majority, never rejected the powerful combination of stereotypes interwoven so deeply into the modern history of São Paulo. Nikkei artists often looked to their own experiences of ethnicity (as either cutting edge or traditional) for inspiration.[25] Some entered the São Paulo film industry in the sixties and seventies, at times participating in the many erotic films whose story lines used the city as a backdrop. Other Nikkei became involved in politics, and during the dictatorship that began in 1964 there was a boom of Nikkei political leaders at the city, state, and national level.[26] Politically active Nikkei also opposed the military regime, and some joined opposition groups, including armed guerrilla movements, in the hope of overthrowing it.

While many Nikkei saw themselves as part of an ethnic community, others delinked themselves from the institutions of their immigrant parents. The subjects of this book, for the most part, considered themselves community outsiders even though they were seen by many Brazilians as ethnic insiders. The choice to join an armed revolutionary group or perform in an erotic film may thus appear diametrically opposed to the choice of becoming a lawyer, banker, engineer, or businessperson. Certainly historians of the Brazilian dictatorship have treated these choices as opposites. I will make a contrary (and perhaps counterintuitive) argument: that most Japanese-Brazilians had remarkably similar ethnic experiences, independent of their political positions or social and economic choices. Stereotypes of Nikkei, be they guerrillas or ministers appointed by the military, be they farmers or actresses, were constantly implicated in a web of xenophobia and xenophilia. Nikkei often asserted that they were acting not as "Japanese" but as "Brazilians," even as they explained their achievements as culturally tied to an imagined ancestral homeland.

One way of analyzing diasporic ethnicity is as a cultural currency supported by "federal reserve banks" in multiple countries and spent in different ways in different social, cultural, and ethnic spaces. My research suggests that the strategic uses of ethnicity went hand in hand with the broad sentimental understanding of it.[27] São Paulo was filled with ethnic opportunities and constraints since majority Brazilians often presumed that Nikkei, even those on the margins of the "Japanese colony in Brazil," were invested in a notion of Japan as home.[28] While the presumption of diaspora led to discontent among many Nikkei, they did not sit still. Ethnic militancy was supposed to lead to Brazilianness. Ironically, it did the opposite.

Introduction

THE PACIFIC RIM IN THE ATLANTIC WORLD

———•———

The sixties and seventies were Brazil's "Diasporic Decades," and nowhere more so than in São Paulo. During these years Brazil tried to project a bigger role for itself in the world, and descendants of immigrants played an especially active role in shaping international and local connections. Capital from overseas poured into the city, with profits directed both to home in Brazil and to home abroad. Millions of Paulistanos constantly reshaped their identities to take advantage of ethnicities created by immigrant ancestors and Brazilian nationhood. No group more clearly defined São Paulo's Diasporic Decades than the hundreds of thousands of Japanese-Brazilians who became an integral part of life in the city.

As Japan reemerged as an economic powerhouse after World War II, Nikkei throughout the Americas were linked to international capital in ways that changed identity construction. Japan's position on the world stage meant that Nikkei were simultaneously viewed as "radically Other" and as part of a "common capitalist identity."[1] When Brazil's military took power in a 1964 coup, the generals and their civilian minions linked Japan with Brazil's "Japanese" just as a generation of Nikkei entered liberal professions. For the many Nikkei youth who had been born in immigrant farming communities, coming of age meant migration to the city of São Paulo for educational and professional advancement.

Generational change among Nikkei became part of a broader reformulation of bourgeois youth as censorship, repression, and mobilization created particular pitfalls and opportunities for all Brazilians. Nikkei (like many other young people), even if they had long hair or listened to rock and roll, generally followed the paths laid out by their parents and the military regime, focusing on individual economic success. For many Nikkei the dictatorship represented an opportunity to take advantage of the Brazilian higher educational system and ascend the social and economic ladder. Staying out of opposition politics was the norm. The dictators argued that success came from conformity and discipline, and Nikkei both created and took advantage of a model minority myth that separated them from participation in activist politics. The variables of generation, international capitalism, and national politics linked the local and the global in intricate ways that shaped Nikkei identity and images of it.

The opportunities for the renegotiation of ethnicity that emerged during the dictatorship stemmed from São Paulo's nineteenth- and twentieth-century economic expansion, which had attracted immigrants from around the world. By the early 1900s São Paulo was a multicultural city with large populations of African, European, Asian, and Middle Eastern descent. By the 1930s, immigrants were at the forefront of political activism in São Paulo, seeking to redraw the society and their space within it. During the sixties and seventies the city grew enormously, at a rate much higher than that of Brazil overall (see table 2). Many Paulistanos saw themselves as situational "hyphenated-Brazilians" and moved fluidly between Brazilian, Paulistano, and Italo-, Afro-, German-, Arab-, Jewish-, or Japanese-Brazilian identities.

Analyzing ethnic identity in São Paulo in the latter decades of the twentieth century is useful for understanding Brazil more broadly. People migrated in and out of São Paulo in huge numbers. Politicians, activists, artists, and domestic and industrial workers who lived in São Paulo were often *from* somewhere else, and those who resided in other cities often spent formative years in São Paulo. Television and movies flowed from São Paulo to the rest of the country. Advertising produced primarily for the city's residents was used throughout the country because most markets were too poor to receive individual attention.

Many Paulistanos saw their city as a dynamic example that an otherwise static Brazil should follow. The vibrant ethnicity of São Paulo thus seemed at odds with a broader national culture that often denied the importance, or even existence, of ethnicity. If we attempt to generate demographic statistics about Japanese-Brazilians, the competing ideologies become clear. Brazilian censuses, for example, have never allowed for ethnicity, rather grouping all

TABLE 2. Population distribution, São Paulo state, 1940–80

Year	Rural	Annual % Change	Urban	Annual % Change
1940	4,012,205		3,170,051	
1960	4,789,488	0.89	8,021,703	4.75
1980	2,844,334	−2.57	11,191,754	1.68

Source: Instituto Brasileiro de Geografia e Estatística, Evolução da População Residente: Brasil, Estado de São Paulo, Grande São Paulo, 1960, 1980.

citizens into six "color" categories based on a respondent model: white, black, yellow, mixed, indigenous, no declaration.[2] Brazilian census data thus makes it difficult to garner much sociological data on the Japanese-Brazilian population. The leadership of the constituted Japanese-Brazilian community, however, twice conducted censuses with the financial support of a Japanese government eager to know about "its" population abroad. The 1958 Japanese-Brazilian community census was published in Japan in two volumes with text in Japanese and English but not Portuguese. The second Nikkei census was conducted in 1987–88 and produced only in Portuguese, evidence of Nikkei identity's new focus on a generation born and raised in Brazil.

The 1958 census counted just over 430,000 Brazilian Nikkei, with some 325,000 living in São Paulo state and about 120,000 in the city. Immigrants were about one-third of the total in 1958 but over the next two decades the population born in Brazil would increase dramatically, as did migration from rural areas to São Paulo city.[3] By 1987 the Nikkei population had grown to about 1.2 million, with the overwhelming majority (887,000) living in the state of São Paulo. Some 326,000 Japanese-Brazilians lived in São Paulo city and another 170,000 lived in the regions immediately surrounding it. Today the numbers are even higher: São Paulo's population of Japanese descent is much larger than that of the major U.S. cities: Honolulu (113,000), Los Angeles (45,000), New York (26,500), San Francisco (15,000), and Seattle (12,000).[4] It is also larger than the entire Peruvian Nikkei population of about 55,000. Outside of Japan, there are more Nikkei in the state of São Paulo than in the rest of the world combined! (See tables 3–5.)

This huge population emerged from a series of contacts between Brazil and Japan that began in 1894 (see table 6). Brazilian coffee planters, preoc-

TABLE 3. Population growth, Brazil and São Paulo (state and city), 1890–1980

Year	Brazil	Annual % Change	São Paulo State	Annual % Change	São Paulo City	Annual % Change
1890	14,333,915		1,384,753		64,934	
1900	17,318,557	1.91	2,282,279	5.12	239,820	13.96
1920	31,652,472	3.06	3,667,032	2.40	57,982	4.51
1940	41,236,315	2.19	7,180,316	2.91	1,326,261	4.37
1960	70,072,417	4.51	12,809,231	7.20	3,781,446	10.99
1980	111,308,732	2.34	25,040,712	3.41	8,493,226	4.13

Source: Instituto Brasileiro de Geografia e Estatística, Evolução da População Residente: Brasil, Estado de São Paulo, Grande São Paulo, 1960, 1980.

TABLE 4. Population growth, Brazilians of Japanese descent, 1958 and 1988

Region	1958	%	1988	%	Annual %
Brazil	105,870	24.61	340,000	28.25	3.97
São Paulo State	255,520	59.38	562,000	45.60	2.66
São Paulo City	50,000	16.27	326,000	25.50	6.45
Total	430,135	100	1,228,000	99.80	3.56

Sources: Instituto Brasileiro de Geografia e Estatística (IBGE), Estatísticas históricas do Brasil (Rio de Janeiro: IBGE, 1987); IBGE, Anuário estatístico do Brasil, 1987–88 (Rio de Janeiro: IBGE, 1988); Centro de Estudos Nipo-Brasileiros (CENB), Pesquisa da população de descendentes de japoneses residentes no Brasil, 1987–88 (São Paulo: CENB, 1990); CENB, Uma epopéia moderna: 80 anos da imigração japonesa no Brasil (São Paulo: Hucitec–Soc. Brasileira de Cultura Japonesa, 1992).

cupied with the transition from African slavery to free labor, became disillusioned with European laborers who seemed more interested in protesting labor and social conditions than in working as replacements for slaves.[5] The landowner's hunt for submissive labor melded well with the Japanese government's desire to export what they believed to be a surplus agricultural population. When the United States banned most Japanese entry with its "Gentleman's Agreement" in 1907, Japan and Brazil removed all administra-

TABLE 5. Population distribution, Brazilians of Japanese descent, 1958 and 1988

Year	Rural	Annual %	Urban	Annual %
1958	263,762		193,207	
1988	124,000	−2.4	1,104,000	5.9

Sources: IBGE, Estatísticas históricas do Brasil (Rio de Janeiro: IBGE, 1987); IBGE, Anuário estatístico do Brasil, 1987–88 (Rio de Janeiro: IBGE, 1988); CENB, Pesquisa da população de descendentes de japoneses residentes no Brasil, 1987–88 (São Paulo: CENB, 1990); Centro de Estudos Nipo-Brasileiros, Uma epopéia moderna: 80 anos da imigração japonesa no Brasil (São Paulo: Hucitec–Soc. Brasileira de Cultura Japonesa, 1992).

tive and diplomatic hurdles to immigration. Between 1908 and 1941 some 189,000 Japanese immigrants settled in Brazil (followed by another 50,000 after World War II), almost all arriving as subsidized labor. Japanese immigrants were well received by many in the Brazilian elite who accepted the Japanese government's claim that its people were the "whites" of Asia. In Japan, there was similar enthusiasm for migration to Brazil, believed to be a country of immense potential wealth.

Japanese immigrants did more than work on plantations. Many Brazilian elites, who had seen first Europe, then the United States as sources of modernity in the nineteenth century, added Japan to this list in the twentieth, following the country's victory over Russia and its subsequent rise to international military, economic, and technological power. In many respects, the experiences of Japanese-Brazilians in the sixties and seventies represented how elites before World War II had imagined what Brazil might become.

The search for modernity abroad to create the Brazilian nation at home is seen clearly in Anita Malfatti's painting The Japanese (figure 6), shown at a controversial 1917 exposition that set the stage for São Paulo's paradigm-shifting Modern Art Week five years later. While most of the fifteen thousand Japanese immigrants who had settled in São Paulo state between 1908 and 1915 were farmers, Malfatti's 1915 image did not portray a rural worker.[6] The subject was confident and dressed for life in the big city in a three-piece suit and bow tie. He was a modern man and a model for other Brazilians.

For elites, the desire to use immigration to import modernity meshed easily with a sense that Japanese were uniquely hard and productive workers.

FIGURE 6. Anita Malfatti, *O japonês* (1915–16).
Used by permission of the Coleção de Artes Visuais do Instituto de
Estudos Brasileiros, University of São Paulo

In the twenties, firms linked to the Japanese government began to purchase large plots of land in areas of São Paulo state where little agricultural development had taken place. The Japanese formed cooperatives that operated networks of distribution, not just production. At the same time Brazilian commercial interests significantly expanded their Japanese market for goods like rice and coffee. Japanese immigrants and their production were crucial to this expansion, since many products traveled via Japanese-Brazilian and Japanese middlemen to Japan for sale. By the 1930s, Nikkei visibility in the Brazilian economy, and Japan's growing international presence, created

TABLE 6. Japanese immigration to Brazil, 1908–79

Years	Number
1908–14	15,543
1915–23	16,723
1924–35	141,732
1936–41	14,617
1942–52	—[a]
1952–59	30,610
1960–69	18,619
1970–79	3,610

Sources: 1908–41: Hiroshi Saito, "Alguns aspectos da mobilidade dos japoneses no Brasil," Kobe Economic and Business Review, 6th Annual Report (1959): 50; Comissão de Elaboração da História dos 80 anos da Imigração Japonesa no Brasil, Uma epopéia moderna: 80 anos da imigração japonesa no Brasil (São Paulo: Editora Hucitec, 1992), table 2, p. 424.
[a]Insignificant because of World War II and its aftermath.

some resentment, and a number of political movements sought to limit Japanese immigration. In the mid-thirties Brazil's elites fought a political and cultural battle among themselves over whether Japanese immigrants would save or ruin Brazil. In 1933, members of the Constitutional Convention, charged with producing what would become the Constitution of 1934, debated Japanese immigration in detail, discussing its relation to imperialism, assimilation, and nationalism. The constitution established a quota system, and while the immigrant stream from Japan slowed between 1933 and 1950, the social place of Japanese and their descendants remained a topic of national political and cultural discussion.[7]

When the proto-fascist Estado Novo (New State) dictatorship was established in 1937, one of its major new policies was the brasilidade (Brazilianization) campaign. This state-driven homogenization program sought to preserve an idealized national identity from the encroachment of ethnicity. New legislation controlled immigrant entry and prevented resident aliens from congregating in farming colonies. Decrees required that all schools be directed by native-born Brazilians and that all instruction be in Portuguese and include "Brazilian" topics. Foreign-language publications had to be accompanied by Portuguese translations, and the Ministry of War began drafting children of foreign residents into the army and stationing them outside the regions of their birth. Speaking foreign languages in public and private was banned, and the Brazilian children of foreign residents were prohibited from international travel.[8]

The brasilidade movement, ostensibly aimed at all foreigners, targeted "resident enemy aliens" when Brazil entered World War II in 1942 on the side of the Allies. Many Japanese immigrants and their Brazilian children were forcibly removed from "strategic areas" along the coast and in major cities, often losing their businesses and land in the process. The reaction of Nikkei to the anti-Japanese movement was to construct a number of new Japanese-Brazilian identities. Some insisted on Portuguese as a language of both internal and external communication and sought to prove their Brazilianness through national loyalty. Others became increasingly "Japanese," often by supporting secret societies linked to emperor worship. These societies garnered wide support after Brazil sent twenty-five thousand troops to Italy in July 1944 and war fever led to intense anti-Japanese propaganda.[9] They grew even stronger after 1945 as postwar ultranationalism mixed with a desire to reinforce a space for Japanese-Brazilian identity.

The most powerful secret society was the Shindo Renmei (Way of the Subjects of the Emperor's League), which became public in August 1945, following Japan's surrender. Its goals were to maintain a permanent Japanized space in Brazil through the preservation of language, culture, and religion among Nikkei and to reestablish Japanese schools. It also denied that Japan itself had been defeated in the war. By December 1945 the Shindo Renmei claimed a membership of fifty thousand and over the next decade supporters would number one hundred thousand. The movement came to the wider Brazilian public's attention when fanatical young members of the Shindo Renmei assassinated, physically abused, or destroyed the homes and fields of Nikkei who admitted Japan's loss in the war, murdering sixteen people and destroying silk, cotton, and mint farms owned by Japanese immigrants and their Brazilian children.[10] By mid-1946 Shindo Renmei propaganda included altered photos of President Harry S Truman bowing to Emperor Hirohito, "press" reports of Japanese troops landing in San Francisco and marching toward New York, and notices that Brazil's recently deposed dictator Getúlio Vargas would be signing surrender documents in Tokyo.

The secret societies were marginalized by the early fifties just as Nikkei began to migrate in large numbers to São Paulo city and establish themselves in the middle classes. At the same time new immigrants from Japan (mainly Okinawa) entered Brazil in significant numbers, intensifying coexisting positive and negative stereotypes.[11] The new immigrants' presence in the ethnically diverse city reinforced memories of the secret societies and by extension Japanese-Brazilians as militaristic, violent, and secretive.[12] For Nikkei, the childhood memory of ethnic violence in their birthplaces was strong, even after they moved to the city.

In the postwar decades Nikkei, like many other ethnic groups, were alternately glorified and vilified by other Brazilians. Many Japanese-Brazilians sought to combat the negative stereotypes by melding commemorations of São Paulo's four hundredth anniversary with those marking fifty years of Japanese immigration in 1958. A huge "Japanese Pavilion" was constructed in São Paulo's Ibirapuera Park and was inaugurated on 18 June 1958, fifty years to the day after the arrival of the first ship bringing Japanese immigrants to Brazil. That day was even decreed a state holiday by Governor Jânio Quadros. As historian Célia Sakurai notes, "from the fifties, the Japanese colony began to gain a different kind of visibility . . . It was no longer the 'Yellow peril' . . . but now a glorification of labor, of the hard work that generates success."[13]

In the 1960s and 1970s positive Nikkei visibility stemmed from economic success and the presence of Japan as a world economic power. Paulistanos came into contact with Japanese-Brazilians, or images of them, constantly. Nikkei were studying in college, were selling fruits and vegetables, were small shop owners and liberal professionals, and were playing roles in advertising and in films. Many held local, state, and national political offices. Popular culture played on the new visibility. One popular song from the fifties told of frugal immigrant farmers driving old trucks who became urban professionals with money to spare and no real sense of how to maneuver a fancy new car in the city.[14] Journalistic articles about São Paulo frequently emphasized the Nikkei presence. The British Sunday newspaper the *Observer* reflected that "office departments seem to be entirely manned by them. . . . [In] horticulture they are brilliant. . . . [On] some days the airport seems to be half-full of them, grasping their identical briefcases, smoking their cigarettes in the stiff style of beginners, posing for numerous photographs."[15]

Nikkei were particularly overrepresented in higher education in the sixties and seventies, making up a little over 2 percent of the population of the state of São Paulo but more than 10 percent of its university students. In 1967, according to the Japanese consulate, there were 40 Nikkei professors in the São Paulo university system as well as graduates numbering 560 engineers, 1,350 physicians, 5 judges, and 450 lawyers. This was in addition to the some 2,900 Nikkei who held university degrees in other areas and 3,300

FIGURES 7, 8. Stamps commemorating Japanese immigration to Brazil,
1958 (Japan) and 1974 (Brazil)

enrolled students.[16] According to Sussumu Miyao's analysis of census and
university entrance data in 1977, 5 percent of all professors and 10 percent of
all students entering São Paulo's universities were of Japanese descent, with
the highest percentage enrolled at the Aeronautical Technological Institute
(Instituto Tecnológico de Aeronáutica, ITA) (15.9 percent), the Getúlio
Vargas Foundation School of Business Administration (12.5 percent), and
the University of São Paulo (12.9 percent). Some 14.6 percent of all students
in the exact sciences were of Japanese descent, with 12.2 percent in the
biomedical fields and 7.4 percent in the humanities and social sciences.[17]

Educational patterns among Nikkei generated much discussion among
elites. Minister of Foreign Relations Antônio F. Azeredo da Silveira used the
numbers of students and professors at the University of São Paulo to hail the
"assimilative power" of Nikkei in a 1978 speech marking the seventieth
anniversary of Japanese immigration to Brazil: "They say that the Japanese
can make pearls like nature, watches like the Swiss, and whiskey like the
Scotch. In Brazil, the Japanese immigrant made himself Brazilian like the
Brazilians!"[18] Not all public comments were as enthusiastic, but the link of
Nikkei to educational achievement was strong. The news magazine Istoé
noted ironically in 1979 that "the Faculty [of Arts and Sciences] starts with
'F,' for Fukuda."[19] Advertisements for preparatory centers that helped secondary school students train for university entrance examinations often featured Japanese-Brazilians. As educated Nikkei became a visible "racial
other," ugly jokes started to circulate: "Guarantee your place at the University of São Paulo tomorrow—kill a Jap today" went one, while another, found

in university toilet stalls, was "as you sit here and shit, it's the books the Japanese hit."

The growing numbers of Nikkei in higher education led to a significant overrepresentation in certain areas of the liberal professions like corporate management (6.3 percent), dentistry (8 percent), economics (9 percent), and chemistry (11.8 percent).[20] While these forms of economic insertion were independent of the authoritarian nature of Brazil's government after 1964, certain regime policies did provide new opportunities. The military was eager to expand law, economics, science, engineering, and medicine as counterweights to the social science and humanities curricula that seemed to lead students to nonproductive dilettantism or, even worse, political activism. University growth was targeted at areas that trained students to develop and produce material goods like refrigerators and televisions that would go with middle-class culture. Into these sectors Nikkei flowed. When University of São Paulo physics professor Shigeo Watanabe was appointed to the National Research Council with much fanfare in 1971, Japanese immigrant parents, most of their children, and non-Nikkei policy makers all agreed that he was a perfect role model for all Brazilians.[21]

Educated Nikkei also became important members of the regime's policy-making apparatus, and their ethnicity was always a point of public comment. Fábio Riodo Yassuda, the former head of São Paulo's Cotia Cooperative, founded by Japanese immigrants, was named minister of industry and commerce in 1969. Press reports hailed the appointment for its importance to relations with Japan and suggested that Brazil's population was changing for the better. Brazil's most widely read newsmagazine, *Veja*, noted that "it took almost three hundred years for the 'Portuguese of Brazil' to consider themselves Brazilians. . . . For the 'Japanese of Brazil' it took much less." This statement was backed up by pictures of families with one "Japanese" and one "Brazilian" parent and a "blond Japanese" child representing "Brazil."[22] Yassuda's brother, São Paulo's secretary of public works, was only one of many Nikkei to hold important public positions. In 1970 the state of São Paulo boasted one federal deputy, three state deputies, eleven mayors, seventeen vice-mayors, twelve city council presidents, and over two hundred city councilmen of Japanese descent.[23]

Nikkei generational change and Brazilian government policies also reinforced economic ties between Japan and Brazil. The government of Juscelino Kubitschek (1956–61) encouraged Japanese investment as part of its import-substitution industrialization (ISI) policy, partly responsible for the establishment of the joint venture Usiminas steel plant in the state of Minas

Gerais in 1958. The following year the Ishikawajima Corporation funded some 70 percent of the Ishibrás shipyard in Rio de Janeiro.[24] Japanese products streamed into Brazil, and vice versa, after the military regime signed a 1967 tax treaty with Japan.[25] Many Japanese corporations located factories in the Manaus Free Trade Zone, increasing the presence of Japanese products in the Brazilian marketplace.

In early 1972, Japanese investment in Brazil was at about 170 million U.S. dollars, behind the United States, West Germany, Canada, Britain, and Switzerland. By the end of the year, however, there was a marked increase to almost 600 million dollars, placing Japan only slightly behind West Germany. That same year Mitsubishi announced a five-year, 1.2-billion-dollar investment, with most of that money for infrastructure and export of raw materials (minerals and food). Brazil's trade with Japan also expanded massively, from 3 percent of the total in 1960 to 6 percent of a much larger total in 1971.[26] In 1960 45 Japanese companies were operating in Brazil. By 1970 that number had jumped to 113 and by 1976 to 537. In the 1970s Japan ranked as the third-largest direct investor in Brazil, at nearly 2.8 billion dollars.

Japan's growing economic ties with Brazil were the result of a number of factors. At the global level, Japan's huge capital reserves needed to be invested overseas and Brazil, with its raw materials and potential for growth, was a logical choice. Investment in Brazil also helped Japanese multinationals cut labor costs and export some of their most polluting plants. There was an imagined diasporic factor as well, since "a unique attraction for Japan is the large and influential Japanese-Brazilian community to which it will look for much of its management and clerical force."[27]

This combination of global and local factors was not lost on Antônio Delfim Neto, the economist who was Brazil's minister of finance from 1967 to 1974, following a well-regarded stint as economic secretary for the state of São Paulo.[28] For Delfim Neto, Japanese investment had two advantages: (1) a lack of the imperialist baggage associated with the United States and (2) frequent involvement with minority partnerships. Japanese-Brazilians also made an impression on Delfim Neto: the Nikkei technocrats whom he chose to work in the Finance Ministry to help "reduce investor apprehension" were his "Japanese Team."[29] Paulo Yokota was considered by São Paulo's *Diário Nippak* to be "one of [his] most loyal assistants" and was later named president of Brazil's National Institute of Colonization and Agrarian Reform (Instituto Nacional de Colonização e Reforma Agrária, INCRA).[30] Brazil's "Japanese Team" did not go unnoticed in Japan. In a 1976 meeting at Aka-

FIGURE 9. Brazilian stamp commemorating
the visit of Crown Prince Akihito in 1967

saka Palace in Tokyo between Brazilian president general Ernesto Geisel and
Japanese prime minister Takeo Miki, the latter commented (much to the
general's delight) that the number of Nikkei in positions of political power
was an indication that in Brazil "there is no racial prejudice."[31]

The ties between Brazil and Japan, and their linkage to Japanese-Brazilians,
allowed the military regime to hail its special relationship with Japan.[32] In
1967, and again a decade later, Crown Prince (now Emperor) Akihito's visits
to Brazil were highly visible and carefully orchestrated, including meetings
with the president and leading members of the Japanese-Brazilian community (see figure 9). In 1967, some twenty-five thousand people greeted the
royal couple on their arrival from Tokyo, and newspapers estimated that one
hundred thousand people surrounded their hotel in downtown São Paulo
hoping for a glimpse.[33] When Japan's Prime Minister Tanaka visited Brazil in
September 1974, he and President General Geisel both commented on the
special relationship between the "two countries[, which] are ready to develop
closer ties and more harmony."[34] When the Brazilian leader visited Japan two
years later, he left with a promise of 3 billion dollars in aid as well as Japanese
investment in a number of heavy industrial projects.[35]

The transnational discourses about trade, investment, migration, and people were linked to local discourses that were critical to creating identity. The
military government took great care, as did all regimes before and after, to
protest any suggestions that Brazil was not a "white, modern nation" of
which Nikkei were an integral part.[36] A plan to send a group of children of

Japanese mothers and African-American servicemen to the Japanese-founded colony of Tomé-Açu (some 400 kilometers north of the Amazonian city of Belém do Pará) was rejected after the Brazilian government defined the orphans as "undesirables."[37] While politicians in Japan believed that these "mixed" children would fit perfectly in "mixed" Brazil, Brazilian politicians and Nikkei elites alleged that the plan made their country a dumping ground for nonwhites.

These minor tensions, however, did little to weaken the growing relations between Japan and Brazil. Sérgio Mendes performed his "Latin rock" to sold-out theaters in Japan, and his interviews with the Japanese press were relayed immediately back to Brazil.[38] Other cultural products also strengthened ties: Brazilian films were frequently sent to Japan, and in 1968 the Brazilian government sponsored a Carnival parade that brought three thousand people to the streets of the port city of Kobe to watch some of Rio de Janeiro's most famous samba schools.[39] In the city of São Paulo, "Japanese" products (made in both Japan and Brazil) became increasingly common.

Japanese goods, presumed to be superior to locally made ones, led many Brazilians to associate the same qualities with Japanese-Brazilians. Brazilian newspaper and magazine articles about the 1970 World Exposition in Japan frequently suggested that high-tech gadgets would flow into Brazil via its Nikkei community.[40] Exotic and subservient female sexuality was also associated with Nikkei. In many cases, the images were combined. Take, for example, an advertisement for imported Yamaha motorcycles (figure 10). The image was of a naked white woman lying on the seat of a motorcycle and the tag line "Have her at your feet" with a prominent Japanese translation under it.[41] Few, if any, readers could understand the Japanese script (which was a faithful translation of the Portuguese), but the presence of Japanese letters next to a Japanese motorcycle sold in Japanese-Brazilian dealerships spoke to quality of technology, an image nearly as powerful as that of the naked woman.

A similar set of ideas lay behind the advertisements that surrounded Varig Brazilian Airline's first direct flights to Japan in 1968. The promotional event for the inaugural flight showed President General Arthur da Costa e Silva and his wife standing with Japanese-Brazilian stewardess Takeo Ouchi dressed in an outfit worthy of Carmen Miranda, including a fruited headdress! Mrs. Costa e Silva (who flew to Japan on that flight) and Ms. Ouchi could be termed traditional, and the imagery found in advertising for Japan Airlines (JAL) in Brazil was similar, focusing on the attention businessmen would receive from women (figure 11).

FIGURE 10. *Fairplay: A Revista do Homem* 34 (1969).
Both the Japanese and Portuguese captions read, "Have her at your feet"

Aqui começa
o Japão da Japan Air Lines

FIGURE 11. Advertisement for Japan Airlines
service from São Paulo to Tokyo (1968).
The caption reads, "This is where the Japan
of JAL begins"

The stamp commemorating that first Varig flight to Japan also suggested a sexual diaspora (figure 12).[42] A woman in traditional Bahian dress and a kimonoed geisha represented how the two different countries were coupled by African and Asian sexuality and the modern airplane overhead. The advertising jingle created to promote the new service used "a Rip-van-Winkle-like Japanese folk tale that almost all Japanese learn as children" mixed with images of Brazilian national identity.[43] The lyrics and music, written by Archimedes Messina, won the prize in 1970 for "Brazilian Jingle of the Year." It was performed by Rosa Miyake, host of the Rede Record television network musical show *Images of Japan*. To this day the Varig jingle is sung at Japanese-Brazilian festivals.

URASHIMA TARO
Urashima Taro, a poor fisherman
Saved a turtle
And it, as a reward, took him to Brazil!
To the enchanted kingdom
He fell in love and stayed here

FIGURE 12. Stamp (1968) commemorating that
first Varig flight to Japan

He stayed many years, but suddenly
Homesickness came upon him
He received a mysterious chest as a present
When he opened it, what joy
It touched his heart
He found a Varig ticket
And he flew, happily, to Japan![44]

THE JINGLE
Academic lectures always lead to surprises, especially when audiences have lived experiences with the research that I am presenting. Such was the case when I had the pleasure to speak at Unisinos, a large university with a long tradition of historical research in ethnicity, located in the city of São Leopoldo, in the state of Rio Grande do Sul. During my talk I showed a slide of the 1968 Brazilian stamp commemorating Varig's first flight to Japan. At the conclusion the professor Maria Cristina Martins approached me with a huge smile. "Your talk brought back memories for me," she said. "Did you ever hear the advertising jingle that Varig produced for the flight?" I said no and to the delight of the group, she sang the entire song, which she had not heard for decades.

The mixture of technology, ethnicity, and sexuality were not confined to motorcycle and airline advertising. An advertisement for a shirt that could

O amor
nasce
do
oriente

"Mulher bonita? Ah, tem que
ser japonêsa! Ela tem
cabelos lisos, os olhos
meigos e é muito amorosa."

Aduato Serapião de Oliveira,
25 anos, linotipista

FIGURE 13. "O que é mulher bonita?"
Realidade, October 1967, 92–101.
The title reads, "Love Is Born in the East"

"go around the world" without being ironed showed a man dreaming of his international experiences. His fantasy was a geisha who appreciated the technological quality of his shirt because she was modern and who was sexually subservient because she was traditional.[45] In Japanese-Brazilian beauty contests young women were hailed for maintaining Japanese ethnicity and giving off a special Brazilian sensuality.[46] An article on male ideas of beautiful women in the widely read magazine *Realidade* (which had a format similar to *Life*) used six examples, including the expected "blonde" and "mulata." Aduato Serapião de Oliveira, a twenty-five-year-old linotypist, told of his fantasy: "A pretty woman? Ah, she must be Japanese! She has straight hair, sweet eyes, and she is very loving" (figure 13).

Advertising using images of Japanese-Brazilians, which became common in the sixties and seventies (and has continued to this day), was a constant point of ethnic interrogation. Advertisements fell into three broad categories: Japanese companies in Brazil focused on the "Brazilianness" of Nikkei,

Japanese-Brazilian firms promoted a "natural" Nikkei ability to improve Brazil, and non-Nikkei firms marketed intelligence and high productivity by conflating Japan and Nikkei. Representative of the first type was a 1972 Sony advertisement for recording equipment with the tag line "Who would have guessed? Sony is even teaching Portuguese in Brazil!"[47] This was similar to a 1978 Ishibrás advertisement created to take advantage of the publicity surrounding the seventieth anniversary of Japanese immigration to Brazil. It showed a child's face, emphasizing his "slanty" eyes, along with the sentence "They believe in Brazil with their eyes closed." The second type can be seen in an advertisement for CEAGESP (Companhia de Entrepostos e Armazéns Gerais de São Paulo, a Japanese-Brazilian agricultural cooperative and distributor) which claimed that "the arrival of Japanese in Brazil led to a great future." Advertisements for Anglo, a firm that prepared students for university exams, were typical of the third type. They showed a group of Nikkei students: "They are already known for being intelligent—Anglo helps to get it [a degree and being known as intelligent]." The Atlantic Petroleum Company took a similar approach. Its cartoon mascot, a small karate master, claimed that he, like the firm, was stronger than he appeared: "If you are not the biggest, you have to be the best" (figure 14).[48]

The presumed bond between Japan and Japanese-Brazilians via industrial discipline and high-quality products was not only seen in commercial advertisements. A propaganda film on personal hygiene produced by the military used "Japanese" (read Japanese-Brazilian) characters to show viewers a model of how proper Brazilians should act. A government advertisement for savings accounts used a drawing of a samurai and text in Japanese and Portuguese to inculcate values of economy: "Those who are perseverant, organized, and provident deserve to make more from their savings account. And they will."[49]

During the sixties and seventies images of Japanese-Brazilians were omnipresent in São Paulo. Residents of the city met real Japanese-Brazilians who were part of its industrial and commercial expansion. They saw Japanese-Brazilians in advertisements for banks, laundry detergent, and insect repellant, all asserting that "Japanese" were modern, hard-working, and serious Brazilians. Nikkei actors performed in art films and in erotic comedies. Children who watched television (and in Brazil the numbers were huge) were enthralled by the arrival in 1964 of the live-action series National Kid, which created a generation that sang along with the Japanized English of the theme song "Nationaro Kiido, Kiido, Nationaro Kiido . . ."

The popular São Paulo music group Premeditando o Breque was formed

FIGURE 14. Advertisement of the Atlantic
Petroleum Company, 1968. The caption reads,
"If you are not the biggest, you have to be the best"

in the mid-1970s but, because of censorship, only released its first record in
1983. They played their own version of the "Nationaro Kiido" theme song as
part of their repertoire. And when the group sang its anthem to the city, "São
Paulo, São Paulo," the lyrics about a stroll through the megalopolis were not
surprising:

> It is always lovely to walk
>> in the city of São Paulo
> The weather fools you, life is money,
>> in São Paulo
> The blond Japanese
> The darkish Northeasterners of São Paulo
>> Punk babes
> The Yankee way of São Paulo.[50]

A scene from the 1979 Bruno Barreto film *Amor Bandido* drove home the
point. A man arriving in Rio de Janeiro by plane is asked by his taxi driver

about São Paulo. The response, "Same as always. Lots of rain, lots of Japanese," certainly drew the same comfortable laugh from the audience as it did from the character in the film.[51]

SOME ORIENTING COMMENTS

While pre-1950 Japanese immigration and Japanese-Brazilian ethnicity have comprised a small but vibrant area of research in Brazil and Japan for many decades, later periods have received far less attention.[52] The Brazilian state was deeply focused on questions of national identity formation during the early twentieth century, and immigrants were always connected to this issue. Given the two hundred thousand Japanese immigrants who settled in Brazil between 1908 and 1940, the integration of the newcomers and their descendants was viewed by academics as a policy question. The focus of research was on government reports, immigration policy debates, newspapers, and books. In the immediate postwar period, studies of Brazilians of Japanese descent focused on two issues: the Shindo Renmei and identity "problems" among the Nissei generation.[53] After 1960, from the state perspective, Nikkei had become Brazilian citizens and did not merit much mention. Ignoring Nikkei was also part of the post–World War II idea that race and ethnicity in Brazil were only functions of class, and research attention was thus oriented toward the economically disenfranchised. More recently, scholarship on the military dictatorship has understandably focused on politics and not ethnicity.

The paucity of research on ethnicity during the Brazilian dictatorship also indicates the unique ways that race and ethnicity are understood in Brazil. Japanese-Brazilians had little to gain by asserting their minority status in a country where "minority," "oppressed," and "impoverished" were part of the same equation. Majority Brazilians had an equal stake in publicly dismissing Nikkei ethnicity, even if they commented on it constantly. By asserting that Japanese-Brazilians were not "real" minorities (i.e., not impoverished), one could continue to use a series of stereotypes about Nikkei with impunity. While it is understandable that Brazilian academics have followed these lines, it seems that scholars of Brazil from other countries have as well. In fact, in spite of academic cautions that Brazil is a place of particular racial transience, Japanese-Brazilians are often treated as a monolithic community, in the rare cases when they appear in academic discussions.

The lack of scholarship is also related to how the dictatorship is remembered in Brazil. Brazilians often say that "Brazil is a country with no historical memory," and the 1979 judicial decision to grant amnesty to all those accused, or potentially accused, of political crimes (including state torture) during military rule is often pointed to as an example. This rejection of memory has been particularly noticeable as former militants have come into positions of political and economic power since the return to democracy in 1985.[54] At the same time, certain sectors of popular culture have turned the period into either a joke (as did the 2003 film *Casseta e Planeta: A Taça do Mundo é Nossa*) or marketing strategy (Burger King's 2005 entrance into the Brazilian market with an advertising campaign using fast food "guerrillas" taking to the street "in revolution" against the "dictatorship" of hamburger choices—eating at Burger King was thus a "democratic" act). The "Brazilianization" of the memory of the dictatorship also includes a rejection of the period's violence, of which Japanese-Brazilians, as I will show, were often considered the most extreme purveyors. As a result, studying ethnicity as part of the memory of the dictatorship has not taken place.

My research, however, moves in a different direction by analyzing ethnic phenomena that occurred during the dictatorship but were not the result of it. Why did so many films include Japanese-Brazilian actors and actresses? Why were the Brazilian press and police so focused on Japanese-Brazilian militants? Why did a guerrilla group kidnap the Japanese consul in São Paulo to trade for a militant known as "Mário the Jap?"

To understand the unplanned effect of certain policies on ethnic identity, I have dug into a variety of sources that often elude the gaze of scholars.[55] These include films (including notes scribbled on video cassette boxes and in the margins of scripts, publicity posters, and audience reactions), oral histories, wanted posters, advertisements, photographs, and police reports. The richness and often unusual nature of these sources demanded that I add some of the techniques of anthropology and cultural studies to traditional historical methods of document analysis. Finding sources, be they the ones above or newspapers, government records, and diplomatic correspondence, was for me always an adventure. Thus I have tried to offer readers insights into where and how I found sources, and how the experiences of discovery may have influenced my analysis.

The words "memory" and "remember" appear frequently in this book, and readers should be aware that the subjects of this volume, even when public or semipublic figures, rarely speak about their ethnicity to the public.[56] Repeatedly they expressed surprise at my questions, and published interviews confirmed that this surprise was genuine and not a stock response. In this regard the responses I quote do not seem to conform to Alice and Howard Hoffman's archival memory concept whereby recollections "are rehearsed, readily available for recall, and selected for preservation over the lifetime of the individual."[57]

My questions led to the reconstruction of memories. Indeed, rebuilding *political and artistic* activism in a context of *ethnic* militancy often led to a kind of warped nostalgia for a past that was created via my interventions. Thus in this book I am not trying to piece together a factual chronology of events. Rather the oral histories, together with many other sources, have helped me to analyze the ethnic scenarios that prodded an always fluid notion of national identity in a city where hundreds of thousands of people considered themselves, and were considered, both nonnormative and the best Brazilians of all.

The first section of *A Discontented Diaspora* investigates artistic militancy, mainly in film. It begins and ends with two movies shown at the Cannes Film Festival, Walter Hugo Khouri's *Noite Vazia* (1964) and Tizuka Yamasaki's *Gaijin* (1980). In these chapters I trace the continuity between many different kinds of films by analyzing scripts and images as well as published documentation.[58] I conducted oral histories with some of the actors and directors and I found published interviews with others. That said, my attempts to get information were far from completely successful: some participants had died and others were unreceptive to my approaches. Films including Nikkei characters helped to spread ideas of Japaneseness and its link to Brazil among significant sectors of the population. Nikkei actors and actresses constantly bumped up against presumptions about their identities just as did most Nikkei. This helps to explain why the Japanese-Brazilian political activists who are the focus of the second part of the book had such similar experiences to performers examined in the first part.

The chapters on political militancy form a kind of prosopography, or collective biography, of Japanese-Brazilian activists. Almost all were born in rural areas with large populations of Japanese immigrants. As children they had intense experiences hearing about violent secret societies. Most moved to São Paulo city for education and there sought to assert their Brazilianness. While the specific stories of political activism diverge from the norm in Japanese-Brazilian life, readers will see that the images that surrounded Nikkei militants were extraordinarily similar to those of nonmilitants. For this section I was able to conduct numerous oral histories, find a wide range of documentation from the press and the government, and to consider a historiography in which images of Japanese-Brazilians are frequent.

The final chapters of the book are about three individuals. Two died decades ago, and my focus is on how they were remembered. The third person is Shizuo Osawa, the famous (or infamous) Mário Japa (Mário the Jap). My ability to conduct many hours of interviews with Osawa was the result of a personal connection that gave me an introduction and the former guerrilla's confidence that his comments would not end up as lurid stories in the popular press. Osawa, who had been interested in Japanese-Brazilian ethnicity since his youth, was a particularly perceptive interlocutor.

•••

This book began with the famous advertisement "Our Japanese are more creative than everyone else's Japanese." The slogan plays with ideas of race, nation, and ethnicity in a way that allows for multiple interpretations. This became clear when I showed it to a large class on comparative race relations that I taught as a Fulbright Fellow at the University of São Paulo in 2001. I began with a simple question about the phrase—who were "our Japanese" and who were "everyone else's Japanese?" The students all agreed that "our Japanese" were Brazilian and that the Brazilian nation was represented by the word "Japanese." While the majority of students saw this as a positive representation, Nikkei students noted that denominating "Brazilians" as "Japanese" suggested that Nikkei were simultaneously Brazilian and foreign. There was much less agreement on the meaning of "everyone else's Japanese." Some students thought this was a comparison to other Latin American Nikkei, notably those in Peru and Paraguay. Others thought it meant "Japanese" from Japan. But what made "our Japanese" "better" or "more creative" than everyone else's? Here the answers from my students were consistent—Japanese (from Japan) were techno-nerd automatons, and Japanese-Bolivians and Japanese-Peruvians were "Indianized." Japanese (from Brazil), however, kept their hard-working Japanese side and added to it a creative Brazilian side. For my students the only thing odd about the advertisement was that we were discussing it in class. Japan was so deeply embedded in Brazil that it required no attention.

1.

Brazil's Japan

Film and the Space of Ethnicity, 1960–1970

Prior to 1960, Nikkei did not appear in many Brazilian movies. Yet as they became increasingly visible in São Paulo's urban landscape, this changed. In the sixties, a generation of Japanese-Brazilians began to seek more mainstream outlets for their artistic impulses, just as non-Nikkei filmmakers became enthralled by the countless Japanese films shown in São Paulo, from samurai epics to art films to soft-core pink movies (*pinku eiga*).[1] These films reinforced a strong imaginary of Japan which was made more volatile by the city's large population of Japanese-Brazilians.[2]

Beginning about 1960 dozens of Brazilian films included Asian or Asian-Brazilian characters in story lines that used ethnicity as a critical component of national identity formation. While viewers tended to see the characters as confirming their essentialist ideas about Nikkei, actors and actresses viewed their participation as a break with the closed ethnic communities of their immigrant parents. These artists sought to be understood as "Brazilian," an idea as essentialized as that of the "Japanese" identity that they struggled against.

Brazilian films that included Nikkei characters varied widely in style and theme. Some, like Walter Hugo Khouri's *Noite Vazia* (*Empty Night*, 1964) and Tizuka Yamasaki's *Gaijin: Os Caminhos da Liberdade* (*Gaijin: The Roads to Free-*

dom, 1980) competed at the Cannes Film Festival. Others, like Carlos Reichenbach's *O Império do Desejo* (*The Empire of Desire*, 1980), had limited international exposure but were renowned in Brazil.[3] Still others were part of a popular erotic genre, including *Reformatório das Depravadas* (*Depraved Girl's Reform School*, 1978), *Ninfas Diabólicas* (*Diabolical Nymphets*, 1978), and *O Bem Dotado: O Homem de Itu* (*Well Endowed: The Man from Itu*, 1979). A number of documentaries explored issues of acculturation in the Nikkei community.

My goal in this chapter and the next is to use motion pictures—the stories, the images, the publicity, the characters, the actors and actresses, and the filmmakers—and the public discussions about them, to examine how ethnicity related to changing notions of nation in São Paulo. Films both promoted and reflected a new sense of São Paulo as a uniquely "Japanese" city and are examples of the "identities in motion" concept explored by Daniel Linger in his anthropological work on Brazilians in Japan and by Peter X. Feng, a scholar of Asian-American film in the United States. For Feng, "The continual repetition of history by cinema reveals anxiety about historical truth: that is, history must be continually repeated so as to persuade us to the legitimacy of the status quo, but the continued repetition suggests that history is actually a construction that can be contested."[4] In the city of São Paulo, I propose, identities did not just repeat and move, they simultaneously sprinted and ponderously ran the marathon. Nikkei identities as imagined by the majority and as practiced by the minority were filled with the oppositions of Brazilianness and foreignness. Characters were iconic and written to be "pure Japanese" even while the actors and actress imagined themselves as representing "pure Brazilians." Thus the artists' statements to me about their intent were often at variance with the films' apparent themes. Japanese-Brazilian characters or themes reaffirmed and challenged identities just as new questions about the nation emerged during Brazil's dictatorship and clashed with equally vibrant concerns resulting from generational change among Nikkei.

The six very different films that I examine represent a variety of genres and chronological moments. Two were released in 1964, the first year of the dictatorship, while the others appeared in the late seventies and early eighties, as the military regime began its "abertura" or political opening. One is a classic art film, one is a popular comedy starring a beloved Brazilian comic actor, and one is a well-known and highly regarded "ethnic film" that continues to have an impact on how Nikkei are seen and how they see themselves. Two others are in the erotic category and use sexual stereotypes to focus on ethnicity.

In spite of the stylistic and thematic differences, these films are easy to link. All show the tension between the traditional notion of São Paulo as a melting pot and the increasing assertions of ethnic pluralism that began in the 1960s. As the children and grandchildren of Japanese immigrants became a familiar part of the human landscape, Nikkei characters were normalized. These images were reinforced in other areas of visual culture such as advertising and *telenovelas* (television soap operas). Portrayals of São Paulo often included Nikkei and were broadcast throughout Brazil. *O Grito* (*The Scream*), shown on the Globo television network in 1975 and 1976, included fashion model and cover girl Midori Tange, who also appeared in a number of other widely watched telenovelas. Harumi Ishihara, another model, appeared in *Salário Mínimo* (*Minimum Wage*, 1979). Perhaps the most prominent roles for Nikkei were in the Bandeirantes network soap opera *Os Imigrantes* (*The Immigrants*, 1981), which ran for 333 episodes and, not surprisingly, had an entire story line about Japanese immigrants and their children.[5]

During the sixties and seventies Nikkei also became an important trope in cinematic visions of São Paulo. Actresses like Tange, who played good girls in small parts on television, got the chance to play bad girls in bigger parts in films like *Belinda dos Orixás na Praia dos Desejos* (*Belinda dos Orixás on Desire Beach*, 1979) and *Desejo Violento* (*Violent Desire*, 1978). Célia Watanabe went from a model on whom a viewer's gaze briefly fell in print advertisements to an actress whose every movement was explored in film.

Films including Japanese-Brazilian characters brought the Discontented Diaspora to the surface. Filmmakers were surprised that Nikkei actors and actresses did not know how to "act Japanese." The players were unhappy with characters that were insufficiently "Brazilian." Non-Nikkei Brazilian filmmakers looked to Japanese film for inspiration and began to link Japanese art (from Japan) with their own Brazilian art that included "Japanese" (from São Paulo). "Japan in Japan" became "Japan in Brazil" as homages to Japanese cinema were contextualized by many directors' experiences with Brazilians whom they often considered to be authentic Japanese. By the mid-1970s Nikkei had become a comfortable and regular part of São Paulo's cinematic landscape.

Portrayals of Japanese-Brazilians were not simply consumed by the majority. Nikkei performers were deeply engaged in film and, in many cases, so was the Nikkei viewing public. Film created a forum for militant debate of the disjunction between Nikkei and non-Nikkei interpretations of identity. This was especially the case with female roles. Reviewers tended to see Japanese-Brazilian women as uniquely beautiful and sexy. Viewers wondered how the images of bad girls on screen were related to those of good girls in real life. Actresses and actors saw their participation, especially in sexual scenes, as part of a battle against stereotypes. The generation born in Brazil and educated in the city of São Paulo rejected an internal ethnic community insistence on chaste "non-Brazilian" sexual attitudes. Nikkei community leaders publicly hailed the entertainers as ethnic heroes who were winning a fight against discriminatory majority attitudes that had previously kept Japanese-Brazilians out of the mainstream media.[6]

Brazilian films portrayed a particularly potent Japanese sexuality of "competing and sometimes contradictory sexual stereotypes based on nationality."[7] Directors and screenwriters constructed Brazilian Nikkei men as "Oriental" and sexless while portraying Japanese-Brazilian women as "Oriental" and especially available and kinky. Such images had circulated in elite circles throughout the Americas prior to the arrival of the first Japanese immigrants in Brazil in 1908. But Japan's post–World War II reconstruction as a technological leader, and global changes in both forms and speed of information transfer, meant that by the sixties new kinds of transnational ideas about "the Orient" were strongly felt in Brazil. São Paulo became a South American location of what Steven Heine calls "the butterfly syndrome," his term for the many films made in the United States in the fifties and sixties that dealt with Americans in Asia, often focusing on "love affairs between American men and Asian women, usually Japanese, who were alternately put on a pedestal and scorned."[8] Brazilian filmmakers, like the public more broadly, accepted the idea that "Japan" was in "Brazil," and thus São Paulo was portrayed as both a Brazilian and a Japanese city. While American men traveled for love to an Asia an ocean away, São Paulo's men traveled to an Asia just across town.

A sharp division of gender portrayals meant that the few Japanese-Brazilian male roles focused on samurai-like individuals for whom honor, and not sexual activity, was paramount. Yet most portrayals were of women. A global fetishizing of Asian women and a concern that "Brazilian" women no longer played conventional sexual or homemaking roles led some men in São Paulo to imagine that the hundreds of thousands of Nikkei women in the city would be geisha-like in their attitudes. Beginning in the sixties, magazines frequently contained articles in which "Brazilian" men expressed their desires for Nikkei women.[9]

Portrayals of Japanese-Brazilian women often combined the two classic types that Renee Tajima identifies as oppositional in U.S.-made films, the Lotus Blossom Baby (China doll and geisha girl) and the Dragon Lady (prostitute). Japanese-Brazilian female characters were "passive figures who exist to serve men—as love interests for white men" even as their hidden sexual aggressiveness separated them from the open sexual boredom of many Brazilian female characters.[10] The model and actress Harumi Ishihara complained that "the cinema portrays an image of the stereotypical Japanese woman for people, who can only accept her in this way."[11] Actress (and now university professor) Misaki Tanaka was born in Japan and moved to Brazil as a child. She played many "geisha" roles and told me in language more vehement than Ishihara's that "the label that the Brazilian, the Occidental, places on a Japanese woman is that she is submissive. . . . stick a kimono on and you are Japanese . . . and men have the idea that Japanese women will do anything for you, different from a 'Brazilian' woman, whom you have to please."[12]

IDENTITY, CINEMA, AND SPACE

São Paulo's filmmakers and film critics (often the same people) spent a great deal of time watching Japanese films in the neighborhood of Liberdade, São Paulo's "Japantown." In the sixties and seventies Liberdade was home to five Japanese-language movie houses. They served a moviegoing public that developed in rural areas in the twenties and thirties, when Japanese films were shown on mobile projectors that traveled to the plantations where immigrants labored. The Nippaku Cinema-sha (Nipo-Brazilian Cinema Corporation) was founded in the small city of Bauru (state of São Paulo) in 1929 to bring films to rural areas, but by the mid-thirties it had moved its base to São Paulo to serve the growing Japanese population in the city. By the end of the decade a number of other distributors made Japanese films a regular part of São Paulo's cultural landscape, including to broad Brazilian audiences in downtown cinemas.[13]

In 1938, just as Japanese films became more widely distributed, a major shift in national cultural policy, called the *brasilidade* (Brazilianization) campaign, began as dictator Getúlio Vargas succumbed to the political pressure of an increasingly vocal nativist elite. Legislation sought to prevent foreign populations from concentrating in residential communities, to force schools to teach "Brazilian" topics in Portuguese, and to dismantle foreign cultural outlets, including newspapers and film showings.[14] The brasilidade campaign reached its height when Brazil entered World War II as an Ally in 1942, and Japanese immigrants and their Brazilian children became targets of discrimination.[15]

Brazil's "victory" for democracy in World War II helped to topple the undemocratic Vargas regime, and by 1946 the censorship laws had been removed. Japanese film returned in force and by 1950 six different distributors operated in the city of São Paulo. Nikkei traveled to Liberdade to see new releases from Japan, including the Kurosawa tour de force *Rashômon* (1950), which was first presented in a mainstream São Paulo cinema in 1952, attracting viewers from many backgrounds. The Toho Company, Shochiku Films, the Toei Company, and Nikkatsu, Japan's principal film producers and distributors, made Brazil a regular part of their distribution networks in 1958, 1959, 1960, and 1962, respectively. Together they brought thousands of films to São Paulo and sponsored film festivals that featured appearances by Japanese stars.[16]

By the end of the 1950s, Liberdade was a location of great cinematic excitement. Viewers flocked to five different cinemas (each linked to a specific distributor), totaling about four thousand seats, to see films soon after their release in Japan. By 1962 Japanese movies were seen in many São Paulo neighborhoods, and Japanese film festivals sold out at the São Paulo Museum of Art (Museu de Arte de São Paulo, MASP) and at the University of São Paulo cinema.[17] Lines of fans at the mainstream Cine República, Cine Coral, and Cine Esplanada kept favorably reviewed films like Heinosule Gosho's *Corvo Amarelo* (*Kaachan kekkon shiroyo*, 1962) and less critically acclaimed ones like Hideo Gosha's *Espada do Mal* (*Kedamono no ken*, English title: *Sword of the Beast*, 1965) running for months.[18]

In the mid-fifties, a group of non-Nikkei cinephiles began attending showings in Liberdade, often watching the Japanese films without subtitles. One, Ermetes Ciocheti, became an assistant to Walter Hugo Khouri, whose portrayals of Nikkei I will discuss below. In 1963 he and his colleagues appear to have written a study on Japanese film. In the early 1960s critics like Rubem Biáfora and Alfredo Sternheim (both directors as well) began writing about Japanese cinema in *O Estado de S. Paulo*, and Jairo Ferreira did the same for the *Folha de S. Paulo*. Ferreira also published longer essays on Japanese, Brazilian, and international films in the Portuguese-language section of the primarily Japanese-language *São Paulo Shimbun*, which became required reading for Paulistanos interested in film.[19] Biáfora, whose film *O Quarto* (*The Bedroom*, 1968) was highly influenced by Japanese cinema, always "dedicated a few lines to Japanese cinema in his [weekly] column on new releases," and the non-Japanese-speaking audience grew quickly.[20] Sternheim remembers a call from Toho Film's São Paulo manager thanking him for writing "enthusiastically" about Tomu Uchida's *Daibosatsu tôge* (*Daibosatsu*

Pass, 1957 and 1959), released in Brazil as *Espada Diabólica* (*Diabolical Sword*). According to Toho's research, Sternheim's lively reviews in *O Estado de S. Paulo* led to screenings that were "filled with non-Japanese." Sternheim remembers going to the fourteen-hundred-seat Niterói Cinema in Liberdade, where he was amazed to "see the whites, the pale faces, the *white men* [as he called them laughingly in the interview, using the English words] going into that movie house in the Japanese neighborhood."[21]

Japanese films screened in São Paulo were only one component of a visual diaspora that included Japanese films using Brazil as a backdrop. *Rio no wakadaishô* (*Young Guy in Rio*, 1968, dir. Katsumi Iwauchi), was one of many "Young Guy" movies made in the 1960s and 1970s. The "Young Guy" was an Elvis Presley–like character whom many Japanese viewers may have associated with the Brazilian pop idol Roberto Carlos, at the time well known in Japan, where he toured and appeared on television. In *Rio no wakadaishô* the "Young Guy" worked for a shipbuilder in the firm's Rio office. The film's opening in 350 Japanese cinemas in 1968 delighted Brazilian diplomats, who had invested much energy in convincing Toho Films to finance Japanese/Brazilian coproductions.[22] That same year James Bond girl Akiko Wakabayashi (from *You Only Live Twice*, 1967, dir. Lewis Gilbert, a film also widely distributed in Brazil and Japan) starred in the action drama *Sekido o kakeru otoko* (*Diamonds of the Andes*, 1968, dir. Buichi Saito). Filmed on location in Rio de Janeiro in spite of the Andean title, *Sekido o kakeru otoko* was made with the support of the Brazilian Embassy in Tokyo.[23] These films helped to stimulate audiences for Brazilian movies in Japan. The work of director Glauber Rocha was particularly popular and formed part of the canon created by the Art Theatre Guild of Japan, a group credited with "a vital role in the creation of a new consciousness of film history in Japan."[24] The president of Shochiku Films was even honored in São Paulo by the Union of Brazilian Film Producers in 1968 for importing Brazilian films into Japan.[25]

NIKKEI COME TO THE SCREEN

It was in a broad local and international context that Walter Hugo Khouri (1929–2003) made *Noite Vazia* (1964), what many critics considered "the first great Brazilian film."[26] It won every major prize in Brazil in 1964 and 1965, and in 1968 *Filme Cultura*, the journal of Brazil's National Cinema Institute (Instituto Nacional do Cinema, INC), chose *Noite Vazia* as one of the country's ten most important films.[27] *Noite Vazia* launched the careers of numerous stars, and its open portrayals of normative and nonnormative sexuality provoked heated debates. *Noite Vazia* was briefly banned following the military coup of 31 March 1964 for "contributing nothing to the betterment of culture and the morals of the people because of its negative message created by its exploration of sex."[28] Even so, the film competed at the Cannes Film Festival. It did not win a prize since, according to one scholar, the president of the jury, Olivia de Havilland (who had played Melanie, Scarlet O'Hara's best friend in *Gone with the Wind*, 1939), disapproved of the lesbian scenes between stars Odete Lara and Norma Benguell.[29]

Noite Vazia opened in São Paulo in September 1964, during the same week as three Japanese films (and four U.S., two Italian, one English, and a number of multicountry productions).[30] The plot was similar to a number of Khouri's "intimist existential-artsy films . . . where neurotic males exorcise their erotic obsessions," often with Japanese-Brazilian women.[31] Khouri's synopsis of the film was as follows:

> Luís, a bored millionaire playboy. Not content with his family's fortune, [he] goes out most nights with a friend, the tormented Nelson, looking for pleasure and excitement. After visiting a number of bars and clubs where they meet the kinds of people typically found in big city nightlife, they go with two prostitutes they pick up to the millionaire's apartment. The scene promises a wild time, fueled by the search for pleasure at any cost. However, the temperaments of the group clash and the millionaire and one of the women end up torturing each other, revealing their weaknesses and manias. The other couple catches a glimpse of the possibility of pure and authentic love. With daybreak, the tedium and sense of frustration return. The four accept their respective destinies, and that night, full of derring-do but empty, changes nothing in their lives.[32]

Noite Vazia included a long scene in a Japanese restaurant in Liberdade (it was actually filmed in Jabaquara, another neighborhood where many Japanese-Brazilians lived).[33] Khouri had spent a great deal of time in Liberdade and represented himself as a scholar of "Japanese literature, iconography, and philosophy." He connected the size of São Paulo's Nikkei population with his absorption of "much from Japanese cinema and the intimacy of its masters."[34] For Khouri, watching Japanese films in Liberdade, surrounded by Nikkei, was not like watching the same films in downtown movie theaters. He believed himself to be in a kind of Japan and saw Nikkei as a local means of Brazilianizing his global influences. In Liberdade he realized that Japanese films with themes like sex or violence could be interpreted in a Brazilian way.

The "Japanese" scene begins in "Brazilian" São Paulo when Luís (played by Mário Benvenutti) and Nelson (played by Gabriele Tinti) go to a nightclub. There they witness a friend of Luís's parents watching her own husband passionately kissing a young girl. Their titillation increases when they see a beautiful woman sitting alone, but as they consider approaching her, an older man arrives. Nelson miserably comments that "one who is different always has an owner," increasing the pair's desire to "own" something "different." The viewer is surprised by a melodic transition as swing becomes traditional Japanese music. The aural shift is accompanied by a visual one: a restaurant sign in Japanese jerks into a close-up of a grinning fat Buddha. Luis's desire to "own difference" cannot take place in Brazilian São Paulo (represented by the nightclub) but it can in Japanese São Paulo (represented by the restaurant in Liberdade).

Inside the restaurant Luís and Nelson sit down on *tatami* (traditional Japanese flooring made of woven straw). The kimonoed Célia Watanabe, playing a character called only "Geisha," brings appetizers and sake, which she pours with a wicked grin. This is no ordinary waitress, and the dual image of Nikkei women, as sexually voracious yet "servile" (the word used by *Noite Vazia*'s assistant director, Alfredo Sternheim) is clear.[35] As the two men gaze at Watanabe lustfully, the following conversation takes place:

> *Geisha:* The food is coming.
> Luís grabs her hand and starts rubbing it, but she pulls away.
> *Luís:* Don't be like that, come here.
> *Geisha:* No!
> *Luís:* Don't you want to go out with us tonight?
> *Geisha:* I can't.
> *Luís:* But didn't you already go out with Gastão?
> *Geisha:* Not today.
> *Luís:* And you also slept with him.
> *Nelson:* Stop this Luís, don't be like this.
> *Luís:* I will double what Gastão gave you. And you will like it a lot. He says that you are an expert, in certain things that I never saw. You can ask for as much as you want, my dear.

Suddenly Nico (played by Ricardo Rivas), an older man and obviously drunk, walks into the restaurant with two high-priced prostitutes; Regina (played by Odete Lara) and Mara (played by Norma Benguell, considered by many the "Brigitte Bardot of Brazil"). Nico tells the two women that "if you don't like the [Japanese] food, you don't need to complain. We can eat a pizza." Regina responds, "You already knew that we would not like it here," but Nico insists, "[You said] we had to go to a new place. Here we are. New." As Geisha serves the trio the camera focuses on Nico's face. He has the same look of lust as the two younger men when Geisha appeared.

When Nico introduces the two women to Luís, he responds with what appears to be a non sequitur: that he came to the restaurant to "eat raw fish." The scene ends with Nico passed out drunk, leaving Luís and Nelson with Regina and Mara for the rest of the film. Yet there is a visual epilogue—a shot of a low table in the foreground with Geisha's bowed head behind it. A hand throws a wad of bills on the table and then starts to caress Geisha's head and attempts to push it up and down—the camera pulls back and we see that it is Luís's hand. Geisha says, "Sayonara," and Luís responds, "I will be back, my dear."

The sequence of this scene in the narrative arc, in the middle of the film, is meant to move viewers from the general angst of the characters into a space of individual relations. This transition helps to direct the last portion of *Noite Vazia*, where the relationships between Luís/Nelson and Regina/Mara are the focus. Moving from "Brazil" to "Japan" contrasts the idea of a disorderly and mixed up New World, where anything can happen (a woman can watch her husband with another woman in public), with a pure and highly stratified Old World, where the rules are so absolute that even servile gestures are predetermined.

Noite Vazia reminds viewers of the irony of Brazil's national motto, "order and progress," when the country seems to have neither. Liberdade represents a wistful, and unrealizable, desire for the absolute hierarchies of gender, ethnicity, and class. As the protagonists move from the modernity of the Brazilian club into Liberdade's world of tradition, the viewer sees mess versus order, loud versus quiet, and modern women like Regina and Mara (for whom sex is a negotiated commodity) versus traditional women like Geisha (for whom sex should be a pleasurable duty, even if for pay). Relations with the two "Brazilian" prostitutes include fancy meals and extended conversations, but this is not the case with Geisha, who Luís wrongly assumes will sleep with him for enjoyment.

Khouri, a former philosophy student and newspaper film reviewer, directed films that were often filled with strong women and miserable men. Yet in Liberdade the roles were reversed—Luís and Nelson look at Geisha lustfully, without the trepidation they feel around modern "Brazilian" women. This helps to explain the seemingly nonsensical conversation about food. For example, when Luís comments that he has gone to the restaurant "to eat raw fish," the script is playing on the word *comer* (Brazilian slang for "to fuck"). If "eating" is a metaphor for sex, "raw fish" and "pizza" become metaphors for two of São Paulo's largest immigrant descent groups, Japanese and Italians. The two choices, exotic raw fish and comfortable pizza, are easily available.[36] The contrast also symbolizes ideas about ethnicity in São Paulo, since sushi is raw and segmented while pizza is a cooked mixture of ingredients which lose much of their individuality in the process. Indeed, Paulistanos often claim that their pizza is better than that in Italy because it characterizes a culinary *mestiçagem*, while their sushi is especially delicious because it remains authentically and purely Japanese.[37]

The end of the scene, when Luís pushes down Geisha's head in a simulation of fellatio, was an unusual representation in early 1960s Brazilian film. For Khouri this adventurous, yet subservient sexuality was possible only in a Japanese space and Luís and Nelson only consummate their more equal relationships with Regina and Mara by leaving the public Japanese space for a private Brazilian one, a fancy apartment. The film suggests that while Regina and Mara were initially interested in sex for cash, the presumed availability of Geisha makes them patriotically and ethnically jealous. Thus they reject a paying client (Nico) for a less explicitly cash-based relationship with Luís and Nelson. Perhaps they are seeking to save Brazilian men from the corruption of tradition by bringing them into modern sexual relationships?

Alfredo Sternheim, Khouri's assistant on *Noite Vazia* and later a director in his own right, remembers that Khouri's use of Japanese-Brazilians was simultaneously a radical multicultural departure and "filled with prejudice [since directors like Khouri] thought that the Nisei or Sansei could only be treated in film as a geisha, and not as a normal woman with a free or not free sexual life, married or unmarried." Misaki Tanaka, who played one of the geishas in Khouri's *O Prisioneiro do Sexo* (The Prisoner of Sex, 1978), was convinced that Khouri and others who used Japanese-Brazilian characters represented "the desire of the public, of the Brazilian man, to want to have [sexually] at least once in his life . . . a Japanese girlfriend."[38]

Sternheim agreed with Tanaka's interpretation, pointing out that in *Noite Vazia* Geisha was "explored for her Oriental side," a difference, he noted, from his own erotic film *Borboletas e Garanhões* (Butterflies and Studs, 1985), which starred Sandra Midori as "categorically a Brazilian of Oriental origin."[39] Sternheim compared the Brazilianness of the characters in the two films directly to that of the actresses, as if the fiction of the roles and the reality of the actresses were indistinguishable. "I wanted to accentuate [Midori's] fun side because Sandra is a happy person. I wrote the part thinking of her. But Célia [Watanabe] was a very closed person, very rigid and very Oriental. Totally a super Oriental posture. I don't think she had a single Western gesture." Watanabe's scene in *Noite Vazia* remained strong in Sternheim's memory because it had taken far longer to film than anyone had imagined. While Khouri anticipated that Watanabe would play a geisha "naturally," the filming disclosed just the opposite.

Sternheim's focus on the difference between *Noite Vazia* and *Borboletas and Garanhões* should not obscure similarities: both involved encounters in Japanese restaurants in Liberdade in which Euro-Brazilian men and Japanese-Brazilian women explored the possibility of explicit sex. While the fantasy of "having" a Japanese woman was not fulfilled in *Noite Vazia*, it was in *Borboletas and Garanhões*. In that film, the Euro-Brazilian character left his rich, uptight Euro-Brazilian fiancée to find true love and explicit sexual fulfillment with the Japanese-Brazilian Midori.[40]

The portrayals of Japanese-Brazilian sexuality in Khouri's films (and in Sternheim's) reflected widespread São Paulo stereotypes. Perhaps this familiarity explains why I have never found a single academic comment on the role of Japanese-Brazilian characters in Khouri films, whether the appearances are brief, such as in *Corpo Ardente* (*Burning Body*, 1966), where Celso Akira plays a painter of abstract art named Shirakawa and Célia Watanabe is his modern but unspeaking wife, or extended, such as in *O Prisioneiro do Sexo*, about an angst-filled man whose struggles with modern women lead him to Liberdade for violent sadomasochistic relationships with silent geishas played by Sueli Aoki and Misaki Tanaka.[41]

Not only scholars ignored the ethnic images of *Noite Vazia*. Only two of hundreds of newspaper reviews and critiques of the film that I read mentioned the scene in Liberdade, and the longer of the two simply describes "a brief dialogue between Célia Watanabe, Mário Benvenutti, and Gabriele Tinti in Japanese surroundings where the first plays a 'geisha' requested by Mário."[42] A typical article was from Rio de Janeiro's *Diário de Notícias*, which critiqued *Noite Vazia* as "cinema without genuine ethical convictions" and lamented that its brief censure by the military regime gave it an undeserved moral authority. While the review makes no mention of the scene in Liberdade, it sees that "Japanese" space as essential; a photograph of Watanabe as Geisha occupied an entire column in the middle of a five-column report. Many other newspapers used the same photograph, almost always without explanatory caption. One magazine used a photograph four times larger than the accompanying thirty-five word explanation of *Noite Vazia*'s removal from the censored list.[43]

Why would visual imagery in the press coverage of *Noite Vazia* focus on a role ignored in the textual discussion? Certainly the director and producer believed that a photograph implying an exotic sexual liaison would bring an audience to theaters. The public's expectation of, and comfort with, such a relationship is emphasized by the fact that many Brazilian newspapers rejected as too controversial a promotional still suggesting the lesbian encounter between Regina and Mara.[44]

Noite Vazia, in its self-promotion and in the way critics, reviewers, and editors chose to see it, used a visual imagery that linked Brazil to Japan. Japanese(-Brazilian) women were to be consumed visually and physically but not spoken of. Such ideas brought Brazil and Japan into a challenging conversation. Brazilian diplomats in Japan, for example, complained that instead of making "sexual films (like) *Noite Vazia*," filmmakers should "raise the value of the Brazilian man against the (foreign) invader" in the manner of Japanese propaganda films that "raised morale" and were critical to the strength of modern Japan.[45] For Khouri and others, Japan and the films that emerged from it inspired a new way of being Brazilian, allowing challenges to the changes taking place in Brazilian gender relations. As Misaki Tanaka told me, male fans could watch Japanese-Brazilian women on screen and easily assume that in real life "I am also submissive."[46]

It would be a mistake to interpret São Paulo's Japan as linked only to sexuality. Sternheim remembered the adventure of going to Liberdade with Khouri: "The way that the Japanese in Brazil lived in those days fascinated me. And Khouri also had this fascination. We would go drink in a Japanese bar, not a common bar, no, but those bars that they had in Liberdade, with sake and stuff like that."[47] Sternheim also implied that his own minority status was crucial to his experience since it allowed him to be both an insider and an outsider in Liberdade. In our conversation he contextualized his interest in Japan and Japanese-Brazilians by saying that "I am Brazilian, the son of German and Moroccan Jews who came to Brazil."[48]

Reviews of *Noite Vazia* in newspapers and magazines constantly reminded readers of the influence of Japan on Brazilian cinema.[49] The critiques often compared Khouri to directors like Masanori Kakei, Yasuki Chiba, and Yoshishige Yoshida, whose films were shown in São Paulo.[50] A review in the *Jornal do Comércio* was placed next to an advertisement for Toshiro Mifune's *Samurai Pirate*.[51] *Última Hora* reported that Valdir Ercolani, who created the titles for *Noite Vazia*, was "practically assaulted by a mob of fans" when he disembarked at Tokyo airport prior to giving a lecture.[52] The *Diário de São Paulo* complained that Brazil was not ready for a film like *Noite Vazia* but that Japan (like the United States and Europe) was.[53] For critics, Célia Watanabe, the actress who played Geisha, was the physical embodiment of Japan in São Paulo. She had started her career as a model and then was contracted by Vera Cruz Studios because "the beautiful, thin *japonesinha* with the slanty eyes and smooth talk could shake up young people."[54] Perhaps this explains why Ignácio de Loyola, the film critic of *Última Hora*, commented on Watanabe's iconic beauty as more that of a fashion model than that of an actress. Jairo Ferreira's review of *As Cariocas* gave the impression that Watanabe was a star of the film although she was not.[55]

Alfredo Sternheim, who continues to be prominent in São Paulo's movie scene, was an important figure in our story. He explored ideas of Japanese-Brazilian ethnicity as an assistant director to Khouri in the sixties and in his 1980s pornographic films. Between the two genres he wrote and produced the documentary *Isei, Nisei, Sansei* (1970).[56]

Sternheim's memory of how he conceived the documentary provides insight into the ways Japanese culture was represented in São Paulo and the circular relationship between majority and minority ideas of ethnicity and nation. In 1969, Sternheim was asked to produce a cultural documentary for a competition funded by the São Paulo state government. He thought of Japanese immigration as a theme because of his love of the Japanese New Wave films that he saw in Liberdade where he "got to know the Japanese colony."[57]

Isei, Nisei, Sansei takes the position that generational change between immigrants and their children is more than a modification of national identity in a sentimental or psychological sense. Indeed, *INS* explains how generational shifts modified everything from language to religion to sex to work. For example, the film posits that the Issei (immigrant) generation was agricultural and that the Nisei (second generation, first born in Brazil) generation was technological, both areas seen as particularly "Japanese." Yet the Sansei (third generation—children of Brazilian parents and Japanese grandparents) generation was able to free itself from ethnically determined labor and become Brazilian, expanding work vistas, especially in the liberal professions. The images of kimonoed farm workers and hipster youths remind viewers of the change, as does the straightforward narration. The music, which shifts from traditional Japanese to jazz, is an aural reminder of this theme. The immigrant generation is exoticized, and the opening shot, of an elderly kimonoed gentleman in a garden, includes a narration that suggests the discovery of a wild and unknown animal—"This is an Issei—a Japanese immigrant." The urbanization and modernity of Nikkei is represented via shots of an auto mechanic, a secretary working an adding machine in a large office, and a pharmacist; "Nisei have a relation with the new society (in the city) and stop being Japanese."

In Isei, Nisei, Sansei Japanese are transformed into Brazilians, and Brazilians are changed as well. Much attention is paid to Japanese-language classes for "all races" and "Oriental" sports like judo and baseball that are "assimilated by Brazilians." The national-identity punch line is that São Paulo "became a new color" via cultural and biological exchange. While this makes the film different from many cinematic portrayals of Japanese-Brazilians, the documentary does essentialize sexuality. In one scene a beautiful young Nikkei woman bounces down the steps of a Catholic church to meet her eager Euro-Brazilian boyfriend. Another scene portrays the "nightlife and diversions" of Liberdade's restaurants as two kimonoed women serve a Euro-Brazilian man. For an instant we get a glimpse of a non-Nikkei woman, presumably the man's date. But the camera pays her fleeting attention since his pleasure comes from the two geishas—one prepares his sukiyaki as the other kneels by his side and pours his drinks.

COMEDY IN THE COUNTRYSIDE: JAPANESE-BRAZILIANS AS THE BEDROCK OF BRAZILIAN CIVILIZATION

If Noite Vazia and Isei, Nisei, Sansei represented Nikkei for their sexuality, the beloved popular actor Amácio Mazzaropi's rural popular comedy Meu Japão Brasileiro (My Brazilian Japan, 1965, dir. Glauco Mirko Laurelli), focused on Nikkei as rural, hard-working, and family-oriented (figs. 15 and 16).[58] Mazzaropi (1912–81) began his career as a radio performer in São Paulo and in 1950 moved his popular live program to television.[59] In 1952 he made his first film for the Vera Cruz studios and went on to make more than thirty movies that mixed drama and comedy. Mazzaropi produced all his own films after 1958, often writing and directing them as well. Four of his comedies were among the thirty-five Brazilian films with the highest grosses between 1970 and 1984.[60] Nikkei viewers were part of his public and he believed Meu Japão Brasileiro would "pay homage to a public that is increasingly esteeming [Mazzaropi] films."[61]

Meu Japão Brasileiro, completed in 1964 and released in early 1965, was written and produced by Mazzaropi and photographed by Rudolf Icsey, a Hungarian immigrant who was also director of photography for Noite Vazia and a number of other Walter Hugo Khouri films. The title of the film plays on "Brazil's unofficial national anthem," Ari Barroso's Aquarella do Brasil,

FIGURE 15. Promotional poster, *Meu Japão Brasileiro*, PAM Filmes, color, Brasil, 1964. Photo courtesy and used by permission of Museu Mazzaropi/Instituto Mazzaropi (Taubaté, Brazil)

FIGURE 16. Still from *Meu Japão Brasileiro*, PAM Filmes, color, Brasil, 1964.
Photo courtesy and used by permission of Museu Mazzaropi/Instituto
Mazzaropi (Taubaté, Brazil)

which begins with the words "Brasil! Meu Brasil brasileiro" (Brazil, my Brazilian Brazil).[62] Mazzaropi's title thus suggests that "Japan" had replaced "Brazil" as the center of national identity. The film's main character, "Fofuca" (played by Mazzaropi), lives in rural São Paulo state among Japanese immigrants and their Brazilian children. After suffering along with his fellow farmers at the hands of Leão, the local middleman, Fofuca (the word sounds like *fofoca*, or gossip) organizes the Nikkei farmers into a cooperative to fight against the exploitation. This approach, as Stephanie Dennison and Lisa Shaw have explained, was common in Mazzaropi's films, where "cultures familiar to the audience" generated characters that were "always portrayed as an integral part of a special community."[63]

Meu Japão Brasileiro, though a commercial success, is neglected by most scholars of Mazzaropi's work.[64] Like *Noite Vazia*, it starred Célia Watanabe as a character with no personal name; for Khouri she was "Geisha" and for Mazzaropi she was "Nissei." The difference was that while Watanabe had a small part in *Noite Vazia*, she was the young female star of *Meu Japão Brasileiro*, appearing in most scenes and singing one of the songs. Khouri had contrasted modern São Paulo and traditional Liberdade to imply that there were no Japanese-Brazilians, only Japanese in Brazil and Brazilians who desire them. Mazzaropi, however, believed miscegenation would shift an oppressed and backward "Brazilian" rurality into a modern "Japanese" one. The opening of *Meu Japão Brasileiro* makes this clear: a group of Nikkei children walk together up a hill from their homes below while a group of "Brazilian" children walk together down the hill from their homes above. They meet in a space where they learn about the future, the "Escola Rural Mista" (Rural Mixed School). Mixing is not only for little children: the primary love story is an interracial one, and Fofuca manages the local "Nipo-Brasil Boarding House" where he serves Japanese farmers in a kimono.

Fofuca embodies the new and better Japanized Brazil (or was it a Brazilianized Japan as the title stated?). While he speaks only Portuguese, he claims to "understand Japanese" when local farmers complain about exploitation in that language, implying that the sentiments of oppression override the specifics of language. The film's major subplot involves a prohibited romance between the oppressive middleman's son, Mário, and Nissei (Watanabe).

These heroes are contrasted with the villain, Leão. The portrayal of the exploitation of local farmers put the film in step with the military regime, which saw the oligarchic position of landowners as a challenge to its urban-industrial intentions.[65] Yet Leão is not only a class exploiter. He sees interracial relationships as an attack on racial purity. Nissei's fear after her first kiss with Mário is the opposition of his father, a twist on the stereotype that Japanese-Brazilians were a closed community. As Leão says to his son, in a Brazilianized nod to *Romeo and Juliet*, "You should not have gotten involved with that race." This ethnic and generational clash leads to the dramatic apex, when Leão uses the creation of an immigrant-led farming cooperative to rile up local Brazilian laborers, who fear "the Japanese [are] running everything." Fofuca prevents a race war by convincing everyone (but Leão) that social mixing is for the best. For Mazzaropi, the oppositions of rich/poor, powerful/weak, and Brazilian/Japanese would disappear through miscegenation.

Mazzaropi's insistence on the value of mixing does not prevent his script from showing separate ethnic realities in rural São Paulo. Throughout *Meu Japão Brasileiro* the gap between "we the Brazilians" and "you the Japanese" is clear. For example, when Fofuca and the farmers meet to discuss an alternative to selling their produce to Leão, it is a Portuguese-speaking "Japanese" (most Japanese in the film have difficulty with the local language) who

FIGURE 17. Still from *Meu Japão Brasileiro*, PAM Filmes, color,
Brasil, 1964. Photo courtesy and used by permission of Museu
Mazzaropi/Instituto Mazzaropi (Taubaté, Brazil)

suggests a cooperative. Fofuca agrees by slanting his eyes and saying, "I am
not Japanese but I almost am." His speech aimed at convincing the farmers
to join the cooperative starts with "My friends, it is a pleasure to see two
distinct races, [pause] men and women, all mixed." It is a good joke since
the audience imagines that the distinct "races" are Japanese and Brazilian,
not men and women.

Meu Japão Brasileiro argues for a glorious, hybridized future, represented by
the marriage of Mário and Nissei as the inevitable result of the childhood
interactions taking place at the "Rural Mixed School." Yet the film also
suggests the explosiveness of Japanese/Brazilian relations in the countryside. This volatility is portrayed in a scene where Nissei happily walks into
the hills to meet Mário. Instead, Leão's older son Roberto appears, falsely
claiming that Mário has rejected his "dear sister-in-law." As Nissei tries to
walk away, Roberto chases and grabs her. Nissei's screams attract the attention of a group of Japanese farmers in a nearby field and as they run to the
rescue, Nissei bites Roberto, allowing her to escape toward the safety of the
arriving farmers.

Roberto, not wanting to show himself as the aggressor, claims he was beaten up by "the Japanese" without mentioning his own actions. These lies convince his father to rile up the local population against the Japanese cooperative so that the old oppressive order can be restored. Leão does more than provoke the locals verbally. When a Japanese immigrant goes to speak to the local priest, who has blessed the marriage of Mário and Nissei, one of Leão's henchmen shoots the padre. Another of Leão's employees then grabs the immigrant as he cares for the bleeding priest and starts shouting that it was the immigrant who committed the crime.

The whole town seems to believe the fiction, and the camera moves from close-up to close-up of "Brazilians" saying "It was the Japanese" and "I saw it, it was the Japanese." "It was the Japanese" quickly becomes "Out with the Japanese," and the cooperative is attacked by an angry mob. Fofuca knows better, "I don't believe that a Japanese would do this," he says. "It's Leão's people who do this to others."

These scenes highlight deeply embedded notions of ethnicity and nation. In some ways the film was antiracist, starkly contrasting "Out with the Japanese" and "I don't believe a Japanese would do this." Yet *Meu Japão Brasileiro* rejects racism as a Brazilian cultural phenomenon. Thus the ethnic and gender violence, and broader discriminatory behavior, can be explained away by naiveté, and the mob's anger can be diminished in an instant.[66] For Mazzaropi, the fury is not real but forced on the locals by the evil Leão, who is a racist and is thus unusual and un-Brazilian. For Mazzaropi and his Brazilian audience, there is no pervasive social problem for *Meu Japão Brasileiro* to comment on.

Meu Japão Brasileiro tangled with Brazil's prevailing foundational myth of racial democracy, most associated with the writing of Gilberto Freyre (1900–1987). Freyre suggested that Brazilian culture was founded on the plantation, where a purported freedom from racial intolerance surged from the exploits of super-sexualized Portuguese men with super-sensualized nonwhite women. If *Noite Vazia* was indebted to the Freyrian view of nonwhite women, *Meu Japão Brasileiro* took a different, but equally Freyrian point of view: that Brazil was a uniquely miscegenated nation free of racism. This theme dominated the marketing of the film. Newspaper advertisements set Mazzaropi's name in faux Japanese letters along with "Japão brasileiro." "Meu" (My), however, was written in a different form, suggesting that the Brazilian Japan was Mazzaropi's and that intermixing would improve the Brazilian race. The promotional trailer lamented that the relationship between Nissei and Mário was a "prohibited romance." São Paulo audiences, witnessing a Nikkei intermarriage rate of around 40 percent, knew that interracial love would prevail. Thus *Meu Japão Brasileiro* was not really the "rebellious cry against the lack of understanding among people" that it claimed to be.[67]

Mazzaropi's intentions were not lost on critics. B. J. Duarte, writing for the *Folha de S. Paulo* opined that "*Meu Japão Brasileiro* looks sympathetically and tenderly at miscegenation in São Paulo's human territory, creating a film filled with love for the Japanese colony and its Niseis assimilated to Paulistana land and customs."[68] Gray (his only name), writing for the Santos newspaper *A Tribuna*, agreed, pointing out that the film both hailed the work ethic of Japanese and "defend[ed] miscegenation."[69]

Reviews of *Meu Japão Brasileiro* paid much more homage to Japan than did the film itself, which shows no indication of Japanese cinematic influence. A devastating, and unsigned, critique in *O Estado de S. Paulo* focused on the quality of Japanese films showing in São Paulo and complained that Mazzaropi did not have the artistic sensibilities of "Tomu Uchida, Eizo Sugawa, Mikio Naruse, Yasujiro Ozu, and Hideo Suzuki," all filmmakers well known to sophisticated Brazilian audiences. *Meu Japão Brasileiro* should have been "a more refined study of the serenity and the efficient labor of the Japanese in Brazil."[70]

Why would the review make such an unfair comparison, especially since Mazzaropi never claimed to make sophisticated films? What are the implications of comparing a Brazilian film, made with Brazilian actors about Brazil, to Japanese films, made with Japanese actors about Japan? The answer seems to be that the cultural categories of Japanese-Brazilian and Japanese were interchangeable in the minds of many reviewers. For critics, Japanese-Brazilians remained wholly Japanese, independent of their birthplace, native language, or citizenship. Even the one bright star in the film, the actress Watanabe, was noted less for her talents than for her nature, since "her beauty and peculiar ease let her escape the ridiculous, even in extremely grotesque situations."[71]

Noite Vazia; *Isei, Nisei, Sansei*; and *Meu Japão Brasileiro* fetishized Japanese-Brazilians in order to suggest that the problem with Brazil was that it was filled with (non-Japanese) Brazilians. Traditional Brazilians might be successful financially (both Luís in *Noite Vazia* and Leão in *Meu Japão Brasileiro* are well-to-do), but their individual triumphs were not earned in a legitimate way. Japanese immigrants, on the other hand, were hard workers, whether as farmers or as lovers, and thus attractive as components in Brazil's future greatness and as sexual partners. The fact that reviews of both films mentioned repeatedly the beauty of Célia Watanabe suggests the extent to which this idea was held. Years later, when director José Adalto Cardoso wanted to make the actor Polêncio into the "new Mazzaropi," he did so with a film that starred Japanese-Brazilian Misaki Tanaka in the principal female role.[72] In Nikkei, Brazilians could see a brighter future.

2.

BEAUTIFUL BODIES AND (DIS)APPEARING IDENTITIES

Contesting Images of Japanese-Brazilian Ethnicity,

1970–1980

———•———

Noite Vazia and *Meu Japão Brasileiro*, among the first films to include extended depictions of Nikkei, were released during the early years of the dictatorship. Yet as the "hard line" military assumed increasing power over the course of the sixties, filmmakers confronted new challenges and created new forums for the circulation of ideas about ethnicity and national identity. In these same years, the urban migration of the children and grandchildren of Japanese immigrants into São Paulo intensified. As Nikkei became visible in most areas of the city's labor and social life, Japanese-Brazilian identity was increasingly interrogated in film.

The sector that grew fastest in the late sixties was the erotic film industry. While many of these films had only modest artistic pretension, others, called "pornochanchada," looked to an earlier generation of light carnivalesque comedies (*chanchadas*) popular in the thirties, forties, and fifties. Many pornochanchadas emerged from São Paulo's "Boca do Lixo" ("Garbage Mouth") movement, itself heavily influenced by the light Italian sex comedies and Japanese "pink" films available on the city's movie circuit.[1] The Boca movement, named after the neighborhood where many production companies were located, was also influenced by aspects of Japanese-Brazilian culture. Some directors and producers had been reading the "national *manga*" that Minami Keizi, the son of Japanese immigrants, had been publishing since the sixties. Keizi was also the editor of *Cinema em Close-Up* (1976–77), a magazine that combined glossy photographs of pornochanchada stars with serious commentary on cinema, martial arts, and the film industry.[2] Today Keizi is a distributor and designer of Brazilian *hentai* (sexually explicit manga) and an astrologer.[3] One of his recent astrological interpretations brought back his memories of the Boca do Lixo.[4]

> Yesterday I went past Triumph Road [in the Boca do Lixo]. Sad and abandoned, the street looked more like a far-away neighborhood, in the periphery where not even the vice-mayor thinks about it. Thousands of memories passed through my head.
>
> The 1960s and 1970s. The road had glamour, an underdeveloped Hollywood. . . . Triumph Road was alive. In the Sovereign Bar [Bar Soberano] the producers, directors, actors, actresses, and extras got together to have a coffee, to eat lunch or dinner, or simply chat. It was the era of pornochanchada, when Brazil produced more than one hundred films a year. The cinema produced on Triumph Road was called Garbage Mouth cinema.
>
> Rio and São Paulo alternated as the centers of cinema. Hunger Alley [Beco da Fome] in Rio and Garbage Mouth [Boca do Lixo] in São Paulo. . . .
>
> . . . Later the cinema decayed. . . . The movie companies moved. . . . Today all that is left are the prostitutes who lived in peace with the famous folks of Brazilian cinema in the Boca do Lixo.
>
> It's garbage. . . . a lot of garbage on Triumph Road.

From their Boca do Lixo base, Brazilian filmmakers sought to emulate Japanese films just as the dictatorship began to allow, and even promote, an erotic film industry through Embrafilme, the national production and distribution organ.[5] Producers, realizing that there was a market for both Japanese films and erotic movies, even tried to fool the public into linking the two. Jairo Ferreira, whose often enthusiastic newspaper reviews legitimized films produced in the Boca, complained that the Kaneto Shindô classic *Onibaba* (1964) had been besmirched by the "sordid mind" of the owner of the Cine Coral (located in the Boca do Lixo), who advertised the Portuguese title as *Onibaba: Diabolical Sex*.[6]

By the early seventies, pornochanchadas were the most popular national cinema in terms of paid viewership, and in 1977 twenty-five of the seventy-six films made in Brazil came out of the "Boca" movement.[7] Pornochanchadas often generated more income than big-budget international films. They were a response, in part, to the censorship of politically themed films and the prohibition on foreign-made pornography.[8] Pornochanchadas also had a thematic link to more mainstream Brazilian films since they often included Japanese-Brazilian characters.

The scholarship on pornochanchada focuses on transgression: audiences viewed the short government propaganda films that by law preceded all feature films, "in sharp contrast to the chaos, individualism, the debauchery and *malandragem* (roguishness) of the pornochanchadas that often followed."[9] Audiences would heckle the propaganda films as part of the fun of watching the pornochanchadas to come, often as part of a double feature with a martial-arts film. Erotic films allowed the mainstream to contravene social norms, and major newspapers reviewed the genre in the same space as releases like *Star Wars* (1977).

Pornochanchada was ethnically transgressive since Japanese-Brazilian characters often appeared in those movies made in São Paulo. Stereotypes of Japanese-Brazilians (and everyone else) were frequent, with Nikkei characters often presented as a challenge to "Brazilian" ones. Nikkei actresses were particularly aware of the stereotypes, especially regarding sexuality. While non-Nikkei directors, writers, and viewers looked to actresses for their "Japanese" sexuality, the actresses saw their roles as proving their Brazilianness by challenging majority and minority notions of modesty. The Japanese-Brazilian imagination of normative Brazilian culture as hypersexual was no less a stereotype than the inverse image about Nikkei. Essentialized hypersexuality was thus a commonality in both Nikkei images of "Brazilians" and Brazilian images of "Japanese."

A TRUE STORY

The Museu da Imagem e do Som (Museum of Image and of Sound) in São Paulo has an excellent archive and library as well as a generous staff. When I told the librarian that my research project included an analysis of images of Nikkei actors and actresses in pornochanchada, she looked at me in surprise. "That's not possible," she said. "Japanese don't do that kind of sleaze. Maybe in their own country, but in Brazil, never."

The list of Brazilian erotic films that include Asian characters is long, but two of the best known are José Miziara's *O Bem Dotado: O Homem de Itu* (*Well-Endowed: The Man from Itu*, 1979) and Carlos Reichenbach's *O Império do Desejo* (*The Empire of Desire*, 1981). Both were box office successes when released, although the first never received critical acclaim.[10] The stars were respected artists with long careers in the mainstream.[11] Both films continue to be shown frequently on television. Carlos Reichenbach remains a vibrant voice in Brazilian cinema and popular culture. In spite of this renown, academic studies have not commented on the presence of Japanese-Brazilians in *O Bem Dotado* or *O Império do Desejo*.

The title of *O Bem Dotado: O Homem de Itu* plays on a popular Brazilian television soap opera, *O Bem Amado*, about the conflict between agrarian and urban life.[12] Like many soap operas and pornochanchadas, *O Bem Dotado* features characters from the countryside who face trials and tribulations in the big city.[13] The story revolves around the virgin Lírio, a shy (and perhaps slightly retarded) hick in his early twenties brought up by a priest in Itu, a small town about an hour by car from the city of São Paulo. Itu became a São Paulo middle-class tourist attraction in the seventies and eighties because of its oversized public objects (e.g., a giant telephone booth) and sales of *tchotkes* (huge toothbrushes and massive combs).

Lírio's relationships with women are naively chaste and filled with romantic love. But when Nair and Zilá, two rich women from São Paulo, arrive in Itu for some shopping, they discover that the town's massive attractions are not limited to manufactured items. Lírio returns to the city as Nair's gardener and boy toy, where he is pursued by women from boss to maid, from neighbors to friends. *O Bem Dotado* revolves around Lírio's sexual exploitation in and by the city and his struggle to return to his pure love in Itu. Lírio's power to resist lies in his special endowment: during the sexual act his partners, who cannot resist the size of his organ, scream, "Mamãe!" (Mommy!), so loud that the ground shakes. Following intercourse, the women are unable to walk comfortably, revealing publicly what they have done privately.

O Bem Dotado includes two Nikkei characters, a brother and sister who work in Nair's home. Kimura is humble and reserved, whether he is working as a chauffeur or as a butler. The role was played by David Yan Wei, who was born in China, migrated to the United States, where he studied theater at the University of Chicago, and then migrated yet again, this time to Brazil. Sueli Aoki (sometimes credited as Suely de Fátima Aoki) played Nice (pronounced "Nisei"), the hardworking and quiet domestic servant. Aoki was born in Brazil of a Japanese father and a non-Nikkei Brazilian mother and had worked as a model and bank secretary before becoming a movie actress.

The Nikkei brother and sister characters are quite different from the other parts written for *O Bem Dotado*. Their stylized manner and clothing implies ethnic difference and emphasizes that they, like Lírio, have been brought up in the countryside. Yet unlike Lírio, Nice and Kimura modernize the home through their efficiency, reminding us of Amácio Mazzaropi's *Meu Japão Brasileiro*. Kimura is also a comic foil, and the film toys constantly with his lack of masculinity. Nice, on the other hand, is a sex object. *O Bem Dotado*'s gender positioning fits easily into the broader trope of Asian sexuality in pornography in the Americas wickedly ridiculed by Glen Pak in the mockumentary *Asian Pride Porno*, starring Tony award–winning playwright David Henry Wang.[14]

When the well-endowed man from Itu arrives at Nair's home, it is Kimura and Nice who are most affected. The demure Nice, opposed to having sex outside of marriage because "it is a sin," becomes sexually voracious. She is the only woman Lírio seduces—in the other sexual encounters it is the women who seduce Lírio. She is also the only one who has sex with Lírio without screaming. *O Bem Dotado* suggests that the naive Lírio is more attracted to Nice, his class, sexual, and rural equal, than the rich women who are using him for his body.

CREATING AN ARCHIVE

While pornochanchadas are receiving increasing attention among scholars of Brazilian film, finding copies of these films is not easy. Many are in 35- and 16-mm reels in archives where access is limited. My breakthrough came when Alfredo Sternheim suggested the Canal X Pornography Superstore/Museum of Erotica that used to be located on São Paulo's Avenida Paulista, the city's Wall Street.

Off I went, armed with a long list of titles and technical data that Rodrigo Archangelo, a student at the University of São Paulo and intern at the Fundação Cinemateca Brasileira, generated for me. I presented the list at Canal X to blank stares—the employees at the superstore had not heard of these films. The owner fortunately came to my rescue. He brought me to a room (films at Canal X are housed in specialty rooms) for "clássicos" (classics) and told me with a laugh that I was the first person to rent one in years. He was not joking. Over the next few months, as I sat on the floor with my computer taking notes from the promotional material on the plastic boxes that covered the films, I would overhear the employees explaining to customers looking at me strangely that I was not a detective or tax agent, just a "gringo pesquisador" (foreign researcher).

I found *O Bem Dotado* quite funny, although my wife (born and raised in São Paulo) thought it was just vulgar. We agreed that the jokes in *O Bem Dotado* played on well-known São Paulo stereotypes of Japanese-Brazilians, continuing the tradition of poking fun at immigrants (notably Portuguese) found in earlier 1950s comic films.[15] The film begins, for example, with Nair and Zilá being driven by the chauffeur Kimura from São Paulo to Itu. Just as Nair comments that "he is the first Japanese driver who knows how to drive

FIGURE 18. Prerelease still from *O Bem Dotado—O Homem de Itu*, 1979.
Reprinted by permission from "Com a casa e as discriminações—
Em busca de um papel," *Arigato* 2.16 (1978)

well," Kimura almost crashes the car. This narrative and visual joke works because of a widespread stereotype that Japanese immigrants and their descendants, with their rural and agricultural backgrounds, became uniquely bad drivers after moving to the city. Kimura is feminized throughout the film. He drives, but badly. He is beaten up by Nair (figure 18). He wears a kimono (like a geisha) and cannot compete with Lírio's virility.

In spite of living in a house with so many horny women, Kimura seems primarily interested in protecting his sister's nonexistent virginity. One scene begins with him dressed in a kimono and holding a long sword, engaging in a weird "samurai ceremony." He completes his ritual and goes on the hunt for the man from Itu who has so upset the household's sexual order. The ceremony, the viewer discovers, takes place just as Lírio is seducing the demure Nice. Kimura's actions seem to make sense. He must protect his little sister and "regain my honor." But the audience soon discovers that Kimura is not angry at his sister's sexual activity. Rather Kimura's besmirched honor can only be regained by "making [Lírio's] the same size as mine" since, as he says angrily, showing his little finger to indicate the size of his penis, "I am like a piece of okra."

There is no doubt that the audience got this joke and laughed. But there were deeper ethnic implications at play. David Yan Wei, the Chinese actor who played Kimura, noted that "there exists some prejudice around the Oriental. His disposition is kind of mystical, and the Occidental sees all Orientals like this." The actor, filmmaker, and critic Jean-Claude Bernardet, today a professor of cinema studies at the University of São Paulo but in the late 1970s the film critic for Última Hora, discussed Kimura's revenge scene in O Bem Dotado in an interview with the Japanese-Brazilian magazine Arigato:

> There are opposite positions—the man from Itu who is well endowed and the Japanese butler who is not. But why did it have to be a Japanese? I get even more concerned because he is the object of the central joke of the film. Like this, it looks a bit racist, even though I cannot say such a thing from just one film. But the truth is that I, the spectator, feel this. The object of the mockery could be played by anyone, so why a Japanese?[16]

Similar ideas about ethnicity were at work in another film that included a Japanese-Brazilian actor. Kazuachi Hemmi, the son of Japanese immigrants, made his living as a professional wrestler on television and performed in a few pornochanchadas. His biggest role was in Jean Garret's Ilha do Desejo (Desire Island, 1974), playing a eunuch who is the island's bodyguard. In an interview with the magazine Cinema em Close-Up, he noted that the character was supposed to be gay and that "when I heard the public say this, I got the message. [The character] came out just exactly as the director wanted, [so] I was happy when people made fun of the character [for being homosexual]."[17]

Sueli Aoki, who played Nice, saw her role in O Bem Dotado in a broader context of Paulistana ethnic relations: "It was not that easy to do the nude scene, since I had been educated in a rigid and moralist way. As a Japanese-Brazilian actress [she described herself using the word descendente, a term used among Nikkei to distinguish between the immigrant and Brazilian-born generations], but mixed [here she used the word mestiça, which is used among Nikkei to mean a child with one "Japanese" parent—either immigrant or Nikkei—and one "Brazilian"], among the Brazilians I am Japanese and among 'descendents' I am considered Brazilian. I am discriminated against from both sides: from one when I want to get a part in a film, from the other because I am an actress."[18]

O Bem Dotado is different from most pornochanchadas in that the primary object of sexual desire is male. As film commentator Gilberto Silva Jr. points out, the poster for O Bem Dotado emphasizes the huge and naked Lírio surrounded by happy and surprised women (figure 19).[19]

While Silva is correct, he, like so many other scholars, has removed the

FIGURE 19. Poster from *O Bem Dotado—O Homem de Itu*.
Photograph by Jerry Dávila. Original in Biblioteca Jenny Klabin Segall
of the Museu Lasar Segall, São Paulo

Japanese-Brazilians from his analysis. It should be noted that the poster
highlights Kimura in the lower-left corner, where the black/white coloring
stands outs from the colorful rest. The eye is further attracted toward
Kimura's image because it is directly below the male star's name. Kimura is
poised to lop off Lírio's penis, a faithful representation of one plot in *O Bem
Dotado*. The poster was used in newspaper advertisements and placed outside of cinemas in downtown São Paulo, where ten of thousands of people
passed it every day. As pedestrians walked down Avenida São João, or as they
read mainstream newspapers, they would have seen *O Bem Dotado* as part of a

FIGURE 20. Photograph of downtown São Paulo movie theater marquees.
Reprinted by permission from "Com a casa e as discriminações—
Em busca de um papel," *Arigato* 2.16 (1978)

larger group of films starring Sueli Aoki, Niki Fuchita, Sandra Midori, Misaki Tanaka, and Midori Tange. Their images and names were splashed in huge letters on theater marquees (such as those in figure 20). In early 1979 those strolling on the Avenida São João would have seen two marquees facing each other on opposite sides of the street: one with Aoki's name and image and another with those of Tanaka.

Cinemas showing erotic films plastered their street entrances with stills far more explicit than the advertising poster above. The stills often included Japanese-Brazilian actresses, even when their roles were minor, such as the use of Misaki Tanaka to promote Ody Fraga's *Reformatório das Depravadas* (*Depraved Girls Reform School*, 1978) or of Sueli Aoki to promote Tony Vieira's *O Matador Sexual* (*The Sexual Killer*, 1979).[20] Reminiscent of how the stills of the Japanese restaurant scene in *Noite Vazia* were used in the press, Nikkei actresses often appeared in magazine photos without their names ever being mentioned.[21] In Antônio Meliande's *Escola Penal das Meninas Violentadas* (*Prison School for Violated Girls*, 1977), Aoki had a small role, but the film poster featured her more prominently than the stars.

Between 1974 and 1981 Tanaka was in eighteen erotic films, and Aoki was in nine others. Most were reviewed in the mainstream press with the "exotic" beauty of the two actresses frequently mentioned.[22] In 1978 Tanaka and Aoki both portrayed geishas engaged in violent sex in a Japanese restaurant in Walter Hugo Khouri's *O Prisioneiro do Sexo*. Yet images of Japanese-Brazilian sexuality, both explicit and potential, were not confined to film: in 1977 Yoko Tani starred in a transvestite show in downtown São Paulo, and Midori Tange played the role of the desirable Shizue in the SBT (Sistema Brasileiro de Televisão) telenovela *O Espantalho*.[23] In 1978, Harumi Ishihara was on the cover of two widely read women's magazines, *Claudia* and *Love Story*.[24] The linkage between sexuality and Japan was so strong that Raffaele Rossi's film *Roberta, a Gueixa do Sexo* (*Roberta, the Sex Geisha*, 1978) had no Japanese-Brazilians in the cast.

MOVING UP?

The owner of Canal X must have been a fan of Sandra Midori, whose work with Alfredo Sternheim I mentioned in the previous chapter. For three of her films he had typed up annotations and attached them to the descriptions of the films on the plastic video box.

The first annotation was on the cover of Garotas Sacanas (Filthy Girls, dir. Alfredo Sternheim, 1985) and was informational: "Sandra Midori, daughter of Orientals, a receptionist at a karaoke club in Liberdade, became famous in national porno in the eighties."

The second annotation was on the box for Senta no Meu que eu Entro na sua (Sit on Mine and I Will Go into Yours, dir. Ody Fraga, 1985). It repeated the information above and added, "She married a really rich American."

The final note came on the box for Orgasmo Louco (Crazy Orgasm, dir. Juan Bajon, 1987). Midori "married a really rich American and lives in a mansion in Los Angeles. She never came back to Brazil."

This plethora of images did not go unnoticed. *Arigato*, a Portuguese-language magazine funded by the *São Paulo Shimbun* newspaper and aimed at a young professional Nikkei audience, published a long article on Nikkei in erotic film. While ethnic magazines in the Americas have tended historically to render public sexuality as an "ethnic problem," *Arigato* focused on how Tanaka, Aoki, and Yan Wei broke sexual and professional stereotypes. The broader São Paulo Nikkei press also hailed the success of Japanese-Brazilian actors and actresses. Articles on Nikkei youth and sexuality often included

FIGURE 21. Misaki Tanaka, publicity photograph. Reprinted by permission from
"Com a casa e as discriminações—Em busca de um papel," *Arigato* 2.16 (1978)

respectful and serious interviews with Nikkei educators, psychologists, and erotic film actresses. A front-page article in the *Diário Nippak* commented without irony that Misaki Tanaka (figure 21), who had acted in *O Bom Marido* (*The Good Husband*, 1978) and *Colegiais e Lições de Sexo* (*School Girls and Sex Lessons*, 1980), was "one of the few descendents to have successfully battled in the world of national cinema without prejudices, playing various roles (just in the past year more than ten films), in addition to fighting for a larger space for Orientals as artists."[25]

Combating stereotypes was important in the erotic films directed by two Asian-born residents of Brazil. Juan Bajon (stage name of Chien Lun Tu) was described in the press as a "Nipo-Filipino" while John Doo, born in Shanghai, had migrated first to Canada and then to Brazil in the late 1950s. Both Bajon and Doo made critically praised films that played much less on ideas about Japanese-Brazilian submissiveness than other films with Nikkei characters.[26] Doo's first film (he made some thirteen) was *Ninfas Diabólicas* (*Diabolical Nymphets*, 1977), a "diabolical erotic" thriller that included Misaki Tanaka and was described by mainstream critics as "Polanski-esque" and as a "do not miss."[27] Reviews focused on the "Asian" feel of the picture, an interpretation that appears based on presumptions about the "Asiannness" of the director. Rubem Biáfora, critic for *O Estado de S. Paulo*, called Doo "a Chinese who seems more like Japanese . . . with the intuition . . . to dive into the fantastic and lascivious world of Japanese legends."[28]

Academics may have ignored the Japanese-Brazilian presence in erotic film, but São Paulo's film critics did not. Jean-Claude Bernardet believed many of the films represented an "appeal to a new (Nikkei) public," the same motivation that Mazzaropi had a decade earlier in making *Meu Japão Brasileiro*. Rubem Biáfora saw things differently. He noticed that while few actresses in erotic films were Nikkei, the numbers of films starring them had grown markedly. He attributed this to the "very professional and serious" approaches of Nikkei actresses, who also had "beautiful faces and bodies."[29]

The attributes of hard work and beauty may seem unrelated, but they are not. The former is a long-standing stereotype of Nikkei throughout the Americas and was frequently referenced by critics, by directors, and by the actresses themselves. Professionalism, seen as natural among Nikkei, was linked to beauty, also seen as natural among the new stars. As Sueli Aoki commented in explaining her difference from non-Nikkei actresses, "[They] only need plastic surgery and to know how to say, 'Hi, How are you,' and nothing else."[30] Tanaka seemed to agree, "It is that old story. . . . [Hiring] a Japanese is a sure bet."[31]

As we saw in the reviews of *Noite Vazia* and *Meu Japão Brasileiro*, film critics focused on Japanese-Brazilian beauty in their publications: Biáfora's negative review of *O Bem Dotado* noted that the film's primary virtue was "the beautiful 'Nisei' Suely Aoki," and that week's film section of *O Estado de S. Paulo* was illustrated with her picture.[32] Tanaka remembers making a film in the 1970s when the director could not explain why her role as the "Japonesa" had been written. Tanaka believed she knew: she was there to be beautiful and exotic, "so that there were not only white girls."[33] Not all actresses, however, saw advantages in Asianness. Minami Keizi reported hearing audience members outside of the Cine Maraba commenting on the performance of Carmen Angélica in *Cangaceiras Eróticas* (*Erotic Bandit Babes*, 1975): "Who is that 'Chinesinha'? . . . or maybe she is a 'Japonesinha.'" His response: "She is neither one nor the other. She is Brazilian, very Brazilian." When he mentioned these comments to Angélica, who performed in more than twenty erotic films in the seventies and eighties, she told him that she had undergone plastic surgery to widen her eyes so that she appeared less Asian.[34]

...

The presence of Japanese-Brazilians in pornochanchada was not limited to films whose main purpose was titillation and comedy. Carlos Reichenbach wrote an Asian character for *O Império do Desejo* (*The Empire of Desire*, 1980), a film acclaimed by the mainstream and artistic press. *Veja*, Brazil's most important newsmagazine, called *O Império do Desejo* "a film in the service of the public," and *Filme Cultura* called Reichenbach a "visionary[,] . . . a complete genius of commercial Brazilian cinema."[35]

Reichenbach was trained at the Escola Superior de Cinema São Luiz, the first film school in São Paulo. He and his fellow students, including a number of Nikkei, watched many Japanese films in the 1960s and 1970s and participated in a movement known as *cinema marginal* or *udigrudi* (a Brazilian deformation of the English word *underground*).[36] Emerging during the darkest days of military repression, around 1968, udigrudi films had characters with no life goals, no problems, and no solutions.[37] This, according to Reichenbach, reflected a generation "brought up in the most violent years of political repression, the sons of the MECUSAID agreement (between the Brazilian Ministry of Education and the USA), which eliminated humanities from the secondary school curriculum."[38]

O Império do Desejo was an intellectual and politically combative pornochanchada, similar in approach to the Japanese New Wave films that so deeply influenced Reichenbach.[39] The seemingly odd pairing of radical politics and explicit sex came about when Reichenbach decided in 1975 to "never make or imagine making a film with a state body" after learning that the Ministry of Culture only awarded prizes to films funded by Embrafilme. Avoiding the government agency led Reichenbach to pornochanchada producer Antônio P. Galante, known as the "Roger Corman of the Boca do Lixo," and together they made three films.[40]

O Império do Desejo tells the tale of two hippies who care for a widow's beach house, where her late husband had gone to meet his extramarital lovers. The beach is home to feminists, fascists, nuts, and beach babes. The "Chinesa," played by Misaki Tanaka, is an explicitly sexual and explicitly political character: she is a journalist for a magazine called "*Proselytize! The sole anchor of antirevisionism in the sea of colonialist exploitation!*" The Chinesa arrives in a *cheongsam* (a Chinese long dress) and a broad-rimmed bamboo peasant hat, and the Maoist and Vietcong references are unapologetic.[41] Viewers interested in film certainly made the connection between

FIGURE 22. Still from *O Império do Desejo*.
From www.contracampo.com.br/36/frames.htm

this character and the French students studying Maoist ideology in Jean-Luc Godard's *La Chinoise* (1967). In that sense, the Chinesa made *O Império do Desejo* both a film about resistance and a parody of the Brazilian Left.

The Chinesa has no given name, making it difficult to divorce this role from Tanaka's others as geishas.[42] The ironic fact that the "Chinesa" is Nikkei arises constantly. She wants to interview one person because he is like a "kamikaze." In her search for the perfect interview she meets a Euro-Brazilian named Di Branco ("White"), described in the press synopsis as "the nice crazy guy, the cannibal of the virgin forest, a type of avenging angel."[43] The relationship that develops between the Chinesa and Di Branco points the viewer toward a Japanese Brazil.

The crucial scene comes when the two enter Di Branco's beach shack. The Chinesa chants revolutionary catchphrases, preaching about "the transforming praxis of the processes of social renovation," but the shack is decorated with odd slogans and Japanese erotic paintings (see figure 22). As the Chinesa and Di Branco fornicate, viewers see that the Chinese cheongsam has been replaced by a Japanese "happy coat" (short kimono). Indeed, a short jacket in Brazil is called a *japona*, and the multiple layers of imagery emphasize the disconnect between the sex and the mocking radical slogans: As the Chinesa reaches orgasm astride Di Branco she shouts with revolutionary fervor, "The movement should always come from below: from below upward!" The Chinesa's on-screen presence ends in an *ofuro* (Japanese hot tub), from which she waves a little red book. As she intones, "The cultural value of a work depends on abandoning in content and form all bourgeois sentiments," the viewer sees that the "little red book" is not Mao Tse-tung's but the Marquis de Sade's.[44]

Reichenbach's portrayal of the Chinesa shares with Khouri and Mazzaropi the use of characters with no personal names. Like Khouri and Sternheim, he was a fan of Japanese cinema. As he noted in a 1985 television interview:

> We were heavily influenced by Ozu, Masaharu Segawa, Shohei Imamura, and other contemporary filmmakers. In a certain way they made sexual films, but politics entered through the back door. Ten years before Ozu was discovered in Europe, we already had access to his films, and we admired him tremendously. In São Paulo these films had been available for a long time, but it was not until later that they fed into a real movement in filmmaking, a young movement called "cinema boca do lixo" which has nothing to do with the way "cinema boca do lixo" is understood today. São Paulo is an international city where all artistic people suffer from brutality. We have a very big Japanese colony, a big Chinese and Korean colony, and because of this Brazil represented the second-largest market for Japanese films. Ninety percent of this market was in São Paulo. Between 1960 and 1970 I must have seen more than five thousand Japanese films. We had four cinemas which only showed Japanese films and I think they really influenced my generation.[45]

Reichenbach's desire to be linked with the Japanese art film movement is seen in *O Império do Desejo*. While Misaki Tanaka believed the producer Galante wanted "naked women to bring in the crowds," both she and Reichenbach saw the "sex scenes as not simply sex. They had a different social connotation."[46] For example, the original title of the film, *Anarquia Sexual* (*Sexual Anarchy*), had to be changed when censors told Galante that the word *anarchy* would not be permitted. Reichenbach suggested *O Império do Desejo* in homage to the Nagisa Oshima film *Ai no corrida* (*In the Realm of the Senses*, 1976), which was given the title *O Império dos Sentidos* ("*The Empire of the Senses*") in Brazil.

The Oshima classic was one of the first sexually explicit foreign films shown in Brazil after censorship laws were relaxed at the end of the 1970s; *O*

Império do Desejo was the first Brazilian film approved without cuts by the Brazilian Censorship Board (Conselho Superior de Censura) under the category "pornographic show." Antônio Galante was no fool: he realized that the wide viewership of Oshima's films in São Paulo would respond to the mocking, "Don't confuse it with the Japanese film" used in the marketing. Linking Reichenbach's *O Império do Desejo* to Oshima's *O Império dos Sentidos* also had a context unknown to the Brazilian director and producer. Oshima's father-in-law had immigrated to the Amazon region of Brazil in the 1930s, and Oshima himself, during a visit to Brazil in 1984, told the monthly Nikkei newsmagazine *Página Um* that he wanted to make a film about the Shindo Renmei movement (see introduction).[47]

When I asked Reichenbach to reflect on the role of the "Chinesa" in *O Império do Desejo*, he was unable to remember Tanaka's name. After a reminder he implied that her role was meant to represent the People's Republic of China, and that only an Asian-"looking" actress would be appropriate.[48] Misaki Tanaka, who had arrived in Brazil as a child from Japan and whose father was a respected journalist in the São Paulo Japanese-language press, saw things differently. She understood her role in *O Império do Desejo* as an attempt to break Brazilian Nikkei out of a position in which "they don't integrate into Brazilian society but they are afraid to say they are Japanese or that they are the children of Japanese."[49]

Misaki Tanaka is a fascinating example of diasporic discontent. Her dissatisfaction with being viewed as Japanese never led her to waver from her insistence that her performances represented her Brazilianness. She began her artistic career as a piano teacher and as a dancer on Brazilian television musical programs like *Japan Pop Show* and *Images of Japan*. In 1975, she entered the University of São Paulo School of Communications and Arts (Escola de Comunicações e Artes, ECA), where she was one of few Nikkei students in radio and television studies (although many Nikkei studied communications at that time). She was recruited into cinema by pornochanchada director Ody Fraga, who "wanted someone with an Oriental face" in his *Macho e Fêmea* (1974). This box office hit starred Miss Brazil 1969, Vera Fischer, who continues to be extremely popular on both big and small screen (figure 23).[50] An entry on Tanaka in the *Enciclopédia do Cinema Brasileiro* describes her customary role as an "Oriental type integrated into Brazilian culture."[51] Integration is a primary plot of Antônio Calmon's erotic comedy *O Bom Marido* (*The Good Husband*, 1978), a film about the importation of Japanese vibrators for Brazilian women, which starred Tanaka as "Tokyo Rose."[52]

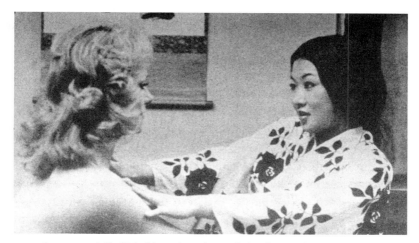

FIGURE 23. Still of Misaki Tanaka and Vera Fischer from *Macho e Fêmea*, 1974.
Reprinted by permission from "Com a casa e as discriminações—Em busca
de um papel," *Arigato* 2.16 (1978)

• • •

Readers familiar with Brazil may have expected Tizuka Yamasaki's *Gaijin: Os Caminhos da Liberdade* (*Gaijin: The Roads to Freedom*) to be the focus of this chapter. *Gaijin*, which competed at Cannes in 1980, is perhaps the only Brazilian film widely remembered as including Nikkei, and it is one of the few Brazilian mainstream movies in which an ethnic minority is both the focus and treated sympathetically.[53]

Tizuka Yamasaki is not Brazil's only Nikkei filmmaker (Olga Futema is well known for her documentaries), but she is certainly the most famous, in large part for her mainstream film and television work. Yamasaki could have been the model for the Sternheim film *Isei, Nisei, Sansei* discussed in the previous chapter. She was born in 1949 in Atibaia (near São Paulo), of Japanese immigrant grandparents and Japanese-Brazilian parents who worked as vegetable farmers. Her name Tizuka, while understood in Brazil to be "Japanese," is instead the Brazilianization of the female name Chizuko, with the final *o*, generally indicating a masculine word in Portuguese, changed to a feminine *a*.

Yamasaki studied cinema at the University of Brasília until 1968, when the institution was closed by the military.[54] She finished her degree in 1975 at the Federal University of Rio de Janeiro, where she studied and apprenticed with Cinema Novo pioneers Nelson Pereira dos Santos and Glauber Rocha.[55]

Gaijin was Yamasaki's first feature film. It had a big budget for the time (about $300,000) and was coproduced and distributed by Embrafilme. The title plays with the Japanese word *gaijin* (foreigner or, literally, "outside-person") and sets up a "them/us" contrast, raising the question of whether the Japanese or the Brazilians are the foreigners. For Japanese-Brazilians who colloquially used the word *gaijin* to designate non-Nikkei, the film pointed to a Brazilian context where Nikkei were *gaijin*. Indeed, the promotional materials for the film made clear the multiple interpretations by playing with Japanese and Portuguese as spoken and as written:

GAIJIN.

UMA PALAVRA JAPONESA.

[A JAPANESE WORD]

UM IDEOGRAMA.

[AN IDEOGRAM]

外人

[GAIJIN]

"DO LADO DE FORA" "HOMEM"

["OUTSIDE"] ["PERSON"]

(Promotional Folder, *Embrafilme apresenta "Gaijin: Os Caminhos da Liberdade,"* "Gaijin," folder P1980–87, Fundação Cinemateca Brasileira, São Paulo)

Gaijin did not receive much support among Nikkei community leaders, and Yamasaki spoke to the press of her dissatisfaction with the refusal of "the colony" to provide production funds and of the Museu Histórico da Imigração Japonesa no Brasil in São Paulo to loan objects from its collection for the film.[56] Yamasaki understood the lack of support as a combination of sexism and generational conflict, but she eventually prodded community leaders to action. When a series of advertisements in Nikkei newspapers for Japanese-Brazilian extras (she needed 600) led to no results, she began going door to door among São Paulo's Japanese prefectural associations and language schools, telling community leaders that if they did not encourage people to participate in the film, "I will put my ten Issei [immigrant-generation] friends in the movie and say that this is how the arrival of the immigrants looked.

Soon they [leaders of Nikkei institutions] got going," fearing that Japanese immigration would not appear large-scale.[57] The Nikkei who took roles as extras in the film, however, were not "authentic" enough for Yamasaki. As Robert Stam notes, she "discovered that she had to use Japanese performers to play the leading roles, since Japanese-Brazilians had developed overly loose 'Brazilian' body language that made them unconvincing as Japanese."[58]

Gaijin is based loosely on stories told to Yamasaki by her grandmother about the immigrants aboard the *Kasato Maru*, the first ship to bring Japanese to Brazil in 1908.[59] The protagonist of *Gaijin*, Titoe (played by the Japanese actress Kyoko Tsukamoto), is a "picture bride" whose arranged marriage (*omiai kekkon*) "officialized" her immigration according to Brazilian legislation that favored "family" entry. Soon after arriving on a São Paulo plantation she becomes pregnant, and the birth of her Brazilian daughter, Shinobu, leads her to stake her future in Brazil, in spite of a terrible marriage.[60]

As the film progresses, Titoe and the plantation's Brazilian bookkeeper, Tonho, played by Antônio Fagundes, become attracted to each other. Tonho becomes politicized and realizes his own complicity in oppressing the foreign (Italian, Japanese, and Portuguese) and native (Northeastern Brazilian) laborers on the plantation. Like Tonho, Titoe becomes aware of her own subjugation in her marriage and in her community's expectations. Titoe and Tonho do not consummate their relationship in the rural space of the plantation. Rather, it is years later in the bustling city of São Paulo, where both go at the end of the film, that they find freedom. Titoe's act of ethnic militancy is to leave her immigrant community and husband, whose refusal to engage in labor activism is portrayed as an inability to stop being "Japanese." Tonho's militancy is different: he has become a labor activist. The director Yamasaki's militancy is different still: her film promoted Brazilianization through interethnic marriage and popular protest. Titoe enters the mainstream by "mixing" with Tonho and thus becoming "Brazilian." As cultural studies scholar Shuhei Hosokawa notes, *Gaijin* is a case study of what might be termed "melting pot nationalism," a position that Yamasaki assumed in discussing the film:

> Now I see how much pressure there was in terms of discrimination from within, in that our parents demanded Japanese behavior, that we speak Japanese, that we not marry Brazilians. In reality we are neither Nisei nor Sansei. We are, before everything, Brazilian citizens. . . . This is our big psychological problem, this racial conflict that is so much part of our generation. The pressure is not just from our parents but from the Japanese community and Brazilian society as well.

But all these problems will persist until we have in Brazil a kind of cultural revolution, or until everything mixes once and for all. Who is a Brazilian? Why only have one type of Brazilian rather than various types? Why do we have to follow the white European or American model?

. . . The "Brazilian," just like the "Japanese descendant," has a prejudice in relation to "the other": the Northeasterner is called *pau de arara*; the Japanese is "Chinese"; the Japanese call the "Brazilian" a "gaijin"; to call someone "Jew" is pejorative. Until now, to be called pau de arara, gaijin, Jew has been terrible because it is a kind of discrimination that comes from the top down. Why not change? I am a "gaijin" and I have lots of pride. I think we have to change these values.

What is missing as well is for descendents to take this position.

I feel great as a Brazilian, and it is really good to have two races.[61]

Gaijin's 1980 mainstream release came at the end of three years of strikes in the industrial cities that surround São Paulo. Like *Eles Não Usam Black-Tie* (*They Don't Wear Black Tie*, dir. Leon Hirszman, 1981), *Gaijin* had a theme of collective action, suggesting that Brazil was near the end of its dictatorship as a political *abertura* (opening) permitted alternative voices to emerge.[62] *Gaijin* attracted attention from a middle class beginning to see itself as part of a broad prodemocracy coalition. Nikkei became more immersed in their past, while non-Nikkei sought to understand what had led Japan (the country) and Japanese-Brazilians to such prominence in the 1960s. *Gaijin* appealed to varied audiences, to the point that even the Chinese ambassador asked for a private showing so he could consider its possible release in his country.[63]

For many viewers in São Paulo, *Gaijin* helped to explain the presence of Japanese products and people in their everyday lives. Japanese multinationals had been expanding rapidly into Brazil since the 1960s, and Japanese goods, from food to televisions, had become common in Brazilian homes. While *Gaijin* was being shown, Japan's relationship to Brazil was constantly in the news. In August 1980, for example, the headlines were about a proposal (later scuttled) to settle 10 million Japanese farmers in Brazil.[64] The following month a "Typical Japanese Food Night" brought food venders from Liberdade to the non-Nikkei neighborhood of Ipiranga and turned out an estimated twenty-five hundred people.[65]

Gaijin's cinematic context included other Asian-themed films, including Francis Ford Coppola's *Apocalypse Now* (*Apocalypse*, 1979), John Berry's *The Bad News Bears Go to Japan* (*A Garotada Vai ao Japão*, 1978), and Yoji Yamada's

Otoko wa tsurai yo: Torajiro junjoshishu (*O Sinal da Felicidade*, 1976).[66] Japanese films continued to play in Liberdade's cinemas, and film critics were as enthusiastic in 1980 as they had been twenty years earlier.[67] Just a few months after *Gaijin*'s release, Oshima's *O Império dos Sentidos* was approved for release without any cuts, soon followed by Reichenbach's *O Império do Desejo*.[68] Anyone going to the Ipiranga Cinema in downtown São Paulo to see *Gaijin* would pass marquees and posters advertising erotic films with Misaki Tanaka, who also appeared in the Yamasaki film.

Many majority viewers saw *Gaijin* as a representation of an "authentic" Japanese immigrant past. The film was received with some ambivalence in the Nikkei community, however, particularly among those Issei (first generation) who attended special showings at São Paulo's Japanese-Brazilian Community Center in Liberdade. These were the only showings in the neighborhood because of Yamasaki's desire to "try to make those more radical Japanese, who have never left Liberdade, change their day-to-day lives."[69] This did not work. Many Japanese immigrants saw the film at the community center, and thus in a separate part of São Paulo from Brazilians (Nikkei and non-Nikkei).

While some Issei were moved by the film and the window opened for younger generations on the immigrant past, many others saw the anecdotes of the Japanese pioneers as banal.[70] Shuhei Hosokawa notes that some Japanese-language articles written by Issei praised Yamasaki's parents more for raising a famous director than they lauded Yamasaki for her achievement. One aspect particularly criticized was the film's suggested romance between Titoe and Tonho.[71] Indeed, the lack of exogamy in the early years of immigration stands in marked contrast to 1980, when close to half of all Nikkei marriages in São Paulo were with non-Nikkei.[72]

In addition, some younger Japanese-Brazilian taste makers were less than enthusiastic about *Gaijin*. Henri George Kobata was a journalist for *Página Um*, a magazine supplement published biweekly by the *Diário Nippak*, which took a progressive position on national politics and Nikkei community matters. He remembers spending long hours comparing Yamasaki's film with Futema's documentary *Retratos de Hideko* (1980), which focuses on three generations of women and argues for a unique Japanese-Brazilian cultural identity.

> For our tastes, Tizuka Yamasaki was trying to make a commercial film. And Olga Futema was engaging in the kind of cinema that was a little more accurate, searching to understand the culture better. Olga's films were much better, in our

opinion, were more important than Tizuka Yamasaki's films. We thought that Olga was more intense, much more profound, more important. And Olga Futema had the life story to make these films. She went out looking for a Nikkei lifestyle, and she kept in touch [with the community], which was not the case for Tizuka Yamasaki. Tizuka Yamasaki never lived in the community, did not know the stories. . . . [This] really sat badly with us, that she came to speak to us only for commercial interests, when we thought she was much more serious as a researcher. To us *Gaijin* was far below our expectations, much less of a film than it could have been. On the other hand, there is that commercial side; she wanted to be on the commercial movie circuit. But from the historical point of view, in terms of content, we were really hurt. We tried to tell her serious stories, and out of the blue she comes in from Brasília, from Rio, saying, "I cannot speak Japanese, I never understood these people, but I am going to make a movie. Can you tell me who I can contact to finance it?" What's up with that! First she should have asked, "Do you want to see the script? Can you help look at the script and see if the historical facts are correct?" But she never once spoke of the script before [asking for help in raising money].[73]

Misaki Tanaka played the role of the immigrant Nishi in *Gaijin*. She also was unhappy with the final product, in part because the relationship between Titoe and Tonho made the film "a little love story. It became something unimportant and sugary." She was surprised at the difference between the final product and the original script written by Yamasaki and Jorge Durán, a Chilean who had lived in exile in Brazil since the early 1970s: "It kept a name kind of like, *The Saga of Freedom*. . . . That's not what it is! This is not what happened to the immigrants in fact. . . . This left me very sad."[74]

Audiences responded to *Gaijin* in very different ways. A number of Issei saw it as falsely "ethnic," while many Brazilian-born Nikkei saw it as truthfully so. Some non-Nikkei Brazilians universalized *Gaijin*, so that it became a nonethnic film about hard work, success, and resistance. For many viewers the "Japanese" plot was mainly an allegory for the rise of the urban metalworkers union in the late 1970s, which would lead, many years later, to Luiz Inácio Lula da Silva's election as president of Brazil.

Following the film's "Brazilian" premiere at the Museu de Arte de São Paulo (MASP), the *Diário Nippak* interviewed a number of people in the audience and found the reception to be entirely positive. Yet while Japanese-Brazilians quoted in the article all commented on issues of "authenticity," non-Nikkei had a different reaction. Filmmaker Nelson Pereira dos Santos, for example, noted that "*Gaijin* is a lesson for all Brazilians and, in spite of the characters being almost all Japanese and descendents of Japanese, I believe that it moves all of us because we are all descendents of immigrants." Luiz Carlos Caversan, a reporter for *O Estado de S. Paulo*, saw *Gaijin* as "an emotional film . . . an epic film. . . . For me *Gaijin* is the film about immigration that has been missing in Brazil."[75] Maria Lígia Coelho Prado, a historian writing some twenty years after seeing *Gaijin*, believed the film was primarily political: "I remember being positively surprised to see, in those years of the dictatorship, a film that ran the risk of having a screenplay with political connotations about the exploitation of rural workers." She focused almost exclusively on broad Brazilian politics, virtually ignoring the film's "ethnic" aspects.[76] The same might be said of film studies scholar Robert Stam, whose excellent *Tropical Multiculturalism: A Comparative History of Race in Brazilian Cinema* mentions *Gaijin* only in a footnote, presumably because it did not deal with Afro-Brazilians and thus fell out of the traditional category of films about "race."[77]

Gaijin's conflation of ethnic integration and political activism was clear in the Embrafilme-distributed promotional material, produced in the form of a top-spiral notepad. Each page had quotes in large font at the top, representing "Japanese" and "Brazilian" ideas about the film ranging from "They fought bravely to realize their dream, their longings, their hopes for easy wealth and a return to Japan" to "defend their rights to the land, acquired through hard work. The right to the fruits of their labor." Ultimately, "*Gaijin* is not a personal idea, it is a story made up of a cast, a technical team, an audience, emotion!" The "notepad" also included comments ostensibly written by the Japanese, Japanese-Brazilian, and Brazilian actors. Compare, for example, the comment of Japanese actress Kyoko Tsukamoto (Titoe): "The integration of two opposing cultures, of Japan and Brazil, is the subject of the film. . . . What we did would be impossible in any other part of the world"; with that of Brazilian actor Antônio Fagundes (Tonho): "My character is an incredible character. Tonho is very representative of the reality in which we live today," a position echoed by Gianfrancesco Guarnieri, the highly politicized actor who played the Italian agitator Enrico. Guarnieri is quoted as saying that "I would call [*Gaijin*] 'national popular' in that it brings our stories to the public in an exciting way." This tension between the universal and the ethnic was, according to Misaki Tanaka, the story behind the film, since Yamasaki suffered "a lot of interference from people who changed some things here and some things there."[78]

Yamasaki focused on the discrepancy between making an "ethnic" film and a "Brazilian" one in her published comments on *Gaijin*: "I do not see cinema as a useful way to deal with the sociological problem of immigrants in Brazil, less still my own existential problems. . . . I assumed that Japanese were not in a different position than other migrant workers. . . . even born in Brazil I am discriminated against, I am seen as a foreigner, visible because of my skin, my style."[79] Yet the contradictions between universal and ethnic do not alter the fact that the film represented the Brazilian dominant myth, that of (in Yamasaki's words) "a mixture of races."

Newspaper reviews portrayed *Gaijin* as both oddly "ethnic" *and* as a uniquely "Brazilian" examination of how miscegenation helped to create the nation. The headline in the popular newsmagazine *Visão* put it succinctly, "Not Japanese and still not Brazilian, descendents search for their cultural identity. A film, 'Gaijin,' may be able to help."[80] Many comments highlighted Yamasaki's "Brazil as *mestiço* nation" message in the text with headlines like "The adventure of the Japanese in our country" or "Immigration as seen by the slant-eyes" along with photographs of Japanese immigrants.[81]

The multiple receptions of *Gaijin* open a unique window on diasporic assumptions in Brazil. *Gaijin* also traveled outside of Brazil, and the Brazilian popular media reported on its reception in the international sphere (see figure 24).[82] In Japan *Gaijin* was viewed as a story of how Japaneseness was lost following migration. Yamasaki was told that distributors were offended by the use of the word *gaijin* in reference to Japanese immigrants. In spite of the awards and the Japanese actors, *Gaijin* was never commercially released in Japan and was only shown at film festivals.[83] In Europe critics applauded the film for its "diasporic sensibilities" but did not see it as Brazilian. At both the Berlin and Cannes film festivals *Gaijin* was incorrectly listed, much to Yamasaki's discontent, as a Brazil/Japan coproduction. While this confusion may have been inspired by the many Japanese actors in the film, Yamasaki believed it was caused by her "Japanese name." This mirrored the misunderstanding she had "always felt in Brazil and [that] led me to make the film. It doesn't matter that I was born in Brazil, because people always call me 'Japonesa.'"[84]

Yamasaki was correct. The Brazilian press played on the idea that *Gaijin* was a foreign film. An article in the *Folha de S. Paulo* hailing the film's chances for a prize in Berlin was placed directly below a large column on a journalist's impressions of a visit to the People's Republic of China, illustrated by a cartoon of a bucktoothed, grinning Maoist worker raising a hammer.[85] The same newspaper illustrated an article on the Cannes prize awarded to Akira Kurosawa's *Kagemusha* with a photograph from *Gaijin*.[86] Imagine how Yamasaki felt when Marcos Vinício, film critic of São Paulo's *Folha da Tarde*, tried to

FIGURE 24. French promotional poster for Gaijin: *Les chemins de la liberté*
Distributed by La Médiathèque des Trois Mondes. Verve Comunicação, 1998–2001.
From www.verveweb.com.br/gaijin2

defend *Gaijin* against critics who rejected it as a Brazilian film by saying, "It could be assimilated as a mestiço film, or binational."[87]

CONCLUSION

Beginning with the release of *Noite Vazia* in 1964, film represented a panorama of how Japanese-Brazilians were imagined in São Paulo. Nikkei characters might be supporters or opponents of the military regime, they might be farm laborers, urban professionals, or sex stars; they might be Japanese- or Portuguese-speaking. Nikkei were simultaneously normative and atypical and thus did not easily fit into the national racial dichotomy of whiteness/wealth/Brazilian and blackness/poverty/Brazilian. Viewers saw Nikkei as diasporic, no matter how much Japanese-Brazilians argued to the contrary.

The discontent was clear in the mid-2005 release of Tizuka Yamasaki's *Gaijin 2: Ama-me Como Sou (Gaijin 2: Love Me as I Am)*, a film about the *dekasegui*, the quarter of a million Brazilians of Japanese descent who migrated to Japan, ostensibly for temporary work, beginning in the 1980s.[88] The film used the original *Gaijin* as a springboard: the main character, Maria (played by the U.S. actress Tamlyn Tomita, who is of Japanese descent), is the granddaughter of Titoe and the daughter of Shinobu. In Japan the gaijin are the Brazilian Nikkei, and the film's production was sponsored by Japanese-Brazilian magazines, Web sites for Brazilians living in Japan, a Chinese fast food restaurant chain, and Petrobrás, the Brazilian national energy company.[89]

A FAILED ACTOR

Scholars make much of the flexibility of racial categories in Brazil, often pointing to studies in which a single person is defined racially in numerous ways. When I heard that Tizuka Yamasaki was holding an open casting call for Nikkei actors and actresses to work in Gaijin 2, I decided to see if I could "pass" as a fifteen-to-twenty-five-year-old Japanese-Brazilian. In the interest of full disclosure, I am of European descent and in the United States I am often demarcated as "white," "Jewish," and "bald." I was also forty years old at the time.

I woke up early on a Sunday morning and joined a long line of fifteen-to-twenty-five-year-old Nikkei. After a while, a few of my linemates began to probe my ethnic background. At first I insisted that I fit the ethnic and age profiles, but I finally admitted that I was neither Nikkei nor fifteen to twenty-five. This led to a confessional moment when a number of my fellow wannabe actors confessed that they were of Chinese or Korean descent and were going make up "Japanese" names to "pass" into the audition.

A member of Yamasaki's crew quickly taught me the limits of categorical flexibility. As hard as I tried, I could not convince her that I was Nikkei, much less a fifteen-to-twenty-five-year-old. So I fessed up and producer Carlos Alberto Diniz (who also produced Gaijin) came to chat. He generously invited me to spend the day watching the casting call together with Yamasaki and her crew. In this process the question of flexibility returned. A woman I will call Chizuko Mori (not her real name!) gave a wonderful reading. Yamasaki complimented her and then asked, "Are you pura or mestiça?" (i.e., are both your parents of Japanese descent or not?). Chizuko paused, clearly trying to figure out the "correct" answer that would get her the part. But that is another story. . . .

In many ways Gaijin (and Gaijin 2) were not so different from Noite Vazia, Meu Japão Brasileiro, or O Bem Dotado. All suggested that "Japan" was in "Brazil" and that sexual mixing would create a new Brazilian race that combined the imagined hard-working community of Japan with the imagined passionate community of Brazil. All played with the idea that ethnicity was biological and that Nikkei were really "Japanese" in spite of where they were born, the language they spoke, and the cultural forums in which they interacted. In the realm of film the circle was complete: there were no Japanese-Brazilians, only Japanese who could produce Brazilian children via miscegenation. Yet the plots were only one part of the story. The actors, actresses, and directors were all fighting for a change. They were ethnic militants trying to dismiss diaspora and create contentment.

3.

MACHINE GUNS AND HONEST FACES

Japanese-Brazilian Ethnicity and

Armed Struggle, 1964–1980

In the decades after World War II, large numbers of Nikkei migrated to São Paulo and, as a result, moved from rural occupations to liberal and administrative professions. Since the city presented many of them a first opportunity for university education, there was great eagerness, and anxiety, to succeed economically and to be accepted socially.[1] As students became more politicized with the beginning of the dictatorship in 1964, some Nikkei began to engage in opposition political activity with their non-Nikkei colleagues. Japanese-Brazilians joined leftist groups for many of the same reasons as others of their generation, but they also had different motives from the majority. Nikkei activists remember their eagerness to prove that they were legitimate Brazilians, but their experiences often reminded them of their difference.

Leftist organizations, like the military regime and Brazilian society more broadly, eagerly sought Nikkei members but assessed them the fee of their ethnicity, understood as hard work, attention to detail, and at times a proclivity to violence. Nikkei did not consciously regard this exchange as demeaning, but the memories of militants suggest a subconscious discomfort with the costs. From code names to action assignments to experiences with state repression, the surplus visibility of ethnicity dogged Japanese-Brazilian activists.

Almost 60 percent of all armed militants were college students or graduates.[2] Most hoped to turn the population against the dictatorship through street protests, the invasion of radio stations to read manifestos, graffiti in public places, and revolutionary pamphlets left at the site of radical actions. The military regime and its police allies responded in an equally public way. Militants were branded "terrorists" and their "expropriations of funds from capitalist enterprises" were labeled "bank robberies." The regime put wanted posters in public places, and the highly controlled and often compliant press ran regular stories on the errors of militant ways. Torture became a state-sponsored method of social control.[3]

Militants and regime actors both believed they were fighting for an authentic Brazil that was threatened by the other. For Japanese-Brazilians the typical categories of militancy (social, political, student, and community) were always intensified by their ethnicity. Many residents of the city of São Paulo thus saw Japanese-Brazilians as more numerous in political activity than the numbers suggest. Nikkei militants were the focus of newspaper articles. They were on the cover of Brazil's most widely read magazine. They were on wanted posters.

In São Paulo, stopping domestic militancy was in the hands of both the military police in the Department of Operations Information–Center of Internal Defense Operations (Destacamento de Operações de Informações–Centro de Operações da Defensa Interna, DOI–CODI) and the civilian police in the São Paulo State Department of Political and Social Order (Departamento Estadual de Ordem Política e Social de São Paulo, DEOPS).[4] Nikkei posed unique challenges to these repressive forces since their militancy rejected an ethnic imaginary that saw Japanese-Brazilians as studious, hardworking, and docile. Rather, Nikkei militants aroused powerful memories of samurai, World War II death marches, and the Shindo Renmei movement of the mid-1940s. Regime agents worried that politicized Nikkei were indistinguishable from their hard-working immigrant families, making them harder to identify and thus particularly threatening.

It is hard to know exactly how many Nikkei were involved in leftist political activity in the 1960s and 1970s although some militants recall "a strong presence in the student movement and later in the urban guerrilla movement."[5] Many hundreds of Nikkei names appear in the police files although this should not suggest that all were militants. Of the 364 cases listed by

Nilmário Miranda and Carlos Tibúrcio as killed or "disappeared" by the military regime, seven are Nikkei.[6] Some militants with whom I spoke made circular references to about thirty people, while others noted the large number of Nikkei activists in both armed and unarmed movements.

How did Japanese-Brazilian militants contextualize their political experiences? How were these young men and women perceived by the Nikkei and non-Nikkei public, the repressive forces, and the Left? This chapter uses political activism to analyze a potent connection between ethnicity, national identity, and diasporic images, foregoing the class-based approach that characterizes many studies of militancy in Brazil.[7] For Nikkei, militancy was in part a search for a space where ethnicity was unimportant. As we have seen in the previous chapters, that space was not easy to find.

Some background on the *luta armada* (armed struggle) is important to understanding Nikkei militancy and the reactions to it. The Brazilian military came to power in 1964 and President General Arthur da Costa e Silva's decree of the Institutional Act 5 (AI-5) in 1968 created what Thomas Skidmore called "a genuine dictatorship."[8] AI-5 closed Congress, sent those accused of "national security" crimes to military courts, and imposed strict censorship on all media. Universities were especially affected because the military believed that impressionable young students provided easy recruits for radicalized older students and professors. Lectures were monitored by DEOPS agents disguised as undergraduates, uncooperative faculty lost their academic positions, and student movements were repressed. These actions further radicalized opponents, and more than a dozen relatively small guerrilla movements emerged. The number of armed activists was small (less than 1,000), and most were in their teens and twenties. They believed robbing banks and kidnapping foreign diplomats were appropriate revolutionary activities, but this created little support among the many Brazilians who considered the militants to be terrorists.[9]

Entry into leftist movements was ostensibly understood, from both within and without, as based on a political ideology of class struggle. While there had been a small Jewish cell in the Brazilian Communist Party in the 1930s and a integrationist "Black Movement" around the same time, Brazil did not have powerful ethnic-based movements in the sixties and seventies. There were no Black Panthers, no Jewish Defense Leagues, and no I Wor Kuens or Red Guards (Asian-American groups in the United States) in spite of the many Afro-Brazilians, Jewish-Brazilians, and Japanese-Brazilians in leftist political activity.[10]

Nikkei students in the fifties and sixties had life experiences quite different from those of their non-Nikkei friends and colleagues. Most had been born in rural communities in the states of São Paulo and Paraná with high concentrations of Japanese immigrants (see map 1). Reared in Japanese-speaking environments, many recalled learning to speak Portuguese only after attending public school.[11] Some recalled being mocked in sexual terms; men for having small penises and women for having vaginas that were "slanted, like their eyes."[12] All remembered conflict over how they would be nicknamed and what their Brazilian names would be after baptism.

The similar upbringing among Nikkei students did not always lead to similar outcomes. Since most saw themselves as part of an imagined "Japanese colony," this helped to create their new urban identities coupled with economic and social mobility. Activists, in contrast, usually considered themselves to be outsiders from the formally organized "colony" of community organizations, newspapers, and festivals. Militancy was not only a challenge to the dictatorship; it was a challenge to the politically and culturally conservative generation of their parents. One generational split was over the choice of marriage partners. During the sixties the overall Japanese-Brazilian intermarriage rate in the city of São Paulo was around 50 percent, with the percentage increasing markedly each decade.[13] Yet among Nikkei militants the rate appears to have been almost 100 percent. Those I spoke with often pointed to their own mixed marriages as evidence of Brazilianness.

I understood that intermarriage was a "trope" in my oral histories since the preinterview chitchat invariably included a question *to me* about my wife's ethnicity. My subjects assumed that she was Japanese-Brazilian, and that this explained the subject of my research. Yet when I responded that she was Jewish-Brazilian, the initial surprise among interviewees was quickly followed by a knowing nod or comment that was based on an expectation of ethnic endogamy, even if the subjects did not practice it themselves. This led to discussions of their own marriages to "Brazilians," a group which neither they, nor me, nor my wife were a part. Exogamy was presented as a form of "ethnic identity freedom" that could not be found in Nikkei endogamous relationships. As one person told me, "In my family there is only one brother who married a Japanese. A Nissei. This was [laughter] the only marriage that did not work out!"[14]

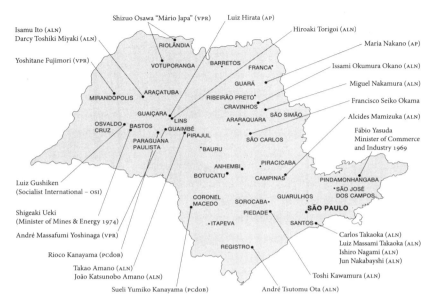

Shizuo Osawa "Mário Japa" (VPR)   Luiz Hirata (AP)

Isamu Ito (ALN)
Darcy Toshiki Miyaki (ALN)
                                                    Hiroaki Torigoi (ALN)
                        RIOLÂNDIA
                                                              Maria Nakano (AP)
Yoshitane Fujimori (VPR)
                        VOTUPORANGA   BARRETOS
                                              FRANCA•   Issami Okumura Okano (ALN)
                                          GUARÁ
                 ARAÇATUBA   Miguel Nakamura (ALN)
   MIRANDÓPOLIS   RIBEIRÃO PRETO•
                              CRAVINHOS   Francisco Seiko Okama
           GUAIÇARA   SÃO SIMÃO
   OSVALDO• •LINS   ARARAQUARA   Alcides Mamizuka (ALN)
   CRUZ BASTOS •GUAIMBÉ
              •PIRAJUL   Fábio Yasuda
       PARAGUANA   SÃO CARLOS   Minister of Commerce
       PAULISTA   •BAURU   and Industry 1969

                   ANHEMBI.   PIRACICABA
                   BOTUCATU•   CAMPINAS   PINDAMONHANGABA
Luiz Gushiken   •SÃO JOSÉ
(Socialist International – OSI)   DOS CAMPOS
                   CORONEL   GUARULHOS
                   MACEDO   SOROCABA•   SÃO PAULO
Shigeaki Ueki   PIEDADE•
(Minister of Mines & Energy 1974)   SANTOS•
                     •ITAPEVA
André Massafumi Yoshinaga (VPR)   Carlos Takaoka (ALN)
                                                   Luiz Massami Takaoka (ALN)
                   REGISTRO•   Ishiro Nagami (ALN)
   Rioco Kanayama (PCdoB)   Jun Nakabayshi (ALN)

   Takao Amano (ALN)
   João Katsunobo Amano (ALN)   Toshi Kawamura (ALN)

       Sueli Yumiko Kanayama (PCdoB)   André Tsutomu Ota (ALN)

MAP 1. Birthplaces of Nikkei militants, São Paulo State, Brazil

THE INTERVIEWER AS SUBJECT

All the former activists who consented to oral histories responded to my request in the same way, saying they were not part of the "Japanese colony" and could not imagine what being Nikkei had to do with their militancy. Each expressed surprise that an "American" would be interested in the topics of militancy and ethnicity.

That is, until they met me. Unfailingly the first question was "Where are you from?" My answers (the United States, Connecticut, Atlanta) were always met with a shake of the head and a more pointed, "I mean, where are you really from?" It did not take long for them to get the answer they wanted: Jewish (a number of interviewees told me they could tell just by looking at me). This led to an immediate sigh of relief: I was not a "real American" but rather one who was "naturally" interested in ethnicity and militancy.

Intermarriage was one way that militants rejected "their" ethnic community. Another way was focusing on a dislike of "Japanese," which meant Japanese in Japan, Japanese immigrants to Brazil, and Japanese-Brazilians who maintained ties to the "colony." For example, Marta Tanisaki, a former Ação Popular member, commented that in rural Brazil "the Japanese are so ugly," an impression she also brought back from her postdoctoral scientific research in Japan. The primary memories that Shizuo Osawa, a former member of the Vanguarda Popular Revolucionária (VPR), had of a trip to Japan were his desire to return to Brazil and "good food," especially *feijoada*, Brazil's national dish. Carlos Takaoka was born in São Paulo city and is the son of a well-known Japanese immigrant painter and Communist Party member. He spent a number of years in jail where torture left him physically disabled. In 1996 he went to Japan as part of the *dekasegui* labor migration of some quarter million Brazilians of Japanese descent. In our conversation he repeatedly connected his experience in prison to his life in Japan, where he found a great deal of "prejudice" against his physical deficiencies.[15] To Takaoka, verbal torture in Japan was like physical torture in Brazil.

Rejecting the "colony" was not the only way Nikkei militants understood themselves. Militants were unusually high achievers even among educationally oriented Nikkei. They had left their rural homes to attend high school in more urban areas and then moved to the city of São Paulo for their university education, often living with older family members and other Nikkei. All remembered having difficulty adjusting to city life. They mentioned seeing television for the first time or having to wear a heavy jacket in São Paulo's cold weather. Many had joined Nikkei Catholic groups as youngsters and continued their participation after migrating to the city. The most important was the Associação Nipo-Brasileira Estrela de Manhã (Morning Star Japanese-Brazilian Association). It was directed in the fifties and sixties by Dom Pedro Paulo Koop, who later became bishop of Lins; in 1959, twenty-two hundred Japanese-Brazilians participated in an Estrela de Manhã conference in the city of Bauru.[16] A number of militants remembered the group as fundamental to their politicization because of priests who saw Catholic doctrine as justifying activism.

Nikkei in São Paulo during the dictatorship confronted stereotypes of themselves as docile and hard-working Brazilians, inclined to violence and passionately loyal to Japan.[17] In the 1960s such images resonated for two reasons. First, economic ascension in education and liberal professions made Japanese-Brazilian success particularly visible. Second, memories of the Shindo Renmei movement were widespread among the educated classes, government officials, and the police. The Shindo Renmei had disappeared by the end of the 1950s, but the memory of it continued in the DEOPS, where officials related it to Nikkei militancy, and in the Itamaraty (Brazilian Ministry of Foreign Relations), where it appeared in the context of repatriation issues and requests that property taken from Japanese citizens by the Brazilian government during World War II be returned.[18]

The Shindo Renmei was also a vivid memory for Nikkei, who discussed it both privately and in the Japanese-Brazilian press. Most of the militants with whom I spoke recalled overheard conversations among their relatives and neighbors about *kachigumi* (Shindo Renmei members). Jun Nakabayashi, a student leader and member of the National Liberation Alliance (Aliança Nacional Libertadora, ANL), made much of his father's *makegumi* (anti–Shindo Renmei) position, while Rioco Kaiano saw her own arrest and torture in the late 1960s in the light of her father's arrest and torture by the DEOPS some two decades earlier for his kachigumi activities.[19]

Nikkei violence was always juxtaposed against the image of docility. Thus Japanese-Brazilian militants, well dressed and polite, often became the anonymous public face of many militant groups in São Paulo. They rented rooms and bought groceries, exploiting the public assumption that one could expect nothing more than studiousness, hard work, and honesty from a well-dressed and soft-spoken "Japanese."[20] Japanese-Brazilians were expected to be reserved, so chatting was never expected. Militants played to the idea that Nikkei were antiyouth; they did not wear wild clothes or counterculture hairstyles; they did not talk too much or play too hard.

There was, however, a violent side to the identity coin. Militant leaders considered Nikkei primarily as soldiers (rather than as revolutionary theoreticians) because they were presumed to follow orders and to "get the job done correctly." An unremarkable twenty-year-old Japanese-Brazilian neighbor could also be the "Japanese terrorist" known throughout the city for robbing banks. The ethnic militancy of Japanese-Brazilian guerrillas was always tempered with the knowledge that much of their activity was successful because of majority stereotypes.

· · ·

Japanese-Brazilians were well-known members of student organizations and militant groups in the sixties and seventies. Mário Tokoro was an engineering student at the Aeronautical Technological Institute (Instituto Tecnológico de Aeronáutica, ITA) and was chosen as class orator for the school's 1965 graduation ceremonies. While Tokoro was not involved in armed struggle, he was a student leader, and the ITA had been targeted by the military regime as a "breeding ground for communists." Just three weeks before graduation, he was taken off a soccer field by an Air Force officer, driven home, given fifteen minutes to pack a bag, and then dropped at a bus station and ordered to leave town, expelled for his political positions.[21] Isamu Ito was elected vice president of the São Paulo State Union of Students (União Estadual dos Alunos) in 1967 and was imprisoned a number of times.[22] University of São Paulo (USP) students Ishiro Nagami and Yoshihiro Ono were killed in 1969 when the bomb-filled Volkswagen they were driving exploded.[23] Yoshitani Fujimori, Shizuo Osawa, and André Massafumi Yoshinaga were members of ex-army captain Carlos Lamarca's Vanguarda Popular Revolucionária. Carlos Marighella's ALN included the Amano brothers (Takao and João Katsunobu), the Takaoka brothers (Carlos and Luiz Massami), Miguel Nakamura, and André Tsutomo Ota.

One method of recruitment into militancy was via ethnic community organizations.[24] For example, a number of Jewish militants were led to political activism by madrichim (counselors) in a São Paulo Jewish summer camp.[25] Nikkei often met in ethnic organizations such as the Estrela da Manhã Catholic group or were recruited by Nikkei friends or family and then agitated together, sometimes by choice and sometimes at the insistence of their superiors. Oscar Akihico Terada and Issami Nakamura Okano, two USP students, were accused of distributing pamphlets and "subversive" newspapers together. Okano was first imprisoned in 1969 and then again in 1974, when he disappeared.[26] Mari Kamada, a member of Popular Liberation Movement (Movimento de Libertação Popular, MOLIPO), was trained by Hiroaki Torigoi. The two were accused of a number of joint actions, from painting revolutionary graffiti in public places to bombing a Sears department store.[27]

Nair Yumiko Kobashi, born in 1947 in a small Japanese rural community in Paraná, was a student at the University of São Paulo and an activist in the Conjunto Residencial da Universidade de São Paulo (CRUSP), the student residence halls. She was also a member of the Communist Party of Brazil (Partido Comunista do Brasil, PC do B) and was imprisoned for almost two years.[28] She believed that "we must have had some [ethnic] identity, or recognized it in some form. I remember the Japanese descendants, for example, [and] and a Trotskyite group with many Arabs. I found it funny; I said, 'Wow, they are all Arabs.' In the case of POLOP [Política Operária; Workers' Politics, Marxist Revolution Organization], there were lots of Jews."[29] Kobashi's memory is confirmed by Alex Polari of the VPR. His memoir mentions a group of Jewish militants known as "The Bund," in homage to the prewar Eastern European Jewish workers movements.[30] Not all groupings were self-created. The filmmaker Olga Yoshiko Futema re-members vividly a conversation with a cadre of the Brazilian Communist Party (Partido Comunista Brasileiro, PCB, different from the Communist Party of Brazil, PC do B), who told her that Japanese-Brazilians never made good militants because they were "too loyal" to their own families.[31]

THE FORCE OF NATIONAL LOGIC

A story was reported to me that I have never been able to confirm. It concerns two Japanese-Brazilian militants who were rumored to have fled to the United States in the late sixties. There they reintegrated into militant activity after being recruited by the I Wor Kuen, an Asian-American militant movement. It was assumed by local leftists that those of Asian descent would choose ethnic politics over class politics. That said, I have never found mention of Japanese-Brazilian militant activity in documentary information from Asian-American movements in the United States, and not a single Nikkei militant with whom I spoke in Brazil had ever head of the I Wor Kuen, the Red Guard Party of San Francisco, East Wind, or any other U.S. Asian-American movement. The story, indepen-dent of its veracity, is important because of the discontent it shows with diaspora: while Nikkei would have no opportunity to join an "ethnic" militant group in Brazil, or be interested in doing so, they were imagined to have to do exactly that in the United States.

NAMING AND IDENTITY

The question of names was important for all Brazilians who belonged to non-Catholic, non-European groups. For many (those of Jewish or Middle Eastern descent, for example), the physical ability to pass in day-to-day society often meant dual names, one for the "home" and another for the "street." A Brazilian of Lebanese ancestry might be known as Daú at home and, because *daú* means "light" in Arabic, have the name Luz (Portuguese for "light") in public. A Jewish-Brazilian might be called Luyba at home and Leony on the street. Yet physiognomy never revealed ethnicity in the two examples above. For Japanese-Brazilians, however, names were a disputed ethnic terrain because they could not be delinked from appearance.

Rioco Kaiano's story is typical. Born in 1948 in Guaimbê (São Paulo state), she became an active member of the Communist Party of Brazil (PC do B). She was imprisoned for more than eighteen months beginning in 1972 after trying to join the organization's attempt to foment a rural revolution in Araguaia, a region in the northern Brazilian state of Pará.[32] Her parents were farmers, her father having immigrated to Brazil in 1918 and mother having done so in 1920, and in her early years she was cared for mostly by her grandmother, who taught her to read, write, and speak Japanese. When she was a child, Kaiano remembers, most people had trouble pronouncing Rioco, her first name, since in Portuguese the final letter "o" is generally reserved for male names. For this reason it is not unusual to find female Nikkei (recall Tizuka Yamasaki from chapter 2) who have had their first names Brazilianized by changing the -ko to -ka.

Many of Kaiano's friends were "Brazilians" (her word) of Italian descent, and with them she spoke Portuguese. She recalled her "identity issues, since all the girls were baptized and I was not [silence]. For me, this was a dilemma, [since] I already felt different because of how I looked, and this made me even more different. . . . this religion thing is really strong, don't you think? It is that old story that I was not baptized, and if you were not baptized, in the minds of these people, you were filled with sin."[33]

Kaiano used her baptism to take the name Laura, which she insisted that her friends use. By linking the ritual to her Japanese language and physical features, she made clear her desire to fit in with "typical" Brazilians. From that point on, her name (like the names of the other children in her family) changed depending on the context. At home she and her sister were Rioco (Kaiano spells her name this way; the academic orthography would be Ryoko or Rioko) and Yoko, while in public they were usually known as Laura and Rosa. With "Brazilians" they introduced each other only as Laura and Rosa although today "Laura has disappeared . . . (because) the question of my identity related to this story of a Japanese name . . . this duality, this dubiousness of the name had to be resolved." Kaiano's comment implies that she could not imagine herself as Laura and that most Brazilians could not imagine her as Laura. Kaiano linked the two ideas in a discussion of name pronunciations. She believed that it was difficult for Brazilians to pronounce her birth name (Rioco) because the final o would indicate a male. It was equally hard for Japanese to pronounce her chosen name, Laura, since the sound of the letter r does not exist in Japanese. No matter which name she used, she became an outsider to one of the communities of which she was part.

In 1964, at the age of fifteen, Kaiano moved to São Paulo to continue her studies. She lived with her grandparents and older siblings in a house bought by Kaiano's father with money he had saved as he rose from farmworker to farm owner. The house itself was a space of multiple ethnic identities since the grandparents, who had immigrated to Brazil as adults, were "very Japanese," while Kaiano and her siblings were Brazilian-born. Kaiano's studies brought her into contact with a range of Brazilians, while her social life was more Nikkei oriented. She participated actively in the Estrela da Manhã Catholic group, where she met Takao Amano, who also became a militant.

For militants names also had special meaning. Remaining hidden, even while in public, was crucial to survival, and all activists lived with numerous names—their home name, their street name, their code name, and their false name. For Nikkei militants this became an extension of an already awkward social scenario.

Ethnic code names were common among Brazilian militants, but they were usually divorced from actual ethnicity. Ladislaw Dowbor of the VPR, for example, had the "Arab" code name Jamil even though he was of Polish ancestry.[34] This also was generally the pattern with Arab-Brazilians and Jewish-Brazilians, whose ethnic given names rarely were coupled to their code names or false names. Iara Iavelberg, a member of the October 8 Revolutionary Movement (Movimento Revolucionário 8 de Outubro, MR-8, a dissident movement from the Brazilian Communist Party, PCB), had a number of code names and false names, but none were identifiably Jewish (e.g., Sarah or Rachel), nor was she ever nicknamed "the Jewess" or anything similar.[35] None of the aforementioned Jewish-Brazilians recruited into militancy in summer camp had ethnic code names, although some had ethnically specific birth names.

Ethnic code names and false names, however, did exist. "Turco" (Turk) and "Alemão" (German) were commonly used, as they are in Brazilian society generally, but they were rarely applied to members of those ethnic backgrounds.[36] Ethnic naming was also related to hero worship among militants. Ivan Seixas, a member of the Tiradentes Revolutionary Movement (Movimento Revolucionário Tiradentes, MRT) who was imprisoned in 1971 at the age of sixteen, recalled that Giap (i.e., General Vo Nguyen Giap) and Ho Chi Minh were code names chosen in homage to communist leaders in Asia, but I have not found a single case of a Japanese-Brazilian choosing one of these names.[37] Ottoni Fernandes Júnior, imprisoned for six years because of his political militancy, relates in his memoir meeting ALN member Aton Fon Filho, whose father was Chinese and whose mother was Brazilian. Fon's "Oriental features" reminded Fernandes of Ho Chi Minh, but there is no indication that the militant saw himself in such a light.[38] Indeed, during Fon's trial no witnesses described him as "Oriental" or "Japanese," although one person did distinguish between the ALN's Takao Amano, "the Japanese," and Fon, "the mixed guy."[39]

Even aggressively asserted ethnic identity among non-Nikkei did not lead to ethnic naming in the context of militancy. Perhaps the most striking example can be found in the case of Carlos Marighella, leader of the ALN. Marighella was born in Salvador, Bahia, of an Italian immigrant father and an Afro-Brazilian mother.[40] Ethnicity was an important part of Marighella's self-image, as he made clear in the following poem:

Hey African-Brazil
My grandmother was a Black Haussa
She came from Africa
On a slave ship
My father came from Italy
Immigrant laborer
Brazil is mestiço
Mixture of Indian, black, white.[41]

While one might imagine such an open assertion of ethnicity would cause comment, the historiography mentions it only in passing, suggesting that Marighella's racial/ethnic background was his militancy.[42] Sílvio Tendler's excellent documentary, *Marighella: Retrato Falado do Guerrilheiro* (2001), unintentionally makes the point. Ethnicity surfaces only three times in the forty-five-minute film. Clara Charf, Marighella's wife and the child of Jewish parents (a point she makes frequently in interviews), first mentions his Italian father and Afro-Brazilian mother.[43] The second reference is by a narrator citing Marighella's comment, "Who am I? I am only a Bahian mulato. Brazil is mestiço." The final reference comes in an interview with Takao Amano, the Japanese-Brazilian who headed the Armed Tactical Group of the ALN. He describes Marighella's philosophy differently than did others interviewed in the film, inserting race and ethnicity as components of the leader's class consciousness: "[Marighella's] fight was against colonialism, for the blacks, for the Indians, for the working class."[44]

Marighella's ethnicity never made him anything less than a "typical" Brazilian, except to the members of minority groups mentioned above. Japanese-Brazilians confronted exactly the opposite scenario, since the majority population insisted on their "Japaneseness." As a result, names had different connotations for Nikkei militants than they did for others. Nikkei false names had to be ethnically specific since they were for public consumption—they were put on official (often forged) documentation that was presented when a militant was stopped by authorities. Under these dangerous circumstances there was a correct assumption that a Japanese-Brazilian without a "Japanese" name would be highly scrutinized.

This distinguished Nikkei from other minority Brazilians whose physical appearance either did not "show" ethnicity or whose "ethnic" appearance was not linked to a specific nation. For example, Jewish- or Lebanese- or Italian-Brazilians could use any false name (except a Japanese-Brazilian one) with impunity, since nothing about their appearance would suggest their ethnic background. Afro-Brazilians were also viewed as "ethnic" but had not used ethnically specific names for hundreds of years. The false name "João da Silva" could work for militants from any of the above backgrounds with one glaring exception, Japanese-Brazilians. Darci Toshiko Miyaki, born in the farming town of Araçatuba more than five hundred kilometers from the city of São Paulo, was a law student at the University of São Paulo when she joined the ALN. Her false name was Luciana Sayori Shindo, not unlike Takao Amano's "Oishi," Hiroaki Torigoe's "Massahiro Nakamura," and Nair Yumiko Kobashi's "Christina Akemi Ueda."[45]

Code names were different from false names. They were used by militants to hide their identities from the authorities and from each other, under the assumption that most people would betray confidences when tortured. While Nikkei chose code names in the same way as other militants, they were often called "Japonês" or "Japa" anyway. Sérgio Tujiwara of the PC do B chose the code name "Horácio" but was called "Japonês," as was Yoshitani Fujimori, who chose the code names "Antenor" and "Edgar," and Koji Okabayashi, whose chosen code name was "Mário."[46] Nair Yumiko Kobashi used the code name "Angélica" but was known as "Japa" or "Japinha," names she remembers with fondness.[47] Alcides Yukimitsu Mamizuka, a student leader at the State University of Campinas (Unicamp) and a member of the ALN who specialized in propaganda activities (and later became president of the Campinas Chamber of Deputies), was called "China," a name used as a synonym for "Japanese."[48]

On the surface using names with a clear ethnic denomination seems a dangerous choice. If the raison d'être of a code name is disguise, why call Nikkei militants "Jap" or "Japanese?" There seem to be two related reasons. First, many Brazilians saw "Japaneseness" as so essential that they could not imagine any Nikkei who was not called "Japa." While this term and others like it (notably *neguinho* [little blacky] and *negão* [big blacky], which are commonly used in Brazil among family members and friends) might appear racist to U.S.-based readers, many Brazilians describe them as simply, and even endearingly, descriptive. This understanding is seen in the surprise with which most people (but not all, as we will see in the next chapter) responded to my queries about their code names: to former militants it was obvious that a Japanese-Brazilian would be called *japa, japinha,* or *japonês.*

A second reason that *japa* continued to be used as a nickname or code name despite its inability to camouflage identity is that hiding the "Japaneseness" of a Nikkei militant seemed a waste of time, whether with a false name, code name, or nickname. As was the case with Japanese-Brazilian performers who were presumed, independent of their acting skills, to be able to play roles only as geishas and Nisei, physiognomy and culture were assumed to make Nikkei undisguisable. Police documentation is filled with witness reports in which only Japanese-Brazilians stood out. These reports often included a witness sheet that described the heights, weights, ages, and races of assailants. Generally the "race" or "color" description was one word: *moreno, mestiço,* or *branco.* Descriptions of Nikkei, in contrast, almost always included the word *elemento,* suggesting a scientific biological understanding of Japaneseness. While *elemento* was often used in criminal descriptions used by the Brazilian police, it did not appear frequently for those accused of political crimes. Thus the ethnic specificity of descriptions like "an element with the characteristics of a Japanese" created a discourse that does not appear to have been applied widely.[49]

A confidential Army report on an ALN training mission to Cuba in 1970 showed that the military knew ten of the fifteen participants only by their nicknames or code names. Seven were undescribed, but three received in-depth treatment that highlighted their ethnic backgrounds:

> Ramon—originally from São Paulo, Jewish descent, white color, blondish, medical student (2nd year in 1968), apparently 25 years old.
>
> Luiz—Armenian descent, white color, ruddy complexion.
>
> Tanaka—originally from São Paulo, Nisei, normal physique, full hair typical of the Japanese race.[50]

Ethnic naming was not only applied to individuals. Sometimes assumptions of group solidarity created a more informal language of difference. Rioco Kaiano and Nair Yumiko Kobashi both remembered with pleasure that when they walked through the University of São Paulo campus with other Japanese-Brazilian activists they were called the "Japanese Army" and the "Vietcong Army."[51] Kaiano's memory both constructed and deconstructed the ethnic meaning of the phrase "the Japanese Army":

> *Lesser:* Did other Nikkei call you and your friends "The Japanese Army"?
>
> *Kaiano:* No, No. She [the one who first called us "The Japanese Army"] died in

Araguaia. She was called Helenira [Rezende de Souza Nazareth]. . . . She was black and she was a strong leader [she was on the directorate of the National Student Union], this woman, from the Faculty of Letters. She was older than me. She was a leader, very charismatic[,] . . . she was nice, she was adorable, she rooted for Corinthians [the São Paulo soccer team associated with the lower classes]. She was a sambista, you know. She was very happy!

Lesser: What did you think when she called you the Japanese Army?

Kaiano: We found it. . . . funny. Because it was . . . funny. It did not have a connotation, you know. She was really tall, black. . . . And we were all short. All little things . . . it's funny because some Japanese women are tall but we were all short. So there was me, Sueli, Nair, Eni, there was another called Nana; we were all short. This was really funny. We would go off to a protest march, there in a line, and she [Helenira] would say, "There goes the Japanese Army." It was like a compliment, to show . . . that we were Japanese women. We were there on the Left, in the struggle. . . . It had another meaning because she often said that we were Vietcong. We were the Vietcong Army because of our physical aspects. I remember that this made us proud, because Vietcong represented to us what a revolution could be. So she sometimes called us the Japanese Army, and other times we were Vietcong.

Kaiano's comments show how ethnic discourses in Brazil functioned. When she discussed Helenira, she represented the physical differences between Nikkei and Afro-Brazilians not only by color but by height, an indicator that would rarely be used to define race, although it might be one of many stereotypes related to ethnicity. Helenira's imposition of distinction on the Nikkei women was acceptable, perhaps because Kaiano saw Helenira's racial difference as similar to hers. As long as both parties in the conversation were minorities, ethnic assumptions about each other were permitted since, it seemed, they did not impose hierarchies. Kaiano was comfortable being labeled a member of the "Japanese Army" even though the actual "army" of Japan in the seventies would be considered a foe by the Brazilian Left.[52] Being called "Japanese Army" was the same as being called "Vietcong," and thus it was linked to a broad notion of revolutionary Asianness.

The same label of "Vietcong" that was remembered with such pride was dangerous for Nikkei militants if it came from agents of the military regime. During one of our conversations Kaiano remembered that an uncle who worked at the *Estado de S. Paulo* newspaper phoned her parents in panic when an article on Vietcong atrocities was placed alongside a photograph of her carrying a poster during a protest. While I could not find the specific article or photo, I did find a 1968 article that suggested that those in the student movement were traitors to Brazil. It linked student protests with a photograph of the Vietcong flag via the headline, "Protest only changes its flag: that of the Vietcong."[53]

Stereotyping often grated on Japanese-Brazilian leftists. Former militants repeatedly told me that they had sought to divorce themselves from the assumption of "Japanese" ethnicity. Marta Tanisaki's story is typical. Her parents had emigrated from Japan to Brazil sometime prior to World War II and she was brought up outside of the city of São Paulo. When she moved to the city she lived in an "ethnic" rooming house which she hated for its Japaneseness, even though "in the end I liked that crappy place." When Tanisaki entered university in 1966, her mother (by then a widow) moved to São Paulo and the two lived together. Like many Nikkei of her generation Tanisaki was bilingual and had both Japanese and Brazilian names—in her official documents she is listed as Marta Masako Tanisaki, but at home she was known as Mate—a nickname for Masako but also a type of Brazilian tea (*chá-mate*).

Tanisaki entered the student movement by volunteering to work in a São Paulo slum. Like thousands of students around Brazil, she became even more active after hearing that Edson Luís de Lima Souto had been killed by police in Rio de Janeiro on 28 March 1968. Lima Souto and other students were preparing a protest march, ostensibly against the badly organized Calabouço student restaurant, as part of a larger movement for educational reform. When military police shock troops were ordered into the restaurant, he was shot in the head and pronounced dead on arrival at a local hospital. The following day fifty thousand people attended his open-casket funeral, then marched through the streets to the Rio de Janeiro Legislative Assembly.

The death of Edson Luís de Lima Souto mobilized students around Brazil. On 1 April 1968, student protesters occupied the University of Brasília; on the same day violent protests erupted in Rio de Janeiro and in all the country's major cities. In São Paulo a huge march took place, ending in front of the municipal theater in the city center. Student action continued over the next months as did increasing military mobilization. Brazilians remember 21 June 1968 as "Bloody Friday," when almost one thousand protesters were imprisoned in Rio de Janeiro after violent conflicts left twenty-three protesters and thirty-five soldiers wounded. During the rest of 1968 Brazilian cities often seemed like war zones, with conflicts between protesters and police, and at time between opposition groups.

It was in this environment that Tanisaki joined the Popular Action (Ação Popular), a group that emerged from the Catholic University Youth (Juventude Universitária Católica, JUC) in 1963. By 1968 the JUC had moved toward a variant of what Jacob Gorender calls "Christian Maoism," and later most of its members joined a wing of the Communist Party of Brazil (PC do B).[54] Tanisaki does not think of herself primarily as "Japanese" or "Nikkei" and does not remember anyone making a specific comment on her ethnicity during her years of militancy. Yet the story of her first assignment by the Ação Popular's Central Committee suggests otherwise. According to Tanisaki, "All the Japanese militants [there were five in the group] from São Paulo were sent out of the state. [We] were sent to Maringá [a city in the state of Paraná with a significant population of Japanese immigrants and their descendants], all us of us." Tanisaki understood this strategy to be protective since "if we went to Ceará [a state in the Northeast with few Nikkei] we would call attention to ourselves." Soon thereafter the group was sent to Curitiba, the largest city in Paraná. Although Curitiba had a large Nikkei population, "how could we agitate in a place where we did not know anyone?"[55] Here Tanisaki makes a subtle point. She believes that she and the other Nikkei were sent to Curitiba to work among Nikkei, but they were unable to do so because the presumed ethnic community did not in fact function as the majority imagined.

THE REPRESSIVE IMAGINARY

Japanese-Brazilian militants were stereotyped by both their comrades and the repressive forces. This was done in a number of ways. The São Paulo DEOPS files were organized in a way that highlighted Japanese-Brazilians as subjects of repression and as individuals to be repressed.[56] The DEOPS topical files were dominated by Shindo Renmei material (some 19 volumes), the largest single group in that collection. Files on individuals, however, were not simply alphabetized by name. Rather they were separated into "Brazilian names" and "Foreign names" without regard to formal citizenship. Nikkei were in the "foreign" category, while the "Brazilian" classification included many immigrants who were not yet citizens, notably recent arrivals from Portugal.

The DEOPS files are filled with references to "Japanese" militants whose real names, false names, or code names were unknown. Those accused often mentioned meetings with unnamed "Japanese" militants, or with militants known only as "the Japanese." During interrogation ALN member Paulo de Tarso Vannuchi mentioned numerous people whom he knew only as "the Japanese."[57] In another case, an ALN attack on two police officers in October 1971 left one of the militants severely wounded. He was taken to a hospital and subsequently arrested by the DEOPS. In his interrogation, he named his partner as "Roberto Japonês."[58] A "Roberto Japonês" also appeared in the testimony of MOLIPO member Mari Kamada, although it is unclear if it was the same person. She said that they had stolen license plates together and was only able to describe him in the most generic terms: "Japanese; round face; short, straight, black hair; not too tall; slightly fat."[59] DEOPS agents appear to have accepted the facelessness of these "Japanese," effectively ending attempts at identification.

Such documentation can be read in a number of ways. Most obviously, the accused could actually have met Japanese-Brazilians whose names were never used or whose code names or nicknames included the word *Japonês*. A different reading, however, might be one of resistance. For example, militants might have been confident that saying, "I met some Japanese," during interrogation would be accepted by repressive forces, especially given the frequent linkage of Nikkei to militancy by the DEOPS. For example, no one ever discovered who "Roberto Japonês" was. Might he, like many unnamed "Japanese" in the files, not be Nikkei at all? Perhaps he did not even exist.

DEOPS

There is much debate about the veracity of information found in the DEOPS archives. While a few scholars appear to take the materials at face value, most researchers understand that "statements" in the files were usually written under the threat of violence or after torture had taken place. Many confessions contain a mixture of accurate and inaccurate information, and I never asked people I interviewed what they said while in custody.

What scholars can do with some confidence, however, is examine the strategic meaning of the massive collection of information by the DEOPS. Interrogation statements followed a careful script in which the accused moved from being conned by political movements to realizing the mistakes she or he had made. A desire for normalcy certainly drove recordkeeping: anyone who examines the DEOPS archives in São Paulo, Rio de Janeiro,

Curitiba, or Belo Horizonte would be impressed by the multiple copies that exist of every item, often all in one repetitive packet.

The discourses of Japanese militancy that circulated in São Paulo were one focus of an all-night conversation I had with Jun Nakabayashi. A law student and political activist in the mid-sixties, he joined Carlos Marighella's Ação Libertadora Nacional and later fled to Chile. He remembered with some annoyance that early political bank robberies did not involve Nikkei, but that police pushed the idea that a "Japanese" was involved. "It appears that there was a person who kind of looked like a Japanese. Now, the person who did those first bank robberies, I knew him later on. He was not Japanese. That person known as 'Japanese' was not a Japanese!"[60] Police insistence on "Japanese" involvement caused consternation among Nikkei, who believed they were being racially profiled by the authorities. The DEOPS files contain numerous robbery cases where witness testimony indicates that one or more of the assailants was of "Japanese" or "Nipponic" descent. The DEOPS, in order to identify these "Japanese," would create a lineup with only one Nikkei, who was invariably identified as the aggressor.[61]

Nakabayashi was arrested (and released) two days before he was to go to Cuba for guerrilla training in April or May 1968. He was surprised to learn during his interrogation that his Cuba trip was unknown to the police, who simply were "looking for a Japanese" and had rounded him up in a broad sweep. He was let go quickly because the police were looking for a thin Japanese and "I was pretty fat in those days."[62] The student Ossamu Nakamura was arrested after showing his legitimate documents at a police roadblock because "[that] Japanese was confused with an ALN militant, Issami Nakamura Okano."[63] Such confusion was common: a newspaper article on bank robberies "committed by a group that included a Japanese" noted that police were focusing on Massafumi Yoshinaga when the person responsible was in fact (so the newspaper claimed) Yoshitani Fujimori.[64]

I do not want to suggest that citizens who witnessed militant activity had ethnic clarity *except* in regard to Japanese-Brazilians. On the contrary, statements often showed phenotypic connections between Japanese and Northeastern Brazilians or Andean peoples. Many Brazilians "saw" Asians and indigenous Latin Americans as similar, a position taken by some early twentieth-century Japanese scholars and diplomats, who claimed that Amazonian peoples were a "lost tribe" of Japanese.[65] Jun Nakabayashi remembered one (non-Asian-descended) militant from the Brazilian Northeast who told everyone that he was "Japanese." This may have been the person that a witness to a robbery described to *O Estado de S. Paulo* in 1968 as having the "body language of a Japanese or a Bolivian."[66] Five witnesses to a 1969 bank robbery provided the following information to police: two said that the robbers were all white, one remembered only a tall Japanese, another recalled a Japanese and a person who "looked Northeastern [and] also white," and the fifth described "an element of yellow color, or better, a Japanese."[67]

In the late sixties an increasing number of crimes, political and otherwise, were attributed to Nikkei, a frightening proposition for many Paulistanos, who believed that Japanese-Brazilians were a paragon of hard work and honesty. ALN member Ottoni Fernandes Júnior wrote that "the repressive forces, the press, and the popular imagination created a myth: that every bank robbery was committed by a Japanese and a blonde woman."[68] In one case the two stereotypes were linked by a gas station manager who insisted that he had been robbed by "a Japanese individual, with a blond beard and moustache, with a beret on his head." The officer in charge assumed the robbery was politically motivated, but the victim later identified the assailant as Francisco José de Oliveira, a non-Nikkei criminal with a blond moustache and beard![69]

The claim that Japanese-Brazilians were involved in political and criminal activity was reinforced by the police and the press. A man whose Volkswagen had been robbed at gunpoint said that the criminal "appeared Japanese." His comments were changed by a law enforcement official, who wrote in his official report that he could "affirm that it was a Japanese person."[70] An early 1966 article in the *Diário Popular* alleged that "Japanese terrorists" were operating in São Paulo and suggested that residents believed that the Shindo Renmei had returned to action.[71] The *Jornal da Tarde* (the afternoon edition of *O Estado de S. Paulo* and the newspaper that police often used to feed information to the public) pointed out that officials investigating militant activity were "confused by witness descriptions of assaults and attacks that always mention the presence of a Japanese." According to the report, new methods had been developed to distinguish one Japanese from another but this had led to a frightening discovery: there were many different "Japanese connected to terrorism."[72] The article itself included four photographs of Nikkei militants, with the wrong names attached to all!

Presumptions of Nikkei revolutionary dynamism stemmed from two very different ideas common among authorities and the general population since the thirties. One was that it was hard physically to differentiate "good" Japanese-Brazilians from "bad" ones (since all Japanese-Brazilians "looked the same"); the other was that Nikkei were especially violent as a result of a heritage of warfare and emperor worship. As a result, wanted posters of "terrorists" had a special resonance when Japanese-Brazilians were included.[73] One lurid and widely distributed wanted poster was designed (I do not know if this was purposeful or not) so that the text drew attention to the headshot photographs of the terrorists below, neatly lined up in rows of eight:

> THE FIVE NAMES ON THIS POSTER RISK PRISON AND DEATH
>
> THE POLICE ARE LOOKING FOR THEM
>
> TERRORISTS ASSASSINS
>
> WANTED
>
> THEY ASSAULT—THEY STEAL—THEY KILL
>
> PARENTS OF FAMILIES
>
> (AND THEY ARE IN HIDING)

The eye is led rapidly by the upside down pyramid to the first line of photographs which included Yoshitani Fujimori and André Massafumi Yoshinaga.[74] Both were dressed in tie and jacket and seem to be posing for school pictures, a difference from most (but not all) of the other photographs of non-Nikkei, which are tight headshots. The *Jornal da Tarde* even illustrated the margin around its reprint of the poster with a machine gun.

The press was obligated to publish the wanted posters, but it also took a cue from them in its own articles on the armed struggle. Reports were often illustrated with photos of Fujimori or Massafumi Yoshinaga, even when the text was unrelated to the two or even the militant organizations to which they belonged. One full-page article published in *O Estado de S. Paulo/Jornal da Tarde* was titled "HERE ARE THE NINETEEN FACES OF TERROR." The largest single photograph is that of André Massafumi Yoshinaga, perfectly centered on the page. Next to him is Yoshitani Fujimori. This was no accident: the text notes that they were "the only two Niseis that appear in the police reports" and that Fujimori was also known as "Edgar, or simply Japanese."[75]

Violence, (in)visibility, and Nikkei ethnicity were frequently connected in press and police reports. In 1970 the largest robbery in Brazilian history, 2.5 million U.S. dollars in cash, took place at the Rio de Janeiro mansion of a woman who was supposedly the lover of former São Paulo governor Adhemar de Barros. A witness described two people, "a man" with a knife and "a Japanese" with a pistol. His study of photographs at the local police station led to the identification, according to the newsmagazine *Veja*, of Carlos Lamarca, "one of the major terrorist leaders in Brazil," and Yoshitani Fujimori, "the Japanese who has been present at the majority of bank robberies in São Paulo."[76] The authorities had no idea if Fujimori was involved in "the majority" of all bank robberies, but they gave this information to the press. Many years later those involved in the actual robbery expressed surprise that Fujimori's name appeared since, they claimed, he was not involved.[77]

The conflation of many Nikkei militants into one created a focal point for witnesses. A soldier who was assaulted and had his weapons taken by four men was asked by police to describe his assailants. Only one person "remained clearly in his memory, the physiognomy of one of them, a twenty-year-old man, of Japanese descent . . . carrying an INA [Indústria Nacional de Armas] machine gun." A witness to a bank robbery in late 1969 could only remember that one militant "was of Japanese descent, carrying a machine gun, but [he could not] retain his physical aspects in his memory."[78] An attack on a Military Police captain in October 1971 led to two descriptions, a vague "moreno" and a "Japanese, fat, using glasses with tinted lenses with a white metal frame," who was carrying a Beretta pistol.[79]

The DEOPS highlighted the participation of Nikkei in political crimes with stories planted in the press. An article on a mid-1969 bank robbery in São Paulo claimed that a single "Japanese" participated "in almost all the assaults and [always stood], machine gun in hand, watching the door." Seventeen-year-old Paulo Falcão was passing by the bank and thought that the militant was a bank guard. Suddenly "the Japanese at the door, with a moustache, goatee, and machine gun called out 'Hey dude, come on inside.' "[80] Another *O Estado de S. Paulo* article on the arrests of six young people for distributing a pamphlet titled "The Paths of the Brazilian Revolution" in front of a São Paulo movie house mentioned only two of the detainees, a French citizen and "a young Nisei, carrying a revolver." The majority of those arrested, presumably "Brazilians" rather than "foreigners," were not singled out for individual mention.[81] A *Veja* article on five militants killed in conflicts with police mentioned only one by name, Hiroaki Torigoi of the MOLIPO.[82]

During the sixties and seventies leaders of the Nikkei community grew increasingly concerned about the effect of press reports on what they always presented as the "Model Immigrant Colony." In 1966 the *Paulista Shimbun* noted that a group of Japanese-born smugglers who acted "with impunity due to the protection from within the Japanese colony" had been reclassified by the DEOPS as "terrorists," casting a political shadow on the community.[83] A few years later, *The Mainichi Daily News* of Tokyo interviewed Nikkei in São Paulo and found that many believed the large number of press reports on Japanese-Brazilian guerrillas was a government message, since "so many Japanese are committing to the guerrilla activity, there is a collective responsibility of Japanese society."[84]

The DEOPS files show the same association between violence, Nikkei guerrillas, and the "Japanese-Brazilian colony" that was found in some segments of the broader population. Those files, essentially a script of the relationship between a repressive state and its nonconformist citizens, alleged that Japanese-Brazilian militants were almost always machine-gun-toting and more violent than the norm. This was different from descriptions of other militants who, while described as generically violent, were usually identified by what they said or how they looked in terms of hair style, clothing, height, or weight, not by the weapons they carried. Phrases like "the Japanese with the INA [a Brazilian-made .45 calibre machine gun]" were typical, and VPR militant Celso Lungaretti remembered how depressed André Massafumi Yoshinaga became when the repressive forces and the press began to claim erroneously that he was the "famous Japanese with the machine gun" who was robbing banks.[85] Witness and police reports almost always described Nikkei as armed and difficult to identify because they all looked the same. This typecasting was similar to a tendency among the DEOPS and the press to define women militants as "blondes," regardless of their hair color.[86] In the press and in DEOPS reports Japanese-Brazilians were *always* described primarily as "Japanese" and gun-toting, suggesting a group rather than individual association to violence.[87]

The presumption of Nikkei brutality is also present in the "fictionalized memoirs" of former ALN guerrilla Carlos Eugênio Paz, where characters named Seishi (who Paz tells readers is Yoshitani Fujimori), Tanaka (Takao Amano), and Osaka (André Yoshinaga Massafumi) are all presented as vicious. Seishi first appears robbing an armed car where he "blows out the front windshield with his FAL [Fuzil Automático Leve, a Belgian-made light automatic rifle]." Tanaka is introduced as the "military commander of the Armed Tactical Group," a position that Amano held in the ALN. He is later described as "the portrait of armed action, who demonstrated more than once his dedication and valor."[88] Paz's fictionalized descriptions of Amano were replicated in the (at least ostensibly) nonfictional arena: a military tribunal in 1971 emphasized in convicting Amano that he "almost always used a machine gun."[89]

. . . But getting him to speak with me about his ethnic experiences in the armed struggle was impossible. When I first called him at his home he turned me down by saying that he had nothing to do with the "Japanese colony." This was something of a surprise since many people had described him to me as "the most Japanese" of the Nikkei guerrillas. After a second phone call I faxed him the questions I wanted to ask but I received no response. One evening, I was waiting at a metro station for my friends Edu and Robi to pick me up for our weekly evening of squash (the sport) and beer (the food). Who was standing there but Takao Amano? I have to admit I debated introducing myself, in my shorts and with my sports bag. I did, and he could not have been nicer. But he still would not, and never did, agree to an interview.

The state discourse of violence was refracted by Nikkei, who often believed that "a tendency to obey, to maintain a certain discipline," made them particularly good at certain military tasks.[90] This idea is similar to that attached to the high casualty rates and medals of valor in the U.S. Army among the segregated Japanese-American 442nd Regimental Combat Team during World War II.[91] In Brazil, Japanese-Brazilian soldiers who fought with the forces of São Paulo state in the "Constitutionalist Revolution" of 1932 against the federal government were portrayed in both the Nikkei and non-Nikkei press as genetically disciplined and loyal, a biological reformulation of Naoki Sakai's formulation that "the history of modern Japan is nothing but a history in which a national community is formed as a community of 'unnatural' death."[92]

Some Nikkei militants rejected the idea that they or their comrades were uniquely violent. Yet they often redirected our conversations toward Nikkei police and military officers, whom they saw as ethnically violent and whose numbers had expanded greatly beginning in the mid-1950s. Our conversations also led to references to Harry Shibata, a Nikkei physician and director of the São Paulo State Forensic Medical Institute (Instituto Médico Legal) in the sixties and seventies. He claimed falsely that a number of militants had died of natural causes or suicides, when in fact their deaths were the result of torture.[93]

I do not want to push my point too far. The idea that certain ethnic groups have particular characteristics is common. In the same way that Nikkei militants referred to the disgraced Shibata, Jewish-Brazilian militants with whom I spoke mentioned Isaac Abramovitch, a colleague of Shibata's who also helped to hide torture by signing autopsy reports and death certificates as suicides. This type of internal linkage can also be found in the discussion by

Alfred Sirkis, a Jewish-Brazilian, of ethnic moments in his memoir *Os Carbonários*. The first took place in 1969 in his opposition to kidnapping the Israeli consul, which he argued could lead to two negative results: (1) Israel might not negotiate for the consul's release and (2) Jewish-Brazilians might consider the action to be anti-Semitic. This, according to Sirkis, led to a heated exchange with another militant who believed that Sirkis's opposition was based primarily on his own ethnicity and his unwillingness to accept being castigated by his "countrymen." Another "ethnic" moment came during Sirkis's participation in the kidnapping of the German ambassador Ehrenfried von Holleben in June 1970. He recalled a conversation with the ambassador over a militant who "looked German" but was actually the son of Polish Jews.[94] The DEOPS, however, were not interested in this aspect of ethnicity when they interrogated the ambassador after his release. Rather, they pressed von Holleben repeatedly about whether a "Japanese" was among his kidnappers, even after he had told them that they all wore hoods.[95]

Why were Nikkei guerrillas perceived and remembered as so violent? One reason was that the cultural continuity between modern Nikkei and historical samurais and kamikaze pilots in a uniquely brutal Japan was reinforced and made real by the Shindo Renmei and images of Nikkei militancy.[96] Nikkei were not only frighteningly violent, they were also frighteningly modern, since Japanese products were known for their cutting-edge technology. Police and press reports describing Yoshitani Fujimori usually mentioned his electronics skills and his propensity for violence in the same sentence.[97] Intelligence agents conflated "Japanese militants" who were citizens of Japan and "Japanese militants" who were Brazilians. The language used to describe the Tel Aviv trial of Japanese Red Army member Kozo Okamoto (who had participated in a 1972 attack on Lod Airport) in *O Estado de S. Paulo* used the same term (*terrorista japonês*) used to describe militant Nikkei in Brazil.[98]

The association of Japan with Brazil via Nikkei led to the preparation of a secret, and wildly untrue, 1972 report by the DEOPS and the Naval Intelligence Center (Centro de Informações da Marinha, CENIMAR), two institutions involved in suppressing militant activity. Titled "Japanese Terrorism in Brazil and Latin America: Revelations and Warnings—Internationalization of Terror," the document claimed that an informant who was "intimately connected to the Japanese in São Paulo" had discovered a plot in which "forty-seven or forty-nine *fanatic* Japanese *elements* . . . will enter Brazil with passports in the names of Japanese mythological 'patriots,' sensitizing the youth of the powerful Japanese colony in Brazil." Linking Japanese technology to Japanese fanaticism, the authors claimed that Japanese Red Army members had invented a way to bring weapons through the airport metal detectors in Brazil. The background material included newspaper articles on the Japanese Red Army and Japanese student movement activities from the United States and France together with notations on the activities of Japanese-Brazilian guerrillas.[99] Yet militant activity among Brazilian Nikkei was generally unknown among the U.S. public and among Asian-American militants in the United States.[100]

One of the guerrillas most associated by the police and press with violence was Yoshitani Fujimori. He had been born in 1944 in the interior of São Paulo in an area of Shindo Renmei activity. He spoke Japanese well and was a member of the VPR. He was killed in 1970, either in a shootout or after being wounded and captured by DEOPS officials involved in Operação Bandeirante (OBAN), a massive state effort, which began in 1969, to wipe out armed resistance.[101] Among Nikkei, Fujimori is remembered as the first to rob a bank. Both Jun Nakabayshi of the ALN and Shizuo Osawa of the VPR, who have never met each other, independently complained to me that because of Fujimori, people in São Paulo thought "every bank robbery was done by a Japanese."[102]

The Brazilian press paid much attention to the "renowned" Fujimori, as he was called by the U.S. State Department, often illustrating their articles with photographs and wanted posters.[103] Academic works also portray Fujimori as violent and courageous. Jacob Gorender's history of the armed struggle uses this phrase: "Fighters like Fujimori, who were hunted like animals, still came out into daylight to protect the pamphleteers and had to fight duels with police patrols."[104] A similar image is proffered in Luís Mir's widely read but unreliable and often undocumented *A Revolução Impossível*: "During the first weapons training session . . . Fujimori shocked everyone with his precision. Chosen to get a car for a bank robbery, he tried to rob a Veraneio (a brand of van) and the driver, a small businessman who was carrying the weeks' salary for his employees, reacted. Fujimori shot him various times. Some militants were shocked. The businessman was not armed."[105]

A newspaper report published many years after Fujimori's killing of the businessman quotes an unnamed ex-VPR member describing Fujimori as "an electronics technician who did not read Marx before entering the guerrilla, where he became enchanted by the weapons, the danger, and by the romantic actions, during which he felt like an audacious gentleman trooper." The reporter himself called Fujimori "a violent man, whose life ended violently." *O Estado de S. Paulo* called him "a cold assassin."[106] Elio Gaspari's four-volume study of the dictatorship mentioned Fujimori twice, once for shooting a military policeman in the back and later for "having two deaths and almost ten armed actions on his shoulders." Gaspari concluded his discussion with Fujimori being killed by police with five bullets to the head.[107]

All reports and everyone with whom I spoke agreed that Fujimori was a dedicated revolutionary. Shizuo Osawa told me that "Fujimori barely ever spoke; he was a soldier ready for action, ready to follow orders." Ex-Army sergeant and VPR member Darci Rodrigues, in an interview during his exile in Cuba, offered a more nuanced view. He called Fujimori "an excellent comrade, serious, disciplined, with a great sense of responsibility and genius that never impeded him being a good *companheiro*, always read to take on the 'hard' jobs."[108] It was this last trait that made Fujimori a particular target of the military state and Lieutenant Colonel Leonidas Pires Gonçalves, commander of one of the units sent to capture Fujimori, called him a "cold bandit."[109]

Fujimori's reputation was consolidated in 1969. Together with Carlos Lamarca, he set up a guerrilla training camp in the Vale do Ribeira, an extremely poor area of the far southern part of the state of São Paulo, near the Japanese agricultural communities in Registro and Iguape. The camp was composed of two farms, together known as the "Núcleo Carlos Marighella." Recruits were brought blindfolded, by a circuitous route. One of these trainees was Shizuo Osawa. After completing the guerrilla training course, Osawa returned to São Paulo in late February 1970 to begin urban operations. When Lamarca heard in April that Osawa had been captured, he ordered the immediate demobilization of the site; most of the two dozen militants in residence were put on a public bus dressed as local farmers and sent away. Eight VPR members remained and became the targets of an intense search by five thousand soldiers, which according to the *Miami Herald* included the dropping of napalm.[110]

The story of how the eight VPR members evaded the thousands of soldiers sent to capture them is the stuff of legend. The battle over how the story is told, which shifts blame from one side to the other, is well documented. Two incidents, remembered in different ways, suggest how ideas about Nikkei ethnicity became embedded in memory. The first episode took place when the eight VPR guerrillas came upon a military police unit. The state version suggests that Fujimori wanted to machine gun them all to death. This, according to a press report, "only did not take place [because he was] contained by his own companions."[111] A VPR manifesto published in September 1970 suggests a more classic military confrontation, where a firefight ended with a number of captured soldiers. The prisoners in hand, Lamarca is said to have made a deal with the lieutenant in charge. The officer would lead them past other patrols in the region, and the guerrillas would escape in return for the lives of all the soldiers. According to a VPR statement signed by Lamarca, the lieutenant did not act in good faith and tried to lead the guerrillas into a trap. The guerrillas understood that if they shot the soldier, or let him go, it would give away their location. A "revolutionary judgment" took place, and most press reports at the time attributed the killing of the lieutenant to Lamarca.[112] Sirkis, however, said that Lamarca told him that "the Jap killed [the lieutenant] with the butt of his FAL, right on the back of the head," an act which shocked Sirkis.[113]

All the versions represent Fujimori as an unsentimental killing machine. The press report had him ready to massacre the soldiers, while his companion Sirkis suggested that Fujimori was prepared to commit a highly violent act which others guerrillas were not. Such ideas are present in Emiliano José and Oldack Miranda's biography, *Lamarca: O Capitão da Guerrilha*, which argues that Lamarca saw Fujimori as a "brother" because he had "the patience of Che Guevara, making him the 'perfect warrior.'"[114]

A second incident also emphasized Fujimori's violence. It involved Second Sergeant Kogi Kondo, a seventeen-year military veteran, who was tried in a military tribunal together with three of the eight VPR guerrillas who had escaped from the Vale do Ribeira: Carlos Lamarca, Ariston Oliveira Lucena, and Yoshitani Fujimori.[115] There is no evidence that Sergeant Kondo was a member of the VPR, or any revolutionary group, so why was he judged together with the militants? His "crime" was the bad luck of being a Nikkei soldier captured by a Nikkei militant.

The story, according to the prosecution, began in May 1970, when Sergeant Kondo joined "Operação Registro," whose goal was to find and destroy the guerrillas' bases in the Vale do Ribeira. On 31 May, a Sunday, Kondo, armed only with a pistol, took a truck and four unarmed soldiers to the Tanaka Fountain, a cistern near their military encampment named after a Japanese immigrant who had settled in the region. As they drove to the Tanaka Fountain they came upon a hitchhiker (Ariston Oliveira Lucena), and Kondo stopped the truck to offer a lift. During the conversation, one of the soldiers, Manoel Carreira, realized that the passenger was armed. According to the court papers, one of the soldiers shouted to Kondo, "It's a terrorist, what do we do?" Lucena pulled his pistol on Sergeant Kondo and forced him to give up his weapon. Suddenly Lamarca and the twenty-six-year-old Fujimori emerged from the woods, carrying machine guns. The militants interrogated the captured soldiers about troop sizes, placements, and weapons and then took their clothing, tied them up, and hid them under a tarp in the back of the truck.

Now in charge and dressed as soldiers, the militants began to drive through the region getting supplies. The truck was stopped at one military checkpoint, where Sergeant Kondo's explanation that Fujimori and Lamarca (now in uniform) were soldiers on an approved mission was accepted at face value. Eventually Kondo and his soldiers were released and Fujimori reportedly called out to Kondo, according to one soldier, "See you later, Sergeant, best wishes to your family," and in the testimony of another, "See you later, Sergeant, give my regards to your wife and children." Kondo was accused of telling those under his command that they should make up a story to hide the "shame" of their kidnapping by the militants.

This prosecutorial narrative led to a number of charges against Sergeant Kondo, including leaving the base with unarmed soldiers, leaving a loaded weapon on the seat of the truck, picking up a civilian, and telling the enlisted men to lie about what happened. Yet one charge did not flow from the narrative and was critical to the case made against Kondo: "[Kondo's] unbelievable passivity . . . helped the terrorist actions. . . . When, on the third stop in the vehicle, Fujimori and Kondo were alone and unarmed in the cab of the truck, he [Kondo] did not try to escape. Finally, he even had a conversation in Japanese [with Fujimori], in a demonstration of quasi-solidarity with the criminal acts of the terrorists."[116] The idea of ethnic solidarity appears throughout the prosecutorial narrative. Emphasis was placed on how Fujimori and Kondo exchanged clothes, while no other garment-trading details are mentioned.

Kondo's response, naturally, tells the story from a different perspective. First, he put Fujimori in charge of the operation, placing the "infamous" Lamarca in the background. Fujimori is mentioned eight times in Kondo's statement, while Lamarca is mentioned only three. Indeed Lamarca disappears from the three-page testimony by the end of the first page. Second, responsibility for the discussion in Japanese is placed squarely in the hands of Fujimori, who Kondo says asked about his family, his parents' occupations, and if Kondo understood why the militants were so passionate about their cause. Kondo told the court he understood these questions but never responded to any of them, or to Fujimori's promise, in Japanese, that no one would be hurt if the soldiers remained calm.[117]

Kondo's voice is important. By placing Fujimori (rather than Lamarca, the real leader of the group) in the forefront, he implied that the soldiers survived because of his ethnic advantage vis-à-vis Fujimori. His conversation with Fujimori suggested a Japanese-Brazilian discourse of immigrant parents and hard work developed in a milieu where identity was based on Japanese names and language. This helps to explain why Kondo describes Fujimori so differently from everyone else: Fujimori is calm (saying that no one needs to be hurt), he is nice (he talks about family and tells Kondo that he kidnapped the soldiers only because "his life was in jeopardy and he wanted to get to São Paulo"), and he is a true Brazilian who would go "forty days without food" in order "to destroy the monetary trusts and improve the situation of the poor."[118]

The Kondo case shows multiple diasporic discontentments. Take, for example, the supposed conversation between Kondo and Fujimori in Japanese. The prosecutorial presumption was that speaking Japanese moved Kondo from the category of loyal Brazilian to foreign combatant. Kondo, on the other hand, suggests that Nikkei ethnicity saved the soldiers because Fujimori humanized Kondo by asking about his family and gave secret instructions (i.e., in Japanese) that no one would be killed, to which Lamarca might not have agreed. Indeed, the disappearance of Lamarca and the implicit appointment of Fujimori as leader were used by Kondo to explain why no violence took place.

The prosecutorial narrative in the Kondo case showed a lack of distinction between Fujimori and Kondo. It emphasized the switching of their clothes and the inability of the soldier at the checkpoint to distinguish the officer from the militant. What the soldier "saw" was a uniformed Japanese driving an army truck, and he never thought to question the authenticity of the "soldiers." Yet the folding of an individual action into a group trait did not diminish the competing visions of Nikkei as overly weak (as Brazilians) and as hyper-strong (as non-Brazilians). The prosecution focused on the lack of manliness in the brief Kondo/Fujimori relationship: they trade clothes and family stories in a secret language that the real soldiers/men could not understand. The machine-gun-carrying terrorist Fujimori was allied to his ethnic brother, the "incredibly passive" Kondo, who received a twenty-two-month sentence.[119] As one colleague pointed out to me, the military proceedings read like a date-rape trial with "Kondo's shame and coverup . . . as well as the implication that he did not resist or [perhaps even] facilitated the tryst!"[120]

The issues of language and passivity that emerged from the Kondo case were replicated in other situations. Both Rioco Kaiano and Nair Kobashi had specific memories about code switching of Japanese words and phrases into their predominately Portuguese conversations. Yet they were careful not to do this in front of non-Nikkei friends at the University of São Paulo. As Kaiano told me, "No, no . . . no. Only when we were in a situation, for example, in my grandmother's house, a family situation, really relaxed. When we were making fun of each other, joking, you know what I mean." Passivity and lack of masculinity were clear in the newspaper reports on the confession of ALN member Takao Amano. The articles focused on Amano's initial resistance to the police (the strong Japanese) that dissipated when he was shown photographs of two companions, one his supposed girlfriend, embracing romantically. Amano was cuckolded and thus emasculated, leading him to reveal to the authorities the truth about his militant actions.[121]

Captive Ethnics

The repressive forces were trained in mental and physical interrogation methods and used ethnicity strategically in the interview room and torture chamber.[122] Japanese-Brazilians were of course not the only victims. Flávio Tavares, a journalist at the influential *Última Hora* newspaper and a militant in the Revolutionary Action Movement (Movimento de Ação Revolucionária), notes in his memoir that he was asked the "vague and absurd" question if Samuel Wainer, the Jewish editor of the newspaper, ever received money from "international Judaism."[123] There was some concern that the brutal death in captivity of medical student Chael Charles Schreier in São Paulo might indicate "the possible revival of anti-Semitism within the Brazilian Armed Forces."[124] Ladislaw Dowbor, of the VPR, reported that during torture he was called a "son of a bitch Pole" but that later, "this same interrogator came to apologize, not for having tortured him, but for having made a slurring remark about his national origin."[125]

The Japanese-Brazilian experience appears to be a magnified example of the relationship between ethnicity and state violence, along the lines (although to a much lesser extent) of the Jewish-Argentine experience of repression during the "Dirty War."[126] Jun Nakabayashi was never tortured, but he was arrested a number of times just for "being Japanese."[127] He recalls that "if there had been a Japanese cop, I certainly would have suffered more. It's interesting today; the black cop represses the black delinquent more violently." Carlos Takaoka did not recall ethnicity as an issue during his five-year imprisonment but asserted that Japanese-Brazilian police were uniquely violent, pointing to a police action led by a Nikkei officer that had killed a group of prison escapees just a few days prior to our interview.[128] Shizuo

Osawa agreed, noting that "in general the Japanese [in Brazil] are on the right and it is the Right that justifies repression [and torture]. . . . the identity of the Japanese who wants to be white . . . this is the other side of their military character, the identity that the Japanese acquire is on the side of authority, allied with authority, defending authority. It is never rebellious!" Rioco Kaiano remembered being interrogated by a Japanese-Brazilian military officer: "he was furious. . . . He was angry because I was shaming the Japanese, because I had gotten involved in subversion, do you understand? . . . He was clearly on the side of repression, of those that defended this position. . . . He was speaking to me as an agent of the repression, but he was shouting with a particular anger and hate for me. . . . He showed a kind of hate toward me because he really felt I had shamed the race."[129] These ideas were not only held among militants. The first Japanese-Brazilian to enter the officer corps of the military police in São Paulo, Reizo Nishi, emphasized the "rigid character" of Nikkei culture and its relationship to his entry into "a perfect organization."[130]

When Nikkei militants encountered non-Nikkei repressive forces, ethnicity almost always came to the fore. Amilcar Baiardi, a university professor and member of the VAR-Palmares, recalls hearing a torture session in March 1973 in which a person was repeatedly shouted at as "Japonês," probably Francisco Seiko Okama, who died as a result of his injuries at the age of twenty-five.[131] Rioco Kaiano recalls that in custody she was forced to prove her loyalty, always in the context of "my parents' being Japanese." Told by interrogators that Brazil had provided her parents a place to live, to make money, and to send her to university, she was advised that if she sang the national anthem she would be released (she did not and was not). In a second imprisonment in the state of Pará, where she had gone to try to join the Araguaia guerrilla movement, she remembers the hood on her head being yanked off and the interrogators seeing her short hair and jeans and saying, " 'Is this a man or a woman? I just don't know what it is.' . . . Then in the middle of this they said something like, 'What is this garbage? Is it a man, a woman, a Japanese?' I don't remember exactly, but . . ."[132]

The families of Japanese-Brazilians militants also had to deal with the state. These encounters help us to understand how the militants themselves explain their straddling of an identity line that rejected "the colony" while fully embracing a supposed Nikkei sense of the importance of family and elders. Militant memories about their parents (in the specific sense) were generally respectful, rarely suggested personal generational conflict, and usually included comments about the "Japanese nature" of the relationship.

At the same time parents were remembered in a manner that subsumed ethnic particularities to a greater notion of Brazilianness. Over and over, former militants painted a picture of their fathers and mothers as both similar and different from the immigrant generation norm: they were politically conservative but supportive of the ideological purity, honesty, and intensity of children. Militants often described their parents as unusual because they allowed the "Brazilianization" of their children by not insisting on Japanese language or participation in Nikkei community clubs and events. This positioning of community rejection as atypical, I must emphasize, was not accurate. Approximately half of all Japanese-Brazilians who came of age in the sixties and seventies would describe their relationship to the formal Japanese-Brazilian community in exactly the same terms as did the militants to whom I spoke.

Ex-militants often inserted the word *samurai* in our discussions, usually in the context of their parents' respect for the political passion of their children. When this word was used, it was invariably followed by a story about an encounter with the agents of repression. It often began with a knock on the door of the family home by a DEOPS officer. In each case, as the militant told it, the father or mother, looking serious and overworked, said they had no knowledge of the whereabouts of a child who had acted so poorly. Sometimes the militant was in the house, in at least one case in plain view, but the parents' position was accepted at face value.

Nair Kobashi's father and sister were once summoned to DEOPS headquarters. Kobashi recalled her sister's description of the meeting: "You should have seen it. Daddy arrived and invited the cops for coffee. . . . I felt like I was going to vomit. And he says, 'No, it's been a long time since I have seen my daughter, especially since I am against what she is doing.'" With that Mr. Kobashi and his daughter returned home and Nair remained in hiding.[133] A similar story is told by Rioco Kaiano, who remembered DEOPS agents surrounding her grandmother's house in 1971. Kaiano told the story of her own arrest with a laugh:

> My grandma insisted on coming with me. She said, "No, you cannot take her," and she stamped her foot on the floor. She made such a scene that the police had to put her in the paddy wagon and bring her along. The whole time she kept saying that I was a young girl, that she would not let them take me anywhere without her knowing where. So they had to put her in the car and she went with me to the OBAN. And then they had to bring my grandma to the cell, to show it to her and they said, "Look grandma. Here is the women's cell and there is the one

for men. She will stay with the women," and then they introduced all the women inmates, can you believe this! And then they had to bring her home and I stayed. But the next day she was there . . . saying I was innocent. . . . then she sent a lunch box with spaghetti because her granddaughter was not going to go hungry.

The story did not end there. In fact Kaiano was released from prison after signing a statement that she would stay with her parents in their hometown far from the city of São Paulo. Kaiano was surprised by this resolution and was told by the DEOPS agent that this was possible because "they were Japanese" and that she would be under the "protection of her brothers, her family." Kaiano understood that the agent "would have a better guarantee that I would not get involved with subversion under the guard of my parents in the interior, rather than staying here in São Paulo."[134] Yet again, ethnicity was the trump card.

4.

TWO DEATHS REMEMBERED

The lives and tragic deaths of Sueli Yumiko Kamayana and André Massafumi Yoshinaga show the multiple ways the majority understood and remembered Nikkei militants in both real and discursive encounters. Kamayana died in 1970, apparently in a firefight with miltary forces, but her death only became widely known in the 1980s. Yoshinaga's image was primarily constructed in the press in 1970, when he renounced his revolutionary activities publicly, becoming a poster boy for the military regime before committing suicide later in the decade. The memories of these two figures are still strong and suggest the most tragic consequences of imposed diaspora identities.

• • •

Little is known about Sueli Yumiko Kamayana's childhood. She was born in 1948 in the small town of Coronel Macedo, about five hundred kilometers west of São Paulo city, where she moved for high school. In 1967 she entered the University of São Paulo (USP), majoring in Portuguese and German and minoring in Japanese, her first language.

Kamayana's friends remember her as quiet and reserved. Rioco Kaiano, who matriculated at the University of São Paulo at the same time as Kamayana, recalls the attraction of someone "from the [rural] interior [of

Brazil], just like me." It was Kaiano who invited the "timid" Kamayana to Popular Action (Ação Popular) meetings and protests. When the pair met Nair Yumiko Kobashi, a member of the Communist Party of Brazil (Partido Comunista do Brasil, PC do B) who was also from a rural, heavily Japanese immigrant community, the "Japanese Army" was born, Kaiano said, because of "me, Sueli, and Nair" (see chapter 3).[1]

The three became fast friends, according to Kaiano and Kobashi, in part because of their shared rural Nikkeiness. "With just us it was common, once in a while, to say some words in Japanese. This was only for us, the manner in which we spoke, this is something only for a Brazilian of Japanese origin, because if we spoke this way in Japan they also [i.e., like "Brazilians"] would not understand." This linguistic pattern was reinforced by time the group often spent at the home Kaiano shared with her grandmother, who "really liked [Sueli] in part because she was Japanese and all that." Kamayana treated Kaiano as an older sister. She would do whatever she was told, leading to her nickname "Zokin," Japanese for dust cloth.

In 1970 Kamayana participated with a group of mainly Nikkei university students in a PC do B training course in the beach town of Ubatuba. She asked to be sent "into the field." Neide Richopo, one of only two non-Nikkei in the course, remembers Kamayana as "one of the most dedicated and fearless" in the group.[2] In late 1971 Kamayana went to Araguaia, in the southern portion of the state of Pará, where she joined about one hundred other militants hoping to mobilize local peasants.[3] One of the leaders was José Genoino (president of Brazil's Worker's Party [Partido dos Trabalhadores, PT] until 2005) and another was Helenira Rezende de Souza Nazareth (see chapter 3). The Araguaia guerrillas were known internationally for the multilingual missives they distributed. In 1974 a massive military campaign began against them. Some sixty militants were killed and twenty others executed after being captured and tortured.[4] The military mounted a cleanup operation to hide evidence of the killings, and most who survived (both soldiers and guerrillas) have been hesitant to discuss particulars since the return to democracy in 1985.[5]

Kamayana barely appears in the accounts of the Araguaia guerrilla written by participants.[6] The few "official" memories, for example at the PC do B Web site, contrast the fact "she was really short and thin" with her ideological certainty and her renowned ability to "quickly learn to work in [an] area, relate well with the local population, and carry a fifty-pound backpack through the forests, hunt, and deal with every situation."[7] Elza Monnerat was one survivor of the army attack. Her recollections of Kamayana focus on the lack of racial distinctions drawn by the local peasantry: "the black Osvaldo and the red-haired Bronca were seen as brothers by many peasants. The presence of the Nisei Sueli . . . did not cause any comment: she was seen as an Indian."[8] Monnerat also highlighted Kamayana's invisibility: while she does not appear as her personal or ethnic self, she remained (like the Afro-Brazilian Osvaldo) an ethnic other vis-à-vis the militants.

Sueli Yumiko Kamayana's death has received far more comment than her life. Fernando Portella, one of the first journalists to bring the story of Araguaia to the public, asserts that Kamayana had an extremely violent response to the military incursion: in spite of being severely wounded, she shot a paratrooper in the face as he tried to help her, and she died in a hail of machine-gun fire that riddled her body with more than one hundred bullets.[9] A slightly different story was told by Hitoshi Kozato, the former *Asahi Shimbun* correspondent in Latin America. He commented to a Brazilian journalist that Kamayana hid a revolver in her clothes before her capture; as she was about to be tortured, she shot the soldier, leading to the fusillade.[10]

Given my discussion in the previous chapter about how Nikkei ethnicity was tied to violence, it is not surprising that press accounts constructed Kamayana this way. A different approach, however, was taken by Pedro Corrêa Cabral, an army helicopter pilot who began to question the morality of the operation in Araguaia some two decades after his participation. His comments to the press, and the publication of his 1993 "novel based on real facts" *Xamboiá: Guerrilha no Araguaia*, caused a public furor. The novel and *Veja*'s cover story on Cabral's admissions, headlined "I saw the burned corpses," continue to be widely quoted on Internet sites, many of which focus on his quasi-mystical interpretation that Kamayana, like a European Catholic saint, remained alive even in death.[11]

Her body was buried in a place called Bacaba, where, under the coordination of the Army Information Center (Centro de Informações do Exército, CIE), interrogation cells had been built. During the cleanup operation [done to hide all evidence of the army massacre], her grave was opened and Sueli's corpse was disinterred. Intact, without clothes, her skin very white, she did not show any signs of decomposition. Only bullet holes. A soldier tried to dig out the cadaver with a shovel but he slipped. He tried again. The same thing. One more time. Sueli's body went back to the grave. Angry, the soldier gave an impatient shout, "Come here, to daddy's arms." He jumped into the grave, put his arms around the cadaver, and brought it up. Out of the grave, Sueli's body was put in a plastic bag and carried to a helicopter. . . . She was brought some one hundred kilometers away, . . . and some Brazilians made a pile of cadavers, all taken from their original graves. Covered with old tires and gasoline, they were burned.[12]

Cabral's fictionalized memoirs claim more insight into Kamayana than most other sources. As did the militant Carlos Eugênio Paz, whose use of the same genre I discussed in chapter 3, Cabral created characters for his novel whose names make absolutely clear the real-life inspiration. In *Xamboiá* Cabral gave Kamayana the name Sueli Ohashi, although this invented "real" name was only spoken by the soldiers who pursued her. When she appeared with her militant companions, she was referred to only as the "Japonesa," reminiscent of how Japanese-Brazilians in film were named.

One scene in the novel took place in the forest as the militants discussed eating a wild female turtle. As the men in the group argued over cooking techniques, the "Japonesa," sickened by the idea of cooking the animal alive, demanded its release. The response was not to call her a squeamish girl. Rather it was entirely ethnic: "What is it, Japonesa? . . . The Japanese eat raw fish, so why are you being snobby about a cooked turtle? How about if we pick up some soy sauce for you?"[13] This scene seems to be a precursor to the end of Cabral's novel, where Sueli Ohashi, like the turtle, is burned alive. Yet her attempt to save the animal can be read in at least two ways: that she did not have a true killer instinct or perhaps that she had a special relation to the natural world. Both interpretations fit well with Ohashi's return from the grave in the novel's climatic scene.

Kamayana was remembered in nonfiction by José Genoino, one of the few survivors of the Araguaia guerrilla.[14] In 1980 he gave an interview to the Nikkei magazine *Página Um*. Both the interviewer, Henri George Kobata, and Genoino hailed Kamayana's bravery, courage, and commitment. Yet, in spite of the points of agreement, the article was in fact a battle over her memory. Kobata referred to her as "Yumiko" or "Sueli Yumiko." Genoino, on the other hand, was quoted only as calling Kamayana "that little Japanese girl [*aquela japonesinha*]." Kobata recalls that "I used bold print [each time I quoted him saying] '**aquela japonesinha**' because I was surprised, even angry, at the distance between Genoino and Sueli. He always called her '**aquela japonesinha**' and he didn't even know how to pronounce her name. They were *companheiros* in the armed struggle and he showed a distance. . . . Not an ideological distance but an ethnic distance. He never called Tião [Osvaldo Orlando da Costa, the Afro-Brazilian member of the group] 'little blacky.' "[15]

Kobata was not a radical ethnic activist, but he found Genoino's language offensive.[16] His anger at Genoino's use of "aquela japonesinha," and his discussion with me about it many years later, suggests that assertions that racialized language in Brazil is simply descriptive, and thus inoffensive, are not always accepted by members of minority groups. Geniono may have chosen his description to show solidarity and to memorialize his dead colleague when speaking to a Japanese-Brazilian reporter. He may also have been using this language without thinking since, as I have shown, the use of the term *Japanese* for Nikkei was widespread.

There are a number of analytical points that emerge from the interview and Kobata's reaction. Regardless of his intent, when Genoino called Kamayana "aquela japonesinha," it reduced her to her ethnicity. This is what offended Kobata, who expected that Kamayana's name would be complemented by her ethnicity, not replaced by it. Genoino's ethnic language was reinforced by gender, since the diminutive would rarely be used for a male companion. For Kobata, Genoino had dismissed Kamayana's participation in the Araguaia guerrilla. Finally, Kobata's article opposes Kamayana both to Genoino and to her own family, who refused to speak to Kobata about the "shameful" subject. Kobata's interpretation, it must be noted, was not the only one. An examination of Kamayana's life completed in 2005, based mainly on interviews, portrays José Genoino as a bridge between two essentialist ethnicities (Brazilian and Japanese), arguing that the Kamayana family only reintegrated the memory of their daughter into their family history following a personal visit from Genoino after his 1978 release from prison.[17]

The memory of Sueli Yumiko Kamayana shows how Nikkei identity construction resonated with broader ideas of Brazilian history. In Cabral's novel and Genoino's interview, Kamayana was only "the Japonesa" or "that Japonesinha." In the reports composed after her death, she was presented as a person who fought and died violently. These descriptions were mirrored by Nikkei themselves. The final issue of *Página Um*, in 1984, pointed to Kobata's article as one of the most important in the weekly's five-year history. In an update to the original article, Kobata pointed out that Kamayana's mother, "in spite of the pain of having lost a daughter in such a cruel way, at times felt that this [appreciating the valor of her death] was a way of accepting the death: She fought until her death for the most important dream in her life."[18] The kamikaze-like "fight until death" was also important to Célia Abe Oi, a journalist with *Página Um* and today director of São Paulo's Museum of Japanese Immigration. She told me, "Yumiko was a hero to us." When I asked what she meant, she explained that Kamayana represented the "samurai way" of taking something to the limit AND a person whose sense of Brazilianness was so strong that she was willing to lose her life for her country.[19]

The different names by which Kamayana is remembered show the complexity of Nikkei life in Brazil. Was she Sueli Ohashi (as Cabral has the military call her) or Yumiko (as Kobata insisted)? Was she "aquela japonesinha" (Genoino), "the Japonesa" (Cabral's fictional militants), a "samurai" (Oi), or a Brazilian? These identity clashes were also evident in the memories of André Massafumi Yoshinaga. Widely known as Massafumi, and nicknamed "Massa" to play on the Portuguese word for "the masses," he was for many years one of Brazil's "most dreaded" militants. He was a poster boy for terror, a handsome young man whose picture on wanted posters reminded the public that danger lurked behind even the kindest countenance.[20]

Massafumi Yoshinaga was born in Paraguaçu Paulista, a small town about one hundred kilometers west of Marilia, along the Sorocabana rail lines. The town had many Nikkei residents, and the Shindo Renmei had been active there in the forties and fifties. His mother, Mitki, had been born of Japanese parents in the agricultural town of Albuquerque Lins, and his father, Kiyomatsu, was a native of Nagasaki. When the family moved to São Paulo, Massafumi Yoshinaga entered high school and became politically engaged.[21]

In 1966 he was elected one of the vice presidents of the São Paulo Union of Secondary Students (União Paulista de Estudantes Secundários). His activism increased after the killing of university student Edson Luís de Lima Souto. Massafumi Yoshinaga participated in protests in the city center and wrote about his experiences in the student newspaper he edited at the Brasílio Machado State High School, located in a neighborhood with many Nikkei. This high school, remembers Nair Kobashi, "had a lot of freedom. From these kinds of schools a lot of people became activists. . . . They were really stimulated to be critical, to participate in the life of the nation."[22]

Massafumi Yoshinaga spent his free time at the University of São Paulo, especially in the CRUSP residence halls that were a center of militant activity. Kobashi remembers this teenage kid and his friends hanging out with university students as "really cute. They were boys. They were really young compared to us because they were in high school, but I had real affection for them, for the disposition they had." Massafumi Yoshinaga himself was "a serious boy, very serious. I found him very reserved. That is what I thought, a serious, reserved person. He was not expansive. I never felt that he was an expansive person. But I think he was a good person, you know. A very serious person, very dedicated to what he was doing. That is what I thought."[23]

Massafumi Yoshinaga became an activist and Popular Revolutionary Vanguard (VPR) member Celso Lungaretti called him "extroverted" and much more interested in working with the masses than "living in hiding like a bandit."[24] Kobashi remembers him standing on a balcony at USP waving a revolutionary banner and encouraging student action. He appears to have joined the VPR in November 1969. Two months later he participated in a bank robbery, and over the next two years the police and press described him as one of the most active militants in the city. He became one of the fifty most wanted militants in Brazil in late 1969, leading the newsmagazine *Veja* to call him "the Japanese who has led a number of assaults."[25]

This history was not much different from that of other wanted Nikkei. What separates Massafumi Yoshinaga is that in July 1970 he surrendered to authorities and publicly renounced his political militancy. Leftists labeled Massafumi Yoshinaga a traitor, although some believed that torture led to his about-face.[26] Others echoed comments like those made by a PCB cadre to Olga Futema about how Nikkei filial loyalty trumped political commitment. They blamed family pressure on the young militant, who they said brought shame on them and the Japanese-Brazilian community. For the government, Massafumi Yoshinaga's renunciation was a publicity coup. The regime used his story to suggest that militant leaders were bandits, not political agitators, and that many subversives were naive youngsters who needed to return to the national fold.

Massafumi Yoshinaga was not the first person to renounce militancy publicly: the five militants in the so-called Marcos Vinícius Group, who had been captured in early 1969 and endured prison and torture for almost eighteen months, had made a public statement just a month earlier. In the months after Massafumi Yoshinaga's renunciation, some thirteen other militants did the same. Many government leaders believed that the recantations would help Brazil's international reputation, although a confidential memo from the U.S. consul general in São Paulo noted that the regime's publicity campaign was "an obvious attempt, perhaps too patent, of GOB [Government of Brazil] authorities [to] counter extremely bad press abroad on the torture issue."[27]

Prior to his surrender, Massafumi Yoshinaga was known to the public as André Yoshinaga Massafumi, "o Massa," because of wanted posters and newspaper articles. On surrendering, however, he became Massafumi Yoshinaga (Yoshinaga was in fact his family name).[28] André, it seemed, represented the Brazilian side which had led him to militancy, but now "Massafumi" reappeared, the good Japanese boy from the good Japanese family.

This multiple imagery may explain why the regime chose to highlight Massafumi Yoshinaga's surrender over all others, with the active participation of the media and a fascinated public.[29] His widely published "letter to the youth" of Brazil urged them to give up militant activity and work with the military regime for "national integration and development."[30]

The letter appeared in Brazilian newspapers with articles on the presentation of the repentant Massafumi Yoshinaga at a press conference on 2 July 1970. The event was held in the auditorium of São Paulo's Public Security Secretariat and attended by more than one hundred Brazilian and international journalists. Colonel Danilo de Sá da Cunha e Melo, secretary of public security, began by distributing a "dossier" constructed to narrate Massafumi Yoshinaga's slide from student to activist to terrorist. On a podium, looking over the solitary Massafumi Yoshinaga seated below, were Danton Avelino, commander general of São Paulo's military police, Leonardo Lombardo, a journalist who was director of public relations for security, and various other civilian, military, and representatives from the São Paulo State Department of Political and Social Order (Departamento Estadual de Ordem Política e Social, DEOPS). Cameras from Brazilian and international television networks whirred and flashbulbs popped continuously.

Questions had been submitted to the regime's press officers in advance and were read to Massafumi Yoshinaga. His answers focused on his militant activities. He confirmed his participation in only one action, attacked VPR leader Carlos Lamarca's mental stability, and claimed that watching the 1970 World Cup soccer tournament on television (held in Mexico, won by Brazil, and used by the government as a nationalist propaganda tool) taught him that "terror is really far from the sentiments of the Brazilian people." What received the most media coverage was Massafumi Yoshinaga's comment that "a life of terror leads to nothing other than prison or the cemetery."[31]

On the surface, the event was about militant politics. Yet Massafumi Yoshinaga could not escape his ethnicity. One of the first questions that the DEOPS chose for him to answer came from a journalist at the *São Paulo Shimbun*. The Brazilian newspapers reported it as follows:

Public Relations Officer: And now a question from the representative of the *São Paulo Shimbun*: Did you participate in the kidnapping of the Japanese consul, Nobuo Okuchi, in São Paulo? [This event will be discussed extensively in the next chapter.]
Yoshinaga: I want to make very clear to the masses, and especially the Japanese colony, that I had nothing to do with the kidnapping of the Japanese consul in São Paulo—directly or indirectly.[32]

Another question was on Nikkei participation in militancy. His claim that the only other Nikkei militant was Yoshitani Fujimori was widely reported, although Massafumi Yoshinaga knew Shizuo Osawa and Nair Kobashi well.[33] This suggests that even after surrendering, he was careful to protect his companions.

By arranging questions about "Japanese" from the *São Paulo Shimbun*, the press officers took Massafumi Yoshinaga out of the category of militant and placed him into the category of "ethnic." This was as much a culturally defined interaction as a conscious strategic decision by the regime. Newspapers referred to the ex-guerrilla as "Nisei" or "Japanese" to emphasize what the photographs made clear. Some reports commented on Massafumi Yoshinaga's old jacket, known as a "japona," a pun that must have been clear to journalists and readers.

Press coverage of the Massafumi Yoshinaga story was massive. Almir Guimarães, a reporter for the popular primetime evening news program *Ultra-Notícias do Dia* on São Paulo's TV Tupi, conducted an almost seven-minute interview that included questions submitted by a number of journalists.[34] Shown at a peak evening hour (7:45) and widely watched, the interview was described by *Veja* as "a first-time event of great political impact."[35] Interest was so strong that German television's *Eurovision* program, broadcast in France, Italy, Spain, Germany, and England, covered the event, and the director later requested permission to film another interview with Massafumi Yoshinaga.[36]

Newspapers and magazines ran full- and half-page stories with large photographs that visually distanced Massafumi Yoshinaga from those to whom he had surrendered. The *Folha de S. Paulo*, for example, used a photograph from early in the press conference. Massafumi Yoshinaga was sitting in a chair bathed in light, alone with a microphone in his hand. Behind him, on a stage or podium, sat "the state," in the person of military and civilian officials, none of them paying much attention. Some wore dark glasses and their features were blurred. Was Massafumi Yoshinaga confessing of his own free will or was this a public reenactment of a torture session? Another photo, taken a few minutes later and published in the *Estado de S. Paulo*, shows the ex-militant standing (he sat only for the first two questions of the press conference) and plays with the same idea of power. He is covered in light, a white scarf draped around his neck and extending the whiteness of his face. Behind him (in the photograph) a shadowy civilian reads a piece of paper, seemingly considering a verdict.[37]

Those who watched the TV Tupi interview may have had a different impression of Massafumi Yoshinaga than those who only read newspapers. Viewers might have been struck by the contrast between the young, long-haired, scarf-wearing Japanese-Brazilian and the two older Euro-Brazilians hovering in judgment behind him. One is in uniform, stone faced, while the other seems to be nodding in agreement with Massafumi Yoshinaga's responses. The journalist Guimarães asked questions aggressively and seemed disappointed at the former guerrilla's lack of revelations.

Massafumi Yoshinaga gave the impression of being in complete control of the interview. When Guimarães asked about his participation in bank robberies, the repentant guerrilla gave a little smile, jerked his finger at the men behind him, and said that he had to "clear that up first with the Brazilian Army." The words were betrayed by his body language—the printed text of his response gave the impression that he wanted to "clear . . . up" his own participation. Watching the tape, however, I had the sense that he was laughing at the military for believing that he was the Japanese-Brazilian involved in so many bank robberies.

In an interview a few days after the press conference, Massafumi Yoshinaga suggested that the São Paulo Japanese community was the reason he abandoned militancy. The newspaper reported that "some elements of the Japanese colony in São Paulo stopped dealing with his family. He wanted to change this—'I made the whole colony feel shame because of one of its descendents. Now, in addition to trying to repair what I did, I want to try to make them proud: to be a good Brazilian, of Japanese descent.' "[38] São Paulo's Japanese-Brazilian newspapers also treated the renunciation as important to the Nikkei community.[39] Massafumi Yoshinaga's concerns about community image suggest a different context for his repeated assertion that his surrender was largely motivated by watching Brazilian nationalism emerge during the World Cup. His assertion of pride in the national team thus might be seen as an attempt to prove that he was a true Brazilian in spite of his "ethnic" ancestry.

Massafumi Yoshinaga's affirmation of his Brazilianness was similar to that of many Nikkei (on both the left and right) who spoke to me about their struggles to be accepted.[40] There is no doubt that the military and the Yoshinaga family discussed "ethnic" issues as part of the surrender. Some commentators saw his pardon and release from prison as his way of becoming "a model child . . . making money to help his family."[41] A message from the director of the Female Regimentation Movement on Mother's Day focused on this idea: "You have returned. Welcome. Human respect has won and you have recognized publicly your error, just as in the Prodigal Son parable."[42] In some press reports, the former militant was referred to by his nickname (Massa) rather than the more formal Massafumi, suggesting familiarity and the return to the national fold. This separated him from most other repentant militants, since public comments on the others rarely mentioned family or filiality.[43]

Why was Massafumi Yoshinaga's repentance so much more visible than that of the other ex-militants? In part it was his reputation as a leader of the VPR, although he and other militants always denied that he was more than a "soldier." He also personified the good Japanese/bad Japanese dichotomy felt so strongly in São Paulo. *Veja*'s cover story on Massafumi, headlined "Terror Renounced," played on this idea by taking a photograph from the press conference and cropping and coloring it half dark and half light to suggest a dual or split personality (figure 25).[44] Since students were portrayed by the regime as both Brazil's future and Brazil's downfall, Massafumi Yoshinaga seemed a perfect public representation of this duality.

On being freed, Massafumi Yoshinaga, like many middle-class Paulistanos, went to the beach. Militants, however, were shocked by what they saw as treason and feared that he might have revealed important information to the government. Shizuo Osawa, a member of the VPR who knew Massafumi Yoshinaga, told me, "No one likes traitors, even if the treason is against an enemy." Osawa's statement implies three different betrayals: the first against the established Nikkei community by joining the VPR, the second against the VPR by surrendering to the military, and the third against Massafumi Yoshinaga's Japanese ethnicity by not following through on his militancy to the end.[45] Olga Futema's memory of Massafumi Yoshinaga's surrender also merged the political and the ethnic. She remembered overhearing her mother speaking to a friend and saying, "What a terrible thing, all of it!" "All of it" suggests that, like Osawa, she saw his entire experience as problematic.[46] Nair Kobashi had a different understanding: "there exists a kind of prejudice about Orientals: when they are not reserved they are kamikaze. The repentance of a person like this causes a certain impact because of the fact that [pause] . . . I really feel bad for him. I think people at the time really rejected those kids [who surrendered], and they should rethink this; they should feel somewhat guilty themselves. [Massafumi] felt rejected by all sides."

Massafumi Yoshinaga found himself friendless. Physical freedom created new demons. Olga Futema remembered thinking that he looked frail in

FIGURE 25. "Terror Renounced," *Veja*, 15 July 1970.
Cover courtesy of *Veja*, Editora Abril

photographs and on television. Nair Kobashi assumed that he had been tortured.[47] He tried a number of jobs, from book sales to market research to real estate, but stuck with none. When his mother died in 1973 Massafumi Yoshinaga's mental health declined. He lived in the lower-middle-class neighborhood of Jardim Bonfiglioli in São Paulo with his widowed father and two brothers, in a "little two-story unpainted house on a street with no name."[48] Nair Kobashi also lived in the neighborhood, but when they saw each other they never spoke:

> I think that his age had a lot to do with his fragility, with not being able to deal with everything in the way everyone wanted him to. I lived at that time in Bonfiglioli . . . and he lived near me after I got out of prison. I saw him and he saw me, but he never came my way. I looked at him but he, you know, he never . . . After prison, after all this [it was] really sad. You know how it is, when you see a person who is totally demolished.

After his mother's death, Massafumi Yoshinaga's uncle convinced him to join Sei-cho-no-iê, a "new Japanese religion" popular among educated Paulistanos, both Nikkei and non-Nikkei.[49] But he did not find solace: from October 1975 to April 1976 he was interned in a psychiatric hospital. After leaving the institution he was "in almost complete isolation, never going out of his house and having no friends."[50] He read the Bible and newspapers, rarely making any comments. In early June 1976, his brother came home to find that Massafumi Yoshinaga had strangled himself with a plastic hose. There was no note or explanation of any kind. While Massafumi's father "threw himself on the ground and prayed in Japanese," the local police delegate who handled the case noted, "I never saw a suicide that attracted so little attention from the neighbors."[51] This was not exactly true, according to Nair Kobashi.

> It was soon after I saw him, and I realized that he lived near my house, that his family lived near my house, that he killed himself. I thought to myself—Poor guy . . . look at how he was destroyed. It is a feeling that I have about certain people, you know? I want to say that. . . . What can I say? In this process, with thousands of problems, you know. Some people do not respond to expectations, of what is expected of them, and this finishes them off. They don't feel capable of living. You know how it is, don't you?

...

André Massafumi Yoshinaga is today forgotten. Sueli Yumiko Kamayana died equally tragically but is remembered. In 1997 a PC do B city councilperson in Campinas argued successfully for a law to rename a series of streets in honor of guerrillas killed in Araguaia and whose deaths had been recognized by the Brazilian state in 1995. One of those streets was named for Sueli Yumiko Kamayana.[52]

5·

How Shizuo Osawa

became "Mário the Jap"

———•———

It would be hard to tell the story of Shizuo Osawa without mentioning how I learned of him. One day, colleagues at the Center for Japanese-Brazilian Studies in São Paulo mentioned their memories of a Nikkei guerrilla fighter from the sixties. They could not recall his name, but they did remember his connection to the kidnapping of the Japanese consul in São Paulo. It did not take long to determine that they were talking about Shizuo Osawa, known more widely by his nom de guerre "Mário Japa," or Mário the Jap (see figure 26).

I began to look for written documentation on Osawa—newspaper stories, police documents, and the like. But oddly neither Shizuo Osawa nor Mário Japa appeared prior to his exile from Brazil in 1970. He was not pictured on wanted posters or mentioned in newspaper articles. Thus much of my search for information was centered in the São Paulo State Department of Political and Social Order (Departamento Estadual de Ordem Política e Social de São Paulo, DEOPS) papers, which I imagined would be filled with information. I went to the São Paulo State Archives to examine the files, and the staff member who took my request disappeared into the bowels of the building. He returned apologetically: there were no files for anyone named

CHIZUO OZAVA

FIGURE 26. Photos of the "good" Shuzuo Osawa
and the "bad" Mário Japa. From Ministério do Exército,
Gabinete do Ministro, Centro de Informações do Exército,
Indivíduos banidos do território nacional, 29

Shizuo Osawa. I asked if he would check again, this time using other spell-
ings like *Osava* and *Chizuo* and reversing the first and last names. Nothing.

Then it hit me. Maybe "Shizuo Osawa" never existed for the DEOPS.
Maybe he was known only as "Mário Japa." I filled out another request slip.
And there he was in multiple files. I had found Mário the Jap.

As I began sifting through the hundreds of pages, I was surprised yet
again. Government forces knew perfectly well that "Mário Japa" was the
code name of Shizuo Osawa. They knew his birth name, his educational
background, and about his parents and family. They were aware of his
political trajectory and that he was an important member of the Vanguarda
Popular Revolucionária (VPR). Yet the DEOPS never created a file for "Shizuo
Osawa." For them "Shizuo Osawa" was nothing more than a code name for
Mário Japa.[1]

Analyzing the meanings of the names "Shizuo Osawa" and "Mário Japa"
led to my second attempt to "know" the subject of this chapter. It began at
an academic conference in Brazil when I commented to a friend how odd it
was that the DEOPS only had records for "Mário Japa." "Mário," exclaimed
my friend with a grin, "He and I were militants together. He's a great guy

and lives in Rio." Within forty-eight hours he had contacted "Mário" and I had an invitation to meet the ex-revolutionary.

I was nervous. I "knew" Shizuo Osawa/Mário Japa mainly from the DEOPS files and contemporary scholarly studies of the Brazilian armed struggle. I had learned that he had been so deeply underground and important in the VPR that neither his companions nor the police discovered his real name until days after his capture. He was married to a former VPR member, Maria do Carmo Brito (code name "Lia"), whom the press had called the "killer blonde." The historiography portrayed Mário Japa as the bravest of the brave, attaching words like "kamikaze" to his name. The secondary literature also focused on his capture following a car accident, making me wonder how postdictatorship public memory fit into the broader stereotypes about Japanese-Brazilians as poor drivers, as I mentioned in chapter 2.[2]

Riding the elevator to Osawa's apartment, I was tense. What should I call him? I rang the doorbell and steeled myself to meet what I imagined would be the machine gun-toting revolutionary. Instead a middle-aged man opened the door and was soon telling me about how his daughter was not taking her studies seriously enough. A friendly woman sat me down and started serving soft drinks and snacks, wanting to know about my family and my children. I had met Mário Japa and Lia.

• • •

The man I met that day in Rio de Janeiro had not always been Mário Japa. Shizuo Osawa was born in 1946 in a tiny farming community in the state of Minas Gerais. He was the third of six children and spent most of his early life in Brazil's countryside, moving every few years as his father, a tenant farmer who had emigrated from Japan, cleared and worked plots of land. As a child Osawa lived primarily in the state of São Paulo. The family moved from Guairá (about 100 kilometers north and slightly to the west of the city of Ribeirão Preto) to Riolândia (at the time known as "Viadinho do Porto") to Cardoso (see map 1 in chapter 3).

In each place Osawa and his family lived among immigrants and their Brazilian-born children.[3] Parents spoke to their children in Japanese, while the children spoke to each other in Portuguese, Japanese, and a mixture of the two. On Sunday, movie day, young Shizuo hopped on a tractor-pulled cart with his family and friends as hundreds of Nikkei converged on a rented warehouse where a white sheet became a screen for Japanese movies. For Osawa the scene remains vivid: "I saw an unbelievable quantity of [Japanese] films. And sometimes they were incredibly violent. Sometimes I had nightmares, being stabbed by samurai, gunfights. . . . and I did not understand anything. I even saw silent films, those Japanese films with those samurais."[4]

Osawa began his studies in Riolândia, walking with his friends for almost an hour to a rural school where the majority of students were the children of Japanese tenant farmers. Osawa's parents, Gentaro and Hamayo, took education seriously, and all the Osawa children went to primary school.

> My father had a strict rule: if his children did well in primary school they could go to
> secondary school (instead of working the land). All of us had to go to primary school,
> and if you were a good student, you could continue. He would pay all the costs,
> tuition, housing, he would do everything. My brother, for example, went to boarding
> school and my father paid. Now if you were a bad student in the early years, you
> would work clearing land [laughter]. That's what happened to my older brother. He
> did not do well in school and went to work on the land. It was a punishment.

Osawa's Japanese-Brazilian identity was formed in a context of forced Catholicism, a religion that Osawa's parents claimed in public "without going to church or anything." In fact Osawa's family was Buddhist, but after World War II and the rise of the Shindo Renmei in the region of São Paulo where they lived, "the repression was so strong that anyone practicing Buddhist rituals was under suspicion." Osawa's Buddhist parents thus became public Catholics. Osawa joked that this was "para o brasileiro ver" (*for the Brazilian to see*), a play on the nineteenth-century expression "para o inglês ver" (*for the Englishman to see*), which referred to the Brazilian state's official prohibition, but tacit acceptance, of the slave trade. The Osawa family's public Catholicism helped to educate their children since in Riolândia there was only one school, and the teacher was the "very Catholic" wife of the local landowner. She insisted on catechism classes and first communion (recall the discussions of Catholicism and baptism in chapter 4). As a result Osawa saw a clear distinction between the Brazilian way (which embraced Catholicism) and the Japanese way (which rejected it).

The distinction between Brazil and Japan in Osawa's mind was not simply religious. It was also the result of the Brazilian state's acceptance of some aspects of ethnic identity preservation, such as allowing birth certificates to reflect whatever names parents chose to give their children. Thus Osawa and his two older brothers were known at home and in their formal documents by their birth names, Koichi, Jundi, and Shizuo. Yet parents and the state had a competitor for identity. The local priest refused to baptize those with Japanese names. Osawa's parents told Shizuo's older brothers to be prepared to provide "Brazilian names" to the priest. Thus Koichi and Jundi were baptized as Nelson and Antônio and came to be known outside of their home by these names. When it was time for young Shizuo to be baptized, "my mother told me that I would need a name and that I would be called Carlos." But the priest never asked for a Brazilian name. As Osawa explained with a laugh, "I don't know why. Maybe he thought that 'Shizuo' was the name 'Jesus' badly pronounced."

Most Nikkei had multiple names that reflected multiple identity spaces. Osawa, however, whether at home, on the street, in church, or in school, was only Shizuo. This relatively consistent identity was challenged when Osawa was ten years old and his family moved to the town of Cardoso, near the border of the state of Mato Grosso. There Osawa went to a school where ninety percent of the students were "Brazilian" (non-Nikkei). Cardoso did not have a secondary school, but the larger town of Votuporanga (about 40 kilometers south of Cardoso and about 520 kilometers from the city of São Paulo), did. Gentaro Osawa found a Japanese family in Votuporanga willing to house his son, and twelve-year-old Shizuo left his family and the ethnic countryside forever.

Osawa stayed in Votuporanga for two and a half years, living with two different Japanese immigrant families. He won a number of awards for his intelligence and studiousness, appearing in the local newspaper and on radio. For the first time in his life Shizuo had a new name, "The Atomic Brain," given to him by a local newspaper in reference to his intellect and to the technology that his ethnicity implied. Shizuo seemed destined for success, but in 1961 the harvest did not go well. Osawa's father decided to leave tenant farming and try life in the city. Gentaro Osawa first went to Ribeirão Preto and then to Santo André, a city of 245,000 inhabitants about twenty-five kilometers from São Paulo (by 2004 it had grown to over 650,000), where he purchased a small store. When he was not in school Shizuo worked with his father, tending the counter where they sold liquor, soft drinks, and snacks. Osawa recalled that:

> It was kind of funny because a famous bandit lived in Santo André and he hid on the outskirts of town [where we lived]. Once in a while he would show up at our store, and he always behaved himself. This business with the Japanese, he really respected us. He held up a lot of stores in the neighborhood, but in our bar he never did anything. [The bandit] robbed a lot of places but he never messed with us. He really respected us. It was there that I began to see this business [of respect for Japanese-Brazilians].

Banditry and marginality led Osawa to recognize that a component of the essentialization of Nikkei was exaltation. While Osawa recounted his memories of adolescence in a broader discussion of his life as a militant, the interactions with the bandit in Santo André did not politicize him. On the contrary, in mid-1962 Osawa started working in an office and attending high school at night. Soon he took a position at a bank and began to study at the Faculdade Casper Líbero, at the time the only journalism school in São Paulo. Each morning he took the train from Santo André to São Paulo for his studies, returning in the afternoon for his bank job. While the journalism students were not particularly ideological, Osawa experienced a personal turn toward the left that he remembers as idiosyncratic:

> It's curious because my trajectory is very different from others in my generation who entered into armed struggle. This is because my evolution was very individual. I read a lot but my consciousness rose because I lived at the bar with my parents and it was really a poor place [where people did not have a lot to eat]. Even in high school I had a certain notion of class difference. For example, I realized that on the bus in rural Santo André I was always the tallest, but in school in urban São Paulo I was always the shortest. Santo André in the early sixties had a very traditional middle class. Small, but very traditional. Very conservative. It was something strange. . . .
>
> For example, I could not go to the fancy cinema in the city, the one where the middle class went, because you had to go in a suit, and I did not even have a sports coat. I mean I did not have the right clothes. This shows what I mean by "traditional" . . . and I think it was there that it all began.

Osawa's mention of height reminds us of a similar memory by Rioco Kaiano in chapter 3. His sense of class differential was reinforced by his fellow journalism students, whom he saw as "more sophisticated (and) snobby . . . I just did not fit in well." He joined the bank workers union and after participating in a strike he was punished with a transfer to Curitiba, the largest city in the state of Paraná. With the forced move, Osawa left school and worked full time at the bank, continuing his activism, especially for salary raises.

Osawa tells the story of his late teens and early twenties as one of class recognition and a move to the political left. When I asked him about his ethnic memories, he claimed not to have any from this period. I was thus surprised when he revealed that he had written an article on Nikkei identity while in Curitiba. The essay "They Want to Be Brazilians" was published in the *Revista Panorama*. It used a psychological approach to ethnicity and identity based on Osawa's reading of the Portuguese translation of the experimental psychiatrist R. D. Laing's *The Divided Self: A Study of Sanity and Madness* (1960). Osawa took the position that dominant societal presumptions that Nikkei were not typical Brazilians prevented many from having sufficiently balanced personalities and from fully becoming Brazilian.

> Born out of this entanglement of repression was a tremendous internal confusion. The perplexity makes them seem adapted. In truth, there is little authenticity in their sentiments and judgments about Western values. They seek to understand their inner selves. Their inhibition has deep roots. In a [Brazilian] world where extroversion is exalted, [Nisei] are, at times, obliged to fabricate emotions and reactions to pretend to a perfect assimilation. This simulation, this ridiculous imitation, ends up worsening conflicts in even the most sensible people.
>
> A permanent constraint in relations among Nisei creates an abnormal isolation. The solitude, the absolute incapacity for communication, is almost totalizing. Some, apparently incoherently, manifest a true aversion to Asians and look for refuge among Westerners.
>
> Highly frustrated, they generally apply themselves to work and study. They hail their capacity to produce and learn. They end up confusing their efforts with privileged intelligence. The average Nisei, however, has an profound lack of general culture. His dedication, in reality, is total submission to the demands of the professor, an attempt to compensate for a functional imperfection. Ease of assimilation is a unilateral vision and the result of excessive optimism related to dangerous resignation. The Nisei are too credulous. Their lives confuse more than they orient.
>
> It is not the time to demand complete adaptation from them. They are still fighting paternal and patriarchal resistance. They do not want formal recognition for their merits, some of which are false. What they need is a deeper understanding, a more authentic affect, and, above all, wise and safe counsel. To repudiate them with ridicule is to scorn their ultimate capacity for production and retard their process of assimilation.[5]

Osawa's article can be analyzed on many levels. First, while academic and journalistic comments on ethnic assimilation were common in the mid-1960s in the nonethnic press, they were rarely written by members of the ethnic communities under discussion. Osawa, then, was perhaps the only Japanese-Brazilian to publish on identity in a non-Nikkei forum in this period. The article was also unusual for its insistence that ethnic integration was not a minority "problem" but a majority one. Yet Osawa declared this from a distance, portraying his subjects as different from himself, never using the words *I* or *we*. In an author's note he even insisted that readers should not connect his own ethnicity with the article itself.

Osawa's ponderings on identity did not make him an active opponent of the military coup in 1964. Indeed, he respected the Brazilian politician Carlos Lacerda (whom he now considers on the "extreme right") and U.S. president John F. Kennedy, whom he wrote about favorably in the *Casper Libero* newspaper, praise he now labels "one of my past shames." Osawa's continued activism in the bank led to yet another transfer, this time to Brasília, but by 1966, at age twenty, he was back in Santo André, his career in finance over. Osawa began tutoring high school students and was one of two hundred young adults to apply for an internship at the Ação Comunitária (Community Action), a project funded by the Rockefeller Foundation working with the poor in Peru, Venezuela, and Brazil. Osawa, one of six people selected, for the first time met university-age students in the humanities and social sciences. He thus decided to try a course at the University of São Paulo (USP), studying philosophy with Marilena Chauí, a professor and public intellectual who would become São Paulo's secretary of cultural affairs after the dictatorship. According to Osawa, Chauí was "a talking machine gun, and I did not understand anything," but this did not discourage him. In sociology classes he met political militants. When he went to Venezuela for an Ação Comunitária conference in late 1967, his colleagues at USP gave him a number of contacts. During his three weeks in Caracas he became increasingly politicized.

On returning to Brazil, Osawa decided to become a full-time student at the University of São Paulo. He joined the VPR as a student activist, and by the end of 1967 he had entered the guerrilla wing. One of his first tasks was to choose a code name so that others could not identify him if they were captured. His choice was *Mário*, a name that, on the surface, appeared innocuous. But from Osawa's perspective it was imbued with deep ethnic meaning.

Mário, I knew him from my hometown. He was a short little Japanese [immigrant] who lived on the streets, always drunk. He went house to house, asking for food and money. And the image of that Japanese was always with me, [he was] completely unadapted. Nothing ever went right for him. I never knew what happened to him. . . . people helped, gave him stuff, but he had no family, nothing. He was abandoned. He was a homeless Japanese on a street that wasn't even a street because it was a rural area. He walked hours and hours just to get a bite to eat. So when I entered the organization [the VPR] I needed to choose a name and for me the symbol of the humiliated, the offended, the person without a future, this was Mário.

Osawa never told his companions about the meanings behind his chosen name. Indeed, when I asked him about the code name he commented that the real Mário was the only thing he remembered clearly from his early childhood in the Japanese rural community in Guaíra. The name Mário, then, was not just a political choice but also a way for a "Brazilianized" Nikkei to keep a link to his ethnic past.

As Mário, Osawa was able to conflate his ethnic background and his political ideology. The name also had strategic uses, because Japanese-Brazilian militants, at least in Osawa's mind, had to hide their documented as well as public identities. "Mário was a name used a lot by Japanese immigrants. So I chose a name that I did not think would be odd, having a 'Japan' called Mário. Imagine if I chose the name Inocêncio. . . . I have, for example, a [younger] brother called Jacinto. . . . but these are names that would attract a great deal of attention if a Japanese used them."

In Osawa's recollection, the interplay of meanings in the code name Mário was fraught with ethnic collisions. He chose it to memorialize a Japanese immigrant but the name floated between majority and minority interpretations since it was innocuous. Osawa's positioning of the code name as the antithesis of his brother's Brazilian name was also striking. On the one hand he saw baptism and his sibling's Brazilian appellation as part of a move toward a fixed national identity. Yet Osawa's belief that his "Japanese name" (Shizou) was accepted by the local priest because it "sounded like Jesus" was linked with his memory of taking a "Brazilian name" (Mário) for the first time in his life, in part to hide his identity.

Osawa's explanation suggests the ethnic terrain on which even the most mundane aspects of Brazilian history can be played out. But the new name was not simply Mário. It was Mário Japa. When I asked Osawa about this, he replied that he had never before been asked about his code name. He then spoke of the essentialized way in which Nikkei were seen in Brazil: "I only chose the name Mário. Japa, to tell the truth, came from my companheiros, who added it to my name. I did not choose it."

Why was "Mário" forced to add "Japa" to his code name? Why would militants in a life or death struggle take a chance on an appellation that "lost all its power as a code name or nom de guerre [because] when people said that the group had a 'Mário Japa' everyone knew that there was a Japanese in the group and, since we [Nikkei] were a minority, it was even easier [for the police to identify us]." When Osawa tried to convince his companions to stop calling him "Japa," even changing his code name to "Fernando," why did they refuse? Clearly, no majority Brazilian could envisage a Japanese-Brazilian as simply Brazilian, and no one could picture "Mário" as anything other than "Mário Japa."

Shizuo Osawa had become Mário Japa, although few knew that the two names were connected. By 1968 he and his radical colleagues were striking fear into the hearts of those who sought to uphold Brazil's status quo. In late July he participated in one of the most audacious acts that the dictatorship had seen: the invasion and occupation of Rádio Independência in São Bernardo do Campo, a large city on the outskirts of São Paulo. Taking control of the broadcast, he read a revolutionary message written by Carlos Marighella, then disappeared into the night. In late 1969 Osawa was sent to Algeria to participate in a guerrilla-training course. After returning to Brazil he and Celso Lungaretti purchased the land that became the Vale do Ribeira VPR training camp discussed in chapter 3.[6]

By the end of 1969 Mário Japa was one of the leaders of VPR operations in São Paulo. He remained in public life as Shizuo Osawa and continued using his real name and documents. Information about his clandestine activities is hard to pin down since he remained unknown to most militants and to the police and soldiers who were searching for either one or many mysterious "Japanese." In his militant guise he had been trusted with a great deal of information because, in Osawa's words, "the Asian [is] the ideal soldier for any general."[7] In his public persona, Osawa was just a quiet, studious-looking "Japanese" young man.[8] Osawa's "typical" ethnic appearance allowed him to buy land for training camps and to rent apartments as safe houses.[9] Martha Vianna, in her authorized biography of Maria do Carmo Brito, Osawa's then militant companion and now wife, emphasizes how ethnicity disguised the militant: "A tranquil smile, few words, a precise and at times biting comment, an Oriental patience and fondness for children, he could be the beloved teacher in a primary school or a perfect spy with his cold blood and self-control in even the most chaotic situations."[10] This outsider's image of Osawa matched the power of a Japanese-Brazilian ethnicity that he said gave him "a tremendous facility in renting houses for companions whom the police were looking for. They [the owners] never asked me for documents, a cosigner, these kinds of things."

In July 1969 the VPR joined the National Liberation Command (Comando de Libertação Nacional, COLINA), to form the Armed Revolutionary Vanguard–Palmares (Vanguarda Armada Revolucionária, VAR–Palmares).[11] This alliance fell apart a few months later, and the VPR was reinvigorated with ex-captain Carlos Lamarca taking a leadership role. Osawa's memory of the VPR, however, did not focus on Lamarca. Rather, it concentrated on a VPR leader and theoretician in São Paulo, Ladislaw Dowbor, known by his code name Jamil. Dowbor was different from many revolutionary ideologues in his belief that oppression was not exclusively class-based.[12] Osawa understood the "Jamil Thesis" to be the result of Dowbor's failed relationship with a Jewish-Brazilian woman whose parents (most of whose family had perished in Poland during the Shoah) sent her to Israel to end the match. Dowbor followed her to Israel, worked on a kibbutz, and learned Hebrew, but the relationship faltered and he returned to Brazil alone, seeing oppression from a number of different angles.[13]

LUNCH AT HOME

Ladislaw Dowbor was the eventual successor to Carlos Marighella as leader of the VPR. He generously spent two hours with me at his home one afternoon. He made me a wonderful lunch and took me to pick up his daughter and her friends from school. Yet he diverted all my questions about the period and his ideology. Indeed, his published autobiography glances over the period 1968–70 (which ended with his being arrested and traded for the kidnapped German ambassador before being exiled to Algeria) in two paragraphs.[14]

THE COSTS OF CUSTODY

When Shizuo Osawa became Mário Japa in late 1967 this was unknown to the state. Authorities only began to learn that Mário Japa was Shizuo Osawa on the rainy night of 27 February 1970. Having gone twenty-four sleepless hours, he decided to drive a load of weapons and revolutionary pamphlets from one hide-out to another when the person assigned to the task did not appear.[15] Driving along the Estrada das Lágrimas (Road of Tears) in greater São Paulo, Osawa fell asleep at the wheel and crashed. In the wrecked car the police found an unconscious Japanese-Brazilian whose documents said he was Shizuo Osawa. To their surprise, they also discovered weapons and VPR propaganda in the trunk. Osawa, now awake, was taken first to an emergency room, then to the local police station and finally to DEOPS headquarters "for treatment."[16]

Osawa had told his parents of his decision to become a militant. Thus they may not have been surprised when, as Osawa tells it, an employee "left the police station, discovered my address, and went there to tell my family," because he found it impossible to believe that the mild-mannered Nikkei accident victim could be a militant. Osawa's father and a lawyer arrived at DEOPS headquarters before Osawa, but it made no difference: after two days Gentaro Osawa was turned away and told that no one with his son's name was there.

Rumors of Mário Japa's arrest began circulating among the VPR leadership when he did not appear at a meeting. Carlos Lamarca feared that under torture he might reveal the location of the Vale do Ribeira training camp. Ladislaw Dowbor agreed: "For us it was a heavy loss because we never expected it. It was absolutely necessary to free [Mário Japa] to save the training area whose location he knew."[17] Dowbor thus sent sympathizers (often nonactivist family members who were allowed visiting hours with prisoners) into São Paulo's Tiradentes Prison to determine if Mário Japa had actually been arrested. There was, however, a flaw in Dowbor's strategy. Since no one in the VPR knew Mário Japa's real name it became impossible to confirm that the prisoner named Shizuo Osawa was in fact "Mário Japa."[18]

The VPR leadership knew that someone named Shizuo Osawa was in custody. They also knew that Mário Japa was missing. They were not sure if the two names referred to the same person. The Osawa family knew that their son was in prison even if the DEOPS denied it. The DEOPS and its head, Sérgio Fleury, knew they had captured someone named Shizuo Osawa with weapons and militant literature, but they had no idea if this was one of the various "Japanese" whose names had appeared in testimony garnered by torturing other political militants. The confusion did not work to Osawa's advantage. Fleury, in fact, thought that his prisoner was the "Japanese" bank robber whom he had been looking for. Osawa remembers being accused of incidents in which he had not been involved: "I suffered a lot. . . . There was this problem . . . when they began to speak of one Japanese, then any Japanese who fell into their hands would pay for all. The same thing happened to a blonde woman, they created this myth of the blonde bank robber, and then any blonde who fell into the hands of the police was lost: she was tortured more heavily. This could really make the torture worse."

Identifying Shizuo Osawa as "Mário Japa" was further complicated by the number of different names that appeared in the government's files. These included Mário Japa, Shizuo Osawa, Chizuo Osawa, Shizuo Osava, Chizuo Osava, Shizuo Ozawa, and Shismo Osava.[19] Even so, Fleury knew that he had captured a revolutionary.[20] Not surprisingly, other units of the government also wanted Osawa, who they believed would lead them to Carlos Lamarca, the most wanted militant in Brazil. When officials from Operation Bandeirantes (OBAN) demanded that Osawa be transferred to their headquarters,

Fleury refused. On 1 March 1970, according to the journalist Antônio Carlos Fon, the OBAN leadership sent troops to invade the DEOPS building to take Osawa by force. As the soldiers searched the office, "Fleury forced 'Mário Japa' to lie down on the floor and jumped on him with both feet, breaking a number of his ribs, so that the military would not be able to torture him and discover where Lamarca was hidden [before Fleury did]."[21]

Fleury's sadism did not prevent Osawa from being tortured. Yet the militant is remembered for his resistance, perhaps because this fits the stereotype of Japanese bravery and loyalty. Osawa rejected the idea that he was braver than others. He told one interviewer that he invented an entire story, with a logic of its own, because no other prisoner could identify him and thus his information could never be confirmed or denied.[22] My conversations with Osawa about his experiences under torture, however, went in an entirely different direction:

> When I was imprisoned, there was that idea that Japanese were bad drivers. So they took that thing, that idea [that I was captured following an automobile accident], and it hurt me a lot. And afterward I thought about this, the reason that I felt so humiliated. But I think it was a personal problem, to be called incapable of doing something [like driving well]. To be accused of being incapable of doing something well, for a young person, it hurts a lot, especially since he thinks he is omnipotent.

After days of torture left him almost dead, he was taken to an Army hospital.

> I had an experience, after the OBAN, when I was really bad off, and they put me in a military hospital. And there, one of the physicians on call, who should not have been taking care of me, but who was a friend of the doctor who was responsible for me[,] . . . one day this physician brought a Japanese to speak with me and we had an interview. He came with that chitchat about how I was shaming the race and all that! And then I started to explain to him what we were doing and that there was no reason to be ashamed. We were not stealing and not trying to make ourselves rich. It was exactly the opposite: we would trade our lives for a cause, for the betterment of society. The two of us had a long conversation. And he came back a number of times. Later I heard about that doctor, that he had changed his opinion. He realized that we were idealists, that it was not at all what he imagined or what he had thought.

I asked Osawa if these conversations spoke to generational change. His reply made clear the essentialist boxes in which many Nikkei operated:

Just like that doctor in the military hospital, [Nikkei] have a tendency to take the opposite extreme [about militancy] because the idea of the militant is so terrible, is so bad, that they were surprised [when they spoke with us]. It is an example of how the Japanese are so ideological! He always thinks the worst of the person who goes outside of the rules! [In the Sansei and Yonsei generations] there is more flexibility. But among Nisei . . . they are really inflexible. He who is excluded, it is because he should be excluded! Japanese, in this sense, are kind of, actually all are, equal. Any person who moves outside the margins, he is radically excluded. They [the Japanese] do not accept much difference.

As the days passed, the VPR decided that it could not take a chance that the imprisoned Shizuo Osawa was Mário Japa and that he would buckle under torture. Given the successful trade of kidnapped U.S. ambassador Charles Elbrick for fifteen political prisoners in early September 1969, the VPR leadership put into operation an already formulated political kidnapping plan. Osawa himself had been part of that discussion, which focused on three groups of potential targets, "big fish" (high-level diplomats), second-level diplomats like consuls, and foreign businesspeople.[23] Osawa's memory of these sessions led to a funny moment when he laughed and told me, his U.S. interviewer, that he thought the victim should be "preferably American," and that he had the name and address of just such a person in his pocket when he was arrested.

The different possibilities were resolved in a VPR document titled "Considerations on the Objectives of a Kidnapping Operation." It outlined everything from targets to strategies for surveillance to escape routes. At the top of the victim list were diplomats from countries with large capital investment in Brazil, including the United States, England, West Germany, and Japan.[24] Israel, with little investment but high visibility, was placed last. The document conflated Brazilian-Jewish ethnicity and Israeli national identity, claiming that in spite of the "political-economic force of [the Jewish] colony," kidnapping an Israeli diplomat might create a reaction "characterized as anti-Semitic," exactly the point that had led to the angry exchange between Alfredo Sirkis and his companion discussed in chapter 4.[25] The VPR document included a number of Nikkei among the top priorities for release: Takao Amano and João Katsunobu Amano of the National Liberation Action (Ação Libertadora Nacional, ALN), Carlos Takaoka of the Communist Party of Brazil (Partido Comunista do Brasil, PC do B), and Alfredo Nozumo Tsukumo of the VAR–Palmares.

The capture of Mário Japa activated the plan. While fifteen militants had been traded for the U.S. ambassador in 1969, the kidnapping of the Japanese consul was primarily to free Osawa. According to Maria do Carmo Brito, the VPR decided that "if they took our Japanese, we were going to take their Japanese," and they targeted Nobuo Okuchi, Japan's consul general in São Paulo.[26] The ethnic reasoning behind the decision was reinforced by São Paulo's position as the largest "Japanese" city in the world outside Japan. Furthermore, kidnapping Okuchi would embarrass the military, since the media would certainly link it to the 1970 International Exposition in Osaka, São Paulo's sister city.

These factors, the militants hoped, would pressure the military regime to trade Osawa for Okuchi. Brazilian foreign minister Mário Gibson Barbosa remembered all of these things in a 2004 interview with historian Jerry Dávila: "The kidnappers had, in my opinion, chosen a Japanese on purpose, I mean to say the consul general of Japan in São Paulo!!! To cause an international problem for Brazil, with an important country for Brazil like Japan. Remember, they did not kidnap some African [laughter]. They wanted to kidnap an ambassador from a nationality that would create an international problem for Brazil."[27]

Gibson Barbosa's language is like that of VPR member Carmo Brito, referring to Okuchi's "nationality" rather than his "nation," thus implying an ethnic/national linkage of Osawa and Okuchi. In its cover story on the kidnapping, Veja, Brazil's most widely read newsmagazine, included a photograph of Osawa in the lower-right corner and a banner on the 1970 Expo in Japan (figure 27).[28]

The kidnapping was easily planned, since the consul's home and work addresses were listed in the São Paulo telephone book. As Okuchi left his office on 11 March 1970, his driver, Hideaki Doi, stopped at what appeared to be an accident. Dowbor recalled the preparations in an interview with the Berkeley, California–based magazine Ramparts that was translated and smuggled into Brazil for circulation among the Left.

> The kidnapping of the Japanese consul was really rather funny. On one side of the place where we seized him is the federal police headquarters; on the other side, fewer than one hundred yards away, is the headquarters of the civil police; on the third side is the district police station; and only fifty yards away is the state security agency! Militarily this type of action is usually very simple. He was in his car with a chauffeur. One person in a Volkswagen began to swerve about the road as if his car were out of control, and he motioned to the ambassador's chauffeur to stop, which of course he did because he didn't want to ram into the VW. Six of

FIGURE 27. "The Consul's Kidnapping:
Reorganized Terror? Desperate Terror?" *Veja*,
18 March 1970. Cover courtesy of *Veja*, Editora Abril

our people stepped in at this point. I was on the corner and explained to the ambassador's chauffeur that he should remain calm. Two people then took the consul and put him into a car and drove away.[29]

Okuchi's three-day captivity was marked by long conversations with Dowbor and fellow VPR member Liszt Vieira, a sociologist and lawyer who had worked as a translator at the U.S. embassy. According to Okuchi's memoirs, the three discussed international politics and the cultural and social differences between Brazil and Japan. One of the consul's recollections was being served "Brazilian food[,] . . . maybe because they knew that Japanese like rice, they frequently served dishes with rice."[30] Perhaps it was the food or maybe it was the chats on international relations, but Maria do Carmo Brito told her biographer that the consul was so impressed with Dowbor and Liszt that he treated the two as "future statesmen."[31]

Much of what we know about the kidnapping comes from Okuchi's published memoirs, a complicated source. Okuchi recounts conversations that took place in English among nonnative speakers but which were remembered years later in Japanese. The original publication was translated into Portuguese and quotes from that version were translated into English for this book. Methodological caveats aside, the conversations appear to reveal something about the ethnic assumptions of the kidnappers, at least in the consul's eyes. Okuchi tried to convince Dowbor and Liszt that, from a negotiating perspective, it was less efficient to kidnap a consul general than an ambassador. The consul reported Dowbor's response: "The consul general of Japan in São Paulo has jurisdiction in the states of São Paulo and Paraná, which contain the largest Nikkei communities. If we had a large repercussion among them as our target, the result would be very efficient." Even so, Dowbor noted that "if our objective were not to rescue Mário, maybe we would have chosen a diplomat from a different country."[32] General Newton Cruz, director of Brazil's National Intelligence Service (Serviço Nacional de Informações, SNI), without knowing Dowbor's thoughts on the matter, made the same connection. He wrote that the kidnapping had two goals, to "traumatize the extensive Japanese colony in São Paulo" and to "sensitize [toward militancy] the racial group of Japanese origin in Brazil."[33]

The public knew nothing of these internal conversations. They did, however, see carefully controlled media coverage. Officials focused on the international embarrassment that the kidnappings had caused and suggested that the militants were anti-Brazilian.[34] Newspaper, television, and radio reports were surrounded by commentary on the Expo in Osaka, the unsuccessful hijacking of a Brazilian airplane from Chile to Cuba, a bomb explosion at the offices of a Rio de Janeiro magazine, and a shootout between police and militants trying to kidnap the secretary of security in Rio de Janeiro. Perhaps the most sensational coverage of the Okuchi kidnapping was in the *Jornal da Tarde*, the afternoon edition of the *O Estado de S. Paulo* and the newspaper most associated with the government: its front pages used large images and headlines like AND NOW, WHAT WILL IT COST TO RESCUE THE JAPANESE CONSUL? or THERE WERE SEVEN MEN, FOUR MACHINE GUNS, AND A KIDNAPPED JAPANESE CONSUL. One story included a sidebar with the Japanese characters for "kidnapping" on each page.[35]

Okuchi's kidnapping left the DEOPS confused. Its initial investigation did not focus exclusively on a political motive for the consul's disappearance, in spite of the previous kidnapping of the U.S. ambassador. Rather, DEOPS officials looked back to the agency's long history of awkward relations with the Nikkei community and proposed two other possible motives: that the image of Japanese-Brazilians as well off had led criminals to kidnap Okuchi for ransom and that the Shindo Renmei, so strong in the late 1940s with its claim that Japan had won World War II, had returned with a splash. While the police were unsure how to test either the political theory or that of a ransom motive, they did have an idea about the third possibility. On the morning after the kidnapping, Kazuo Watanabe, Brazil's first Nikkei judge, received a visit from an official of the Ministry of Justice inquiring about Shindo Renmei activity.[36] According to Veja, Watanabe laughed the man out of his office, noting that even if the Shindo Renmei did exist in 1968, "they would be elderly and, as a result, incapable of an action of this type."[37] The press also wondered about a Shindo Renmei connection, but this idea was strongly rebutted by Japanese diplomats in Brazil.[38] Damon Kanda, the lead reporter for the primarily Japanese-language Paulista Shimbun, had immigrated to Brazil six years earlier from Japan. He remembered thinking the Shindo Renmei thesis was ridiculous but "natural" since "Brazilians did not know anything about the Nikkei community."[39]

The VPR claimed responsibility for the kidnapping on the morning of 12 March by leaving a number of communiqués around São Paulo. A phone call to the Japanese consulate directed representatives to a particular book in a specific bookstore. Another call sent a Jornal da Tarde reporter (the militants, like everyone else, knew that the newspaper was linked to the regime) to a mailbox at a private home. A third was sent to the president of the Japanese Industrial and Commercial Association of Brazil (Câmara de Comércio e Indústria Japonesa do Brasil). Brazilian government leaders focused on the demands in the communiqué, but that was not what most interested me. Rather, it was a sentence unlike any other found in communications regarding kidnapped foreign diplomats: "This act is absolutely not directed against the Japanese people or members of their colony, many of whom are in our struggle or are being tortured in prison."[40] This sentence is crucial: for VPR members, like many Paulistanos, a scenario in which Japan (the country), Japanese-Brazilians (the "community"), and Nikkei militants were not linked was unimaginable.

Okuchi's kidnapping was covered intensely by the press. The prime sources of information were Damon Kanda's reports in the Paulista Shimbun which, like all Japanese-Brazilian newspapers, had two entirely different readerships, those of the immigrant generation who read the Japanese-language sections and those born in Brazil who read the sections in Portuguese. Yet Kanda's reporting created a new readership for the Paulista

Shimbun, as reporters from mainstream newspapers realized that there was news in the news.

The implications of Okuchi's kidnapping change when it is viewed from the perspective of the Japanese-Brazilian press. For example, major newspapers received calls from VPR militants telling them where to find communiqués. The *Paulista Shimbun*, however, was phoned by Japanese-Brazilian federal deputy João Sussumu Hirata, whom the VPR had contacted in an attempt to find a Japanese-language outlet for their messages.[41] The VPR's distance from the Japanese-Brazilian community reflected how divorced they and Nikkei militants were from São Paulo's minority communities. This stood in striking contrast to the DEOPS's belief that Nikkei militants linked the VPR to the Japanese-Brazilian community. Indeed, Kanda remembers being warned that the DEOPS had the *Paulista Shimbun* under surveillance, even though it was one of the few newspapers in São Paulo with which the militants had no direct contact.

The release of the first communiqué, with its dual assertion that the kidnapping was not directed toward Japan and that many Nikkei were involved in militant activity, led to strong reactions from Japanese-Brazilian community leaders. Miyasaka Kunito, president of the América do Sul Bank and the Brazilian Society for Japanese Culture, complained that "it is a shame that there are Nisei and Sansei among the kidnappers, but there will be no problems because we [Nikkei] believe in Brazil." Michiko Murakami, president of the Esperança Women's Benevolent Society, blamed the existence of Nikkei militants on the lack of communication between Japanese-Brazilian children and their mothers, while Caio Mori, president of the United Association of São Paulo, argued, "We do not like to think that some Nisei are behind this but we have heard that there are around three hundred Nikkei participating in counterrevolutionary activities. We would like to say to them that, if they want progress for the country, it is a great error to use violent methods."[42]

Connections between the abduction and Japanese-Brazilian identity also were drawn in the mainstream press, which sent its reporters flowing into Liberdade. According to the *Folha de S. Paulo*, many interviewees refused to believe that the kidnapping was politically motivated, insisting that the perpetrators were criminals looking for a ransom. Others feared that there were Japanese or Nisei among the terrorists.[43] A communal sigh of relief must have been emitted when the *Diário Popular* emphasized with italics that the kidnappers "*had no Nipponic features.*"[44] As Hirochi Inoue, a sixteen-year-old who worked at an electric materials store told the *Folha de S. Paulo*, "My family was really upset when they thought that the kidnappers were Japanese, and they felt ashamed. Now it is much better."[45]

The VPR feared a negative reaction to the consul's kidnapping among mainstream Nikkei.[46] To this end, Ladislaw Dowbor sent a VPR sympathizer unknown to the police to Tiradentes Prison to convince an imprisoned militant to write a letter in Japanese "to the Japanese colony saying that the kidnapping of the Japanese consul had nothing to do with the people of that country and that it was only done to liberate a Japanese revolutionary."[47] While Dowbor's comment was made under duress, it illustrates the different meanings ascribed to the word *Japanese*. It could refer to an ethnic community, to an individual born in Brazil, and to a representative of the Japanese government. Carlos Takaoka, the person asked to write the letter, refused for fear of putting other political prisoners at risk.[48]

In Japan, media coverage was constant. Reporters for Japanese media outlets based in the United States flew to Brazil and daily front-page reports were the rule, not only in elite and popular newspapers but in those devoted to sports as well. Some articles claimed that the abduction had been motivated by anti-Japanese sentiment and Japanese ambassador Koh Chiba begged reporters to interview "common people" in Brazil to counter these ideas.[49] Tokizo Araki, another Japanese diplomat in Brazil who had made a public splash in 1968 when he presented a large bronze plaque commemorating the visit of the crown prince at the inauguration of the Fluminense Futebol Club's new Rio de Janeiro headquarters, also rejected the idea that the kidnapping reflected anti-Japanese sentiments. Readers of Araki's comments in São Paulo's *Notícias Populares* saw them placed next to an advertisement for a Volkswagen truck with a Nikkei farmer standing in front of it and the word "Guaranteed" in large letters.[50]

The sense that Japanese were "guaranteed" may explain Okuchi's apparent involvement in crafting the VPR demands that would lead to his release. During one of their "frequent amiable conversations," the consul and his kidnappers focused on the demand that the regime end all torture.[51] He argued that the militants "must couch their demand in acceptable terms" and then presented them with language about "due regard for justice and prevailing laws." To strengthen his point, he told his captors that "he was particularly interested in points of language because he was thinking of his own chance of release [and] he was willing to die for Japan but not for Brazil."[52] Okuchi's position seems to have resonated: the final set of demands from the VPR appear to have used his language.

Once Okuchi's disappearance had been confirmed as a political kidnapping, Brazil's Foreign Ministry became involved. Foreign Minister Mário Gibson Barbosa recalls a meeting to discuss an official response to the VPR's three major demands: that their revolutionary message be published in the press, that the government release five militants whose names were to be provided, and that the five prisoners be given asylum in Mexico. Barbosa argued vehemently for the primacy of diplomatic protocol and, after much debate, the decision was made to save Consul Okuchi.[53]

It took less than twenty-four hours for the Brazilian government to agree to the VPR's demands.[54] After a series of exchanges, a list of five prisoners (plus three children) was published in the mainstream and Japanese-Brazilian press. For the VPR, guaranteeing Mário Japa's release was no easy matter since it remained unsure of his actual identity and name. As a result, the prisoner exchange list referred to him only as "a Nisei with the nom de guerre Mário," and it was the DEOPS which added Osawa's birth name to the list.[55] Another person on that list, referred to only by the code name *Toledo*, was incorrectly believed to have been in the car accident with Osawa, and the VPR assumed he would confirm Osawa's release.[56] There was a problem, however. The government did not have a prisoner known as "Toledo," and Osawa was again tortured to get this information.[57] At the last minute, after both sides realized that no "Toledo" had been in the automobile accident, another communiqué put the name of Diógenes José Carvalho de Oliveira on the release list since he could identify Mário Japa by sight.[58]

The revelation that a Japanese-Brazilian was among those to be traded for the Japanese consul shocked the public. The *Jornal da Tarde* took the most aggressive approach, publishing an article headlined, PAY CLOSE ATTENTION: THE JAPANESE TERROR.[59] Some Nikkei, knowing the close connection between the DEOPS and the newspaper, feared that the article was a warning that "because so many Japanese are committing to guerrilla activity there is collective responsibility of Japanese society in this case."[60] Tokyo's *Nihon Keizai Shimbun* worried that the revelation would hurt the Nikkei community, while the *Yomiuri Shimbun* suggested that as more Japanese companies invested in Brazil the number of Japanese-Brazilian guerrillas would grow.[61] For Brazilian diplomats in Japan, the attention was embarrassing because "the incident is being watched by the whole Japanese population on their 22 million television sets."[62]

Early in the afternoon of 14 March 1970, President General Emílio Garrastazu Médici signed a decree banning the five militants from Brazil in return for the release of Consul General Okuchi. Later that day television showed the group beginning to assemble at Congonhas airport in São Paulo.

The consul was also watching from captivity, and he saw Osawa, who "looked really beaten up."[63] Included in the group was Madre Maurina Borges da Silveira, a nun whose prison and torture became a cause célèbre and was credited with moving the Brazilian Catholic Church toward a more public position on human rights.[64] At about 5:30 P.M. the Caravelle PP-PDX, well known to the Brazilian public because the same model had been hijacked by militants to Cuba the year before, began its flight to Mexico.

The flight was slow (with four stops), and the consul remained in captivity until it arrived in Mexico City early on Sunday, 15 March. Shizuo Osawa had to be helped off the plane because he had been so badly tortured (the DEOPS claimed that his injuries were the result of his car accident).[65] An Associated Press caption to the photograph of Osawa's arrival made special note that he was "called Mário the Japanese" (see figure 28).

After confirming that Osawa was free, the VPR prepared to release Okuchi on 16 March 1970. Yet his captors noted an unusually heavy police presence on the streets. Okuchi had pressed the phone number of the house where he was held into a note he had written to his wife and this allowed police to find the neighborhood, but not the specific house where he was held. Since the VPR refused to release Okuchi under these conditions, President General Médici ordered the police off the streets. The following day taxi driver Joaquim dos Santos picked up a Japanese man and brought his fare to the requested address, where some one thousand people were milling around.[66] Only *Paulista Shimbun* reporter Damon Kanda recognized the man who stepped out of the taxi as Consul Okuchi.[67]

Later that night, after having been warned by Japanese ambassador Chiba to take "real care in your comments so that we do not exasperate the Brazilian [government]," Okuchi made his first formal statement to some two hundred reporters. Over the next few days, Okuchi would indeed exasperate Brazilian authorities by refusing to condemn the kidnappers and by claiming that he could not remember what any of them looked like. In his memoirs his explanation was that "the man who I had seen had a beard, but in the photos that the police showed he was clean shaven."[68]

The Japanese Socialist Party's Motojiro Mori, a member of the upper house of the Japanese Diet, was also annoyed with Consul Okuchi. He attacked the diplomat for not being more aggressive in seeking information during his captivity and for calling his kidnappers "gentlemanly" afterward.[69] Okuchi paid Mori no heed and repeated his comments in his private discussions with U.S. diplomats. He also looked to the United States for advice on personal security since, following his release, he received a num-

FIGURE 28. Associated Press photograph,
15 March 1970. From 30Z/160/5628, DEOPS Papers,
Arquivo do Estado de São Paulo. Used by permission
of the Arquivo do Estado de São Paulo

ber of threatening phone calls and believed that "perhaps [he was] safe from
the group that had kidnapped him . . . [but that] there were other groups that
would as soon snatch him as anyone else."[70] Indeed, just a month after the
release of Okuchi, the Taiwanese consul general in São Paulo reported that
an "Oriental man" had entered his apartment and tried to "subjugate the
maid by injection in the arm." The woman's screams alerted neighbors, who
called the consul's wife. Entering her apartment, she received a phone call
from a Chinese speaker, who told her that "if [the] consul general does not
leave Brazil by the end of the month, I will kill him and his whole family."
Within twenty-four hours the consul's family had been issued visas to the
United States.[71]

Brazilian press reports after Okuchi's release consistently used language
that blurred the lines between the Japanese consul who was posted to Brazil
and the Brazilian militant who had a "Japanese name" and was called
"Japa." Brazil's Portuguese-language newspapers printed numerous articles

about the stories in Brazil's Japanese-language newspapers.[72] The *Folha de S. Paulo* even illustrated its story on the consul's release with a photograph of the *São Paulo Shimbun*. The same edition of the *Folha* included a long story on a Japanese-Brazilian "genius child" (remember that Osawa had been called the "Atomic Brain") who proudly asked the reporter, "Did you know that a Sansei can be president of Brazil?"[73] The cover of *Veja* (see figure 27 above) included Okuchi, Osawa, and a banner on the Expo across the top that attracted the eye much more than the title of the cover story, "The Kidnapping of the Consul." The article led directly into a report on Expo 70 which suggested (correctly) that the image of Japan as hypermodern and technological had modified the image of Japanese-Brazilians as farmers.[74]

Discourses about ethnicity and nation were not confined to Brazil. In Japan, the news that Okuchi had been traded for Osawa led to discussions of the negative implications of diaspora. Most articles in the Japanese press focused on Osawa and newspapers frequently cropped group photographs of the released militants so that only he appeared.[75] An editorial in *The Japan Times* made a series of DEOPS-like connections between Japanese fanaticism during the World War II era, the Brazilian Shindo Renmei movement in the decade after the war, and Japanese and Brazilian revolutionary movements that emerged in the sixties and seventies: "That there should be persons of Japanese descent in such [terrorist] bands is not surprising when it is recalled that there were extremist Japanese who had refused to believe in Japan's war defeat. Many of them in time turned to hooliganism."[76] An editorial in the *Yomiuri Shimbun* (republished in English in *The Daily Yomiuri*) took a similar position, misquoting Osawa as saying that all Japanese-Brazilians leftists were members of a single guerrilla group which was "determined to achieve revolution."[77] Perhaps this explains why the *Sankei Shimbun* ran an article on the Okuchi case next to another on the arrest of two members of the Japanese Red Army.[78]

Newspapers in Japan also published stories about the stories in Brazilian newspapers, including that mentioned above, subtitled "The Japanese Terror." In one case a Japanese newspaper even quoted a mainstream Brazilian newspaper quoting a Japanese-Brazilian newspaper.[79] While most Japanese-Brazilian militants were the children of rural agricultural workers, they were often portrayed in Japan as coming from "families who play a leading role in the Japanese society in Brazil."[80] These multiple messages reflected the ambivalence with which many Japanese saw emigrants: on the one hand, there was pride in diasporic success; on the other, the "non-Japanese" aspects of diaspora life were precisely what led young Nikkei to antiauthoritarian positions.

In the aftermath of the kidnapping, the Brazilian and Japanese governments assured each other that the events would not hurt "the traditionally friendly relations between our two countries."[81] The Brazilian government did not forget about the militants it had banned, keeping a careful eye on Shizuo Osawa as he followed a brief stay in Mexico with an extended period in Cuba, and then by time in Chile, Portugal, Belgium, and Angola.[82]

Leaders of the Japanese-Brazilian community feared that the kidnapping would hurt their relations with both the Brazilian regime and the Japanese government. Osawa's grandfather went to the Japanese consulate in São Paulo "to ask forgiveness in the name of my whole family for the shame of being a subversive." The consul saw no need for contrition, writing in his memoirs that Osawa's desire to improve Brazil meant that "there is no reason for Japanese of the first generation to lament or consider shameful the existence of Nisei and Sansei activists in guerrilla activities."[83]

Shizuo Osawa remembered Okuchi's postkidnapping refusal to condemn his captors with great pride. In doing this he told me a story in which he constructed Ladislaw Dowbor, who had planned the kidnapping, not as a militant but as an outsider minority: "The police were really mad [at Okuchi] because it was impossible not to be able to describe and recognize Ladislaw. Ladislaw is blond, a type completely different than a normal Brazilian. So it was really easy to recognize him. And he [Okuchi] did not recognize anyone [in the police photos], he did not describe anyone [laughter]. The police were furious: not only did he not collaborate, he did the opposite, he sabotaged the police!"

Okuchi seemed to remember Osawa with equal pride, noting in his memoirs that "Osawa learned from his parents the Japanese hard work ethic. He had respect for Japan and its people. That said, he had the conviction that he was Brazilian, born and raised in Brazil. He thought first in Brazil and fought for this country."[84]

Perhaps because of these sentiments, Okuchi chose a different path than kidnapped diplomats who left Brazil soon after their release. He remained consul general in São Paulo and put the kidnapping behind him.[85] When Osawa received amnesty and returned to Brazil in 1979, he discovered that Okuchi was now Japan's ambassador. This time Osawa took meeting Okuchi more seriously, wanting to "thank him for the attention and worry," but he feared that a meeting "would cause [Okuchi] problems." Osawa, along with Ladislaw Dowbor, finally scheduled a meeting with Okuchi in 1989, when the former ambassador returned to Brazil for the release of his memoirs. The appointment was cancelled when Okuchi fell ill and died soon thereafter. The "Japanese" militant would never meet the Japanese consul.

NAME CONTROL

Damon Kanda, the reporter for the Paulista Shimbun, *told me a story that was never published: At a party in Brasília in the late 1980s, Okuchi met Ladislaw Dowbor, then a civil servant. According to Kanda, the former consul and the former militant shook hands and had a nice chat. I have had many nice chats with Shizuo Osawa, who today controls the meaning of his code name. He insists that his friends call him "Japa," exactly the name that caused such discontent in late 1960s Brazil.[86]*

Epilogue

DIASPORA AND ITS DISCONTENTS

Anyone flying to twenty-first-century São Paulo would be amazed by the images of Japan that he or she encountered on entering the airplane. Much to the surprise of international passengers, Varig, Delta, and other airlines that fly directly to the city have, as a matter of policy, Japanese-speaking stewards. In-flight movies are always dubbed in Japanese, Portuguese, and English. On domestic shuttle flights between São Paulo and other major cities, one often finds on seat backs Semp Toshiba stickers that proclaim, "Our Japanese are STILL better than everyone else's." On the highway from the airport to the city, Bradesco Bank billboards promote international financial services with a kimono-clad Japanese-Brazilian woman. She seems to be pulling her eyes back to make them more "slanty," emphasizing her Japaneseness and suggesting that the "Brazilian" component of Japanese-Brazilianness is problematic. Or perhaps she is a *mestiça*, with one "Brazilian" and one "Japanese" parent. If so, is she trying to return to a fuller Japanese identity which is, as the tag line notes, "So Complete"?

Entering the city, residents and visitors see advertisements for everything from Yakult energy drinks to Nipomed, an insurance company that associates corporate and ethnic stereotypes of quality and honesty. Driving through the downtown, more billboards, this time as part of a joint campaign by the federal government and the Banco do Brasil. They are written in Japanese and use a Nikkei model. Japan and its Japanese-Brazilian corollary are everywhere.

The mixing of the imagined nations of "Japan" and "Brazil" via the imagined community of "Japanese-Brazilians" is not only visual. While Japan today is only the tenth-largest direct foreign investor in Brazil (as compared to third largest in the seventies) the number of "Japanese" products, from automobiles to televisions, is enormous. Walking down busy main streets in São Paulo, residents encounter recent Chinese immigrants and Northeastern Brazilian migrants selling *yakisoba* (a Japanese noodle dish). In middle- and upper-class neighborhoods, and in shopping malls, there are sushi bars. In more modest areas, stores sell "PRODUCTS IMPORTED FROM JAPAN and other countries," in which almost everything on the shelves is from "other countries." Images of Japan and Japanese are in the phone book: pest-control services with names like Tókio, Kioto, Osaka, and Nikkey claim, often in faux "Japanese" script, that they use a special "Japanese method" to kill bugs. Two of the largest extermination firms call themselves "Nagasaki" and "Hiroshima," linking without irony the power of the atomic bomb and their success at getting rid of bugs and rodents. College-preparation courses use Japanese-Brazilians as advertising tropes, today as they did in the sixties and seventies, to suggest excellence, diligence, and success.[1]

A NIKKEI PROTEST

It is late 2003. I am walking down Avenida Paulista and in the distance I see a demonstration blocking the busy avenue. Red flags are waving and yellow-shirted protesters are marching back and forth across the traffic. As I get closer I can read the slogans emblazoned on the flags: "Down with the Dirt Dictatorship" and "Stamp out Stains." Moving nearer I see that the shirts are adorned with the letters O–M–O and that the protesters are all college-aged Nikkei men. A bystander tells me with a laugh that the "protest" is actually an advertisement for the laundry detergent OMO. "Why are all the guys Japanese-Brazilian?" I wonder. Eventually I find myself chatting with the advertising agency representative organizing the "protest." He tells me that the company has chosen Nikkei to represent hard work and quality, people who "get the job done," just like the detergent. "But why men?" I ask. "Don't most laundry advertisements use women?" "Sure," he tells me, "but everyone knows that Japanese women don't work, they just stay at home like geishas."

This book has focused on the 1960s and 1970s, but little has changed in the essentialized way Japanese-Brazilian ethnicity is viewed in São Paulo. Many residents imagine Nikkei men as biologically hard-working and Nikkei women as highly sexualized. Yet something is different in São Paulo: the meaning of "ethnicity." While the descriptive word *Japanese* remains a shorthand reference to a cluster of cultural characteristics that Paulistanos think of as common among members of the group, thirty years of historical experiences have changed the meaning of "typically Japanese."[2] Today residents rarely imagine a relationship between Nikkei and the agricultural countryside, instead relating Japanese-Brazilians with urban liberal professions. They no longer link the country of Japan to Brazil via Japanese immigrants. Rather, the almost 250,000 Brazilian Nikkei temporarily living in Japan, representing that country's third-largest foreign community behind Chinese and Koreans, are at the imaginary forefront.

Another area of change is in ethnic flexibility. While Paulistanos continue to construct all Nikkei as "Japanese," some people of non-Japanese ancestry also perform Japaneseness. Advertisements for low-cost sexual services by "Japonesinhas" can be found in newspaper classified sections and on stickers in phone booths. "Japonesinhas," however, are overwhelmingly non-Nikkei who dress like "geishas" and act in a pseudo-subordinate manner. This form of paid sexual relation has been prominent for at least a decade, suggesting that both providers and clients find some kind of satisfaction. The same theater of Japaneseness can be found in food consumption. Sushi chefs in São Paulo are overwhelmingly from the Northeastern state of Ceará. Their vaguely indigenous heritage leads many Brazilians to say they "look Japanese," especially when wearing headbands emblazoned with rising suns and Japanese letters. What makes "these Japanese" better than "everyone else's" is that they create new and highly Brazilianized styles of sushi.[3] Being "Japanese" is related to dress and action, not to ethnicity in the classic sense. Yet, the nonfluid nature of Japanese-Brazilian ethnicity has not really changed. The consumer market has become comfortable with the idea of "Japanese" who are not of Japanese descent because no one believes that becoming Japanese is possible.

The notion that some 1.2 million Brazilians are "Japanese" has important implications for our understanding of nation, ethnicity, and diaspora. Whereas many scholars have tried to look beyond the nation, my work suggests that the nation continues to be a viable concept in the real lives of real people. While Japanese-Brazilians are part of a nonnormative and discontented diaspora, most Nikkei subjects see Brazil as their national center. Many majority Brazilians, however, continue to imagine that Japan is the "homeland" for Nikkei. While the two nations are created by physical borders, the subjects of this study seem to understand that the diasporic images of people, products, and identities do not always fit together comfortably. National identity and diasporic identity work together, and while there may be points of ethnic commonality between Japanese-Brazilians, Japanese-Americans in the United States, and Japanese-Peruvians, none would ever confuse themselves with the others.

While a discontented diasporic ethnicity is ever present in São Paulo, the relationship between the imposed from the outside and the imposed from the inside is not easy to separate. I have provided evidence that this book's Nikkei subjects resented representations of diasporic ethnicity by majority society and rejected the idea that they were "Japanese." These same people, however, saw themselves as different from normative Brazilians, and their stereotypes of "Brazil" and "Brazilians" as "other" were often as strong as the majority stereotypes of "Japan" and "Japanese."

The discontent with diaspora can also be seen in generational conflict contained in seemingly respectful family relations. In the 1960s and 1970s, the younger generation's overlay of ethnic rejection and cultural and political revolt was equally national and diasporic. Nikkei militants and their parents admired the "samurai" act but were ashamed of each other and on opposite sides of a political/cultural fence. While Japanese immigrants and their Brazilian children seemed to act in very different ways, they shared a convoluted connection to a diasporic identity. In film we saw the same phenomenon but in a different format. Directors and viewers moved from a fascination with Japanese film to a belief that "Japan" was in São Paulo for the taking. This in turn led some actresses to see public sexuality as an assertion of their Brazilianness even as the audience understood their on-film activity as confirmation of their Japaneseness.

These ebbs and flows suggest that non-Nikkei representations of diasporic ethnicity had a deep effect on Nikkei understandings of their relationship with Japan. Their diasporic discontent was that ethnicity did not necessarily involve a positive identification with Japan. In Brazil diaspora culture was as deeply affected by national culture as the other way around. For Nikkei, Brazil was not in the Atlantic World but rather it was a "transoceanic" space where a presumed Pacific ethnicity helped to create national identity.

• • •

Award-winning filmmaker José Eduardo Belmonte's 1997 short 5 *Filmes Estrangeiros* (*Five Foreign Films*) stars Makoto Hasebe as what viewers assume to be a Japanese visitor to Brasília. He meets a number of other foreigners (from Paraguay, France, and an unnamed African country), each of whom speaks loudly to him in Portuguese and calls him "Japonês." Belmonte's muse was his dismay at the many foreigners who came to Brazil and "had dominated the language and thought that this was paradise where racial democracy ruled." In spite of the film's setting in Brasília, the spatial inspiration was São Paulo, where the director lived for many years and where he "saw the intolerance in how people looked at the other, the nuances, the subtleties." The soundtrack to the film is by Pato Fu, a Brazilian rock band whose lead singer, Fernanda Takai, is described on the band's official Web site as having "half slanty eyes because her paternal grandparents are Japanese" and whose English-titled song "Made in Japan" is sung in Japanese. Belmonte chose the music because it was "kind of globalized to mix various sounds and create a certain ambiguity."[4] 5 *Filmes Estrangeiros* ends after the "Japonês" murders the foreigners who have tormented him, shouting in Portuguese, "I am not Japanese!"[5]

Notes

PREFACE AND ACKNOWLEDGMENTS

1. Patai, "Minority Status."

PROLOGUE

1. Museu Virtual Memória da Propaganda, www.memoriadapropaganda.org.br/. In 1977 Japanese technology giant Toshiba purchased the majority of shares in the Sociedade Eletro Mercantil Paulista (Semp), a Brazilian corporation founded in 1942. This created Semp Toshiba.
2. The term Nikkei might translate as "of the family," but it is used by people of Japanese descent throughout the Americas.
3. Queiroz, "Nacionalidade," 98. The textbook in which this story is reprinted is a staple of Portuguese-language training in the United States.
4. Brazilian travelers wrote frequently about their visits to Japan. See Lesser, Negotiating National Identity, 147–66. São Paulo is also the world's largest "Italian" city outside of Italy and the world's largest "Lebanese" city outside of Lebanon.
5. Mirsky, "Big Dig."
6. Fairplay: A Revista do Homem 34 (1969): 61.
7. Weinstein, "Racializing Regional Difference."
8. Zilbovicius, "Modelos de produção."
9. Bamerindus Bank advertisements found in numerous editions of Veja between 1975 and 1992. A similar idea was found in the 1990s slogan for SABESP (Companhia de Saneamento Básico do Estado de São Paulo; Basic Sanitation Company of the State of São Paulo), São Paulo's sanitation utility, which proclaimed that its "service was so good you would think [the company] was founded by Japanese."

10. This is a simplification of the concept of the "Rhizome" explored in the introduction to Deleuze and Guattari, *Thousand Plateaus*.

11. Butler, *Freedoms Given*; Dzidzienyo, *Position of Blacks*; Hanchard, *Orpheus and Power*; Warren, *Racial Revolutions*.

12. "Vale a pena ser brasileiro?" *Realidade*, November 1966, 51–59; "Os estrangeiros (um fato): Mesmo? (uma questão)?" *Realidade*, November 1966, 171–89.

13. Ropp, " 'Nikkei' Negotiation."

14. Borstelmann, *Cold War and the Color Line*, 37–40.

15. Speech of Acylino de Leão, 18 September 1935, República dos Estados Unidos do Brasil, *Annaes da Câmara dos Deputados: Sessões de 16 a 24 de setembro de 1935* 17 (Rio de Janeiro: A Noite, 1935), 432.

16. Ribeiro, *Brazilian People*. The original is Ribeiro, *Povo brasileiro*.

17. Borrie, *Cultural Integration of Immigrants*; Marcos Chor Maio, "Brasil no 'concerto' das nações"; Maio, "UNESCO and the Study of Race Relations."

18. Diégues, *Imigração, urbanização e industrialização*; Saito and Maeyama, *Assimilação e integração*. Another socially ascendant neighborhood, Pinheiros, was the site of the distribution center of São Paulo's largest Japanese-Brazilian agricultural cooperative and also had significant numbers of Nikkei residents. See Petrone, *Pinheiros*.

19. Dirlik, *What Is in a Rim?*; Hu-DeHart, "Latin America in Asian-Pacific Perspective"; Lavie and Swedenburg, introduction.

20. This complicates Homi Bhabha's contention that, for the colonized, "to be Anglicized is to be emphatically not English," since Nikkei non-Brazilianness was often a virtue; Bhabha, *Location of Culture*, 87.

21. These two ethnic groups are also linked to contemporary nations primarily because of political disputes. For an examination of the widespread consumption of Arabness in Brazil, see Karam, *Another Arabesque*.

22. This relationship changed markedly in the late 1980s, when Japanese legislation opened up labor options for all those of Japanese descent. By 2000 some 200,000 Brazilians were living in Japan, ostensibly as temporary laborers. See Lesser, *Searching for Home Abroad*.

23. Louie, *Chinese across Borders*, 23–26.

24. Lye, *America's Asia*, 5.

25. "A poesia do abstrato," *Veja*, 21 October 1970, 88; "O novo e o clássico," *Veja*, 28 October 1970.

26. Hirabayashi, "Pathways to Power," 41.

27. Radhakrisnnan, "Ethnicity in an Age of Diaspora," 121, 125; Brubaker and Cooper, "Beyond Identity," 4. A fascinating recent study is Siu, *Memories of a Future Home*.

28. Many immigrant groups in Brazil defined themselves as "colonies," in part because all settlers in the nineteenth and early twentieth century were considered *colonos* (land laborers).

INTRODUCTION

1. Palumbo-Liu, *Asian/American*, 341.
2. For a discussion of the rise of racial statistics in Brazil, see Dávila, *Diploma of Whiteness*, 52–62.
3. Centro de Estudos Nipo-Brasileiros, *Pesquisa*, tables 2.1 and 2.3, 19–20; Comissão de Recenseamento da Colônia Japonesa, *Japanese Immigrant*, table 1, "By State, Region, Município—Generation, Residence, Sex," 6–7. For an analysis of issues related to the Brazilian census, see Nobles, *Shades of Citizenship*.
4. Spickard, *Japanese Americans*, table 2, 162–63. U.S. Census data for 2000 found at factfinder.census.gov/home/saff/main.html?—lang=en.
5. Holloway, *Immigrants on the Land*, 36, 48.
6. Malfatti painted *O japonês* in New York but only exhibited it in Brazil, where it was purchased by Mário de Andrade. He considered it one of Malfatti's finest works and wrote to her about the painting with some frequency. See Andrade, *Cartas a Anita Malfatti*, 47, 65, 66, 88, 116. See also Miceli, *Nacional estrangeiro*, 103–23; and Batista, *Anita Malfatti*. The painter also explored Asian themes in her *Boneca japonesa* (1914–15?), *A chinesa* (1921–22), and *A japonesa* (1924).
7. Lesser, *Negotiating National Identity*, chap. 4.
8. Decree Law 1.545 (25 August 1939), arts. 1, 4, 7, 8, 13, 15, 16.
9. Brazil's large populations of Italian and German descent were formed primarily in the nineteenth century and were usually considered "Brazilian" during World War II. Japanese immigrants, who had arrived largely in the twenties, were marked as "foreigners" and thus were particular targets of nativist attitudes. See Cytrynowicz, *Guerra sem guerra*.
10. Lesser, *Negotiating National Identity*, 136–46.
11. Between 1953 and 1959 over 30,000 new Japanese immigrants settled in Brazil, followed by another 16,000 in the next decade. Over 81% of all Japanese emigrants between 1952 and 1965 settled in Brazil. Flores, "Japoneses"; Nakasumi and Yamashiro, "Fim da era," table 2, 424; Sims, "Japanese Postwar Migration."
12. See former foreign minister Oswaldo Aranha's agreement with General José Maria de Vasconcelos about "the danger of the growth of the Japanese colony in Brazil"; handwritten note of Oswaldo Aranha to General José Maria de Vasconcelos, 1951 (no exact date), OA cp 1951.00.00/, Série: cp—Correspondência política, microfilm roll 26 fot. 85–87, Oswaldo Aranha Papers, Centro de Pesquisa e

Documentação História Contemporânea do Brasil, Fundação Getúlio Vargas, Rio de Janeiro [hereafter CPDOC].

13. Sakurai, "Fase romântica."

14. Premeditando o Breque, "Marcha da Kombi."

15. Perrott, "Brazil's Reckless Dash."

16. Japanese Consular statistics reported in American Consulate General in São Paulo to U.S. Department of State in Washington, D.C., "Status of Japanese Colony in São Paulo," 2 October 1970, pol. 23–10 Brazil, box 2133, NWDPH 2, National Archives and Record Center, Washington, D.C. [hereafter NARC]. Tomoo Handa reports that by 1965 10% of all students in São Paulo's universities were Nikkei; Handa, *Imigrante japonês*, 792.

17. Miyao, "Posicionamento social," 94–96.

18. "Conferência pronunciada por Sua Excelência o Senhor Ministro de Estado das Relações Exteriores, Embaixador Antônio F. Azeredo da Silveira, por ocasião da abertura do Simpósio Sobre os 70 Anos da Imigração Japonesa," Brasília, Câmara dos Deputados, em 16 de maio de 1978, Série Ministro das Relações Exteriores, Conferências 1974/75, AAS MRE ag 1974.05.27, CPDOC. My thanks to Jerry Dávila for sharing this document with me.

19. *Istoé*, 1 February 1979. Fukuda is a family name. The article generated a number of racist letters which garnered responses in the Japanese-Brazilian press; "Essa invasão japonesa!" *Diário Nippak*, 7 February 1979.

20. Miyao, "Posicionamento social," 99.

21. One of Watanabe's best-known policies was to search São Paulo's poverty-ridden public schools for mathematical talent. According to Watanabe, between 1977 and 2005 more than 200 talented students had the chance for higher education in math and sciences because of this program. See *Folha de S. Paulo*, 1 August 2005.

22. *Veja*, 19 November 1969.

23. American Consulate General in São Paulo to U.S. Department of State in Washington, D.C., "Status of Japanese Colony in São Paulo," 2 October 1970, pol. 23–10 Brazil, box 2133, NWDPH 2, NARC. Sussumu Miyao found that Nikkei representation in São Paulo politics was about the same as the percentage of Nikkei in the overall population; Miyao, "Posicionamento social," 98. On the first postwar Nikkei politicians in São Paulo, see Sakurai, "Fase romântica."

24. Torres, "Brazil-Japan Relations."

25. Banco do Brasil, *Brasil*, 30–33.

26. *Business Latin America*, 8 March 1973.

27. "Japan's Yen for Brazil," *Brazilian Information Bulletin* 11 (1973): 12. Roett, "Brazil

and Japan." For a postmilitary period study, see Hellerman, *Japan's Economic Strategy in Brazil*.

28. Antônio Delfim Neto became ambassador to France in 1974, returning to Brazil in 1979 as minister of agriculture and then minister of planning; Skidmore, *Politics of Military Rule*, 69–71.

29. *Página Um* of the *Diário Nippak*, 8 March 1980.

30. "Participação dos descendentes no novo governo," *Diário Nippak*, 28 March 1979.

31. Secret memo, "Primeiro encontro de cúpula entre o Presidente Ernesto Geisel e o Primeiro Ministro Takeo Miki," 17 September 1976, Akasaka Palace (Tokyo), Geisel Archive, EG pr 1974.03.18, Serie: PR—Presidência, roll 2 fot. 0707–2099 and roll 3 fot. 0001–1780, F-1902–1904, CPDOC.

32. Letter of Consul Fausto Cardona, acting consul general of Brazil in Japan, to Toshinari Okano, general director, Yomiuri Television Broadcasting Corporation, 19 March 1968, Consulado Geral Cobe 84/28/3/1968, Cobe Ofícios, January–April 1968, Arquivo Histórico Itamaraty, Brasília [hereafter AHI].

33. See *Folha de S. Paulo* and *O Estado de S. Paulo*, 25 and 26 May 1967. A longer discussion of the visit is in Handa, *Imigrante japonês*, 776–80.

34. Speech of President General Geisel at the dinner welcoming Prime Minister Kakuei Tanaka at the Palácio Itamaraty, 16 September 1974. In Ministério das Relações Exteriores, *Resenha de política exterior do Brasil* 11, July, August, September 1974, 13–15.

35. Nester, *Japan and the Third World*, 261.

36. Memo of Francisco José Novaes Coelho (Embassy in Tokyo) to Itamaraty (Rio de Janeiro), 11 July 1966, MDB—Ofícios Recebidos—Tokyo, 1960–67, box 98, AHI.

37. Ambassador to Japan Alvaro Teixeira Soares (Tokyo) to Minister of Exterior Relations José de Magalhães Pinto (Rio de Janeiro), 3 April 1968, Secção de Correspondência Especial—Tóquio Ofícios, 1968–70, AHI. See also *Mainichi Daily News*, 24 February 1968.

38. Ambassador to Japan Alvaro Teixeira Soares (Tokyo) to Itamaraty, 28 March 1968, Tokyo, Cartas Telegramas, 1968, AHI.

39. Memo of Alvaro Teixeira Soares (Brazilian Embassy in Tokyo) to Itamaraty, 26 March 1968, EM 26/3/1968 (3478), Tokyo, Cartas Telegramas, 1968, AHI; *Kobe Carnival 1968*.

40. "O país do século XXI," *Veja*, 18 March 1970.

41. *Fairplay: A Revista do Homem* 34 (1969), inside front cover and 61.

42. A general study of stamps produced during the dictatorship is Cyrelli de Souza, "Selos postais."

43. Roth, "Urashima Taro's Ambiguating Practices."

44. The original jungle can be found at jovempan.uol.com.br/jpamnew/opiniao/consultores/consultores—all.php?id=14&last—id=5182&act=sim.

45. *Revista Manchete*, 24 April 1965, 105.

46. Japanese-American magazines ran articles on these beauty comments, which then returned to Brazil to reinforce Brazilian sensuality as a diasporically positive Japanese attribute. See the October 1952 cover of *Scene: The Pictorial Magazine* and numerous other issues.

47. *Realidade*, January 1972, 119.

48. The images were at times mixed with mockery. A 1977 television advertisement for Lares home pressure cookers had the Japanese-Brazilian character pitch the product by changing all his l sounds to r's, with the tag line, "See, I can't rearry say Rares . . . [Viu? Não consegue farar Rares . . .]," 59-Lares-Televisão–Novembro 1977–(17584), Arquivo da Propaganda (São Paulo).

49. A collection of films, copied on videotape, made by the Assessoria Especial de Relações Públicas (AERP, 1968–73) and Assessoria de Relações Públicas (ARP, 1974–78) were generously given to me by Carlos Fico. This was the same material he used in his book on Brazilian propaganda, *Reinventando o otimismo*.

50. Premeditando o Breque, "São Paulo, São Paulo," from *Quase lindo* (Lira Paulistana/Continental, 1983), 1.30.404.009.

51. *Amor Bandido* (1979), dir. Bruno Barreto.

52. A sample of research on this topic is Ando, *Estudos socio-históricos*; Cardoso, *Estrutura familiar* (1995); Carneiro, *Imigração e colonização*; Müller and Saito, "Memórias do I Painel Nipo-Brasileiro"; Diégues, *Imigração, urbanização e industrialização*; Lobo, *De japonez a brasileiro*; Saito and Maeyama, *Assimilação e integração*; Sakurai, *Romanceiro da imigração japonesa*; and Yamashiro, *Trajetória de duas vidas*.

53. Willems and Saito, "Shindo Renmei"; Maeyama, "Ethnicity, Secret Societies and Associations"; Miyao and Yamashiro, "Comunidade enfrenta um caos"; Tigner, "Shindo Renmei"; Miranda, *Shindo Renmei*; Neves, *Processo da "Shindo-Renmei"*; Cardoso, "Papel das associações juvenis," "Estrutura familiar" (1972); Saito, *Japonês no Brasil*.

54. Chu, "When Revolt Hit Rio."

55. Meihy, "Oral History in Brazil."

56. Some excellent research on these topics can be found in James, *Dona Maria's Story*; Spitzer, *Hotel Bolivia*; and Bal, Crewe, and Spitzer, *Acts of Memory*.

57. Hoffman and Hoffman, *Top of Form Archives of Memory*, 145.

58. Following the work of some film scholars, I have used "reviews as important sources of information about reception"; Klinger, *Melodrama and Meaning*, 69.

1. Turim, "Erotic in Asian Cinema," *Films of Oshima Nagisa*.
2. For another local example of volatility see the discussion of Buenos Aires in Moya, *Cousins and Strangers*, 226–35.
3. Yamasaki is also spelled "Yamazaki" in some documents and scholarly articles. I have chosen to use "Yamasaki" because that is how the director spells her own name in promotional materials for her films. Reichenbach is one of the filmmakers whose biography was commissioned by the state of São Paulo as part of its "AplausoCinemaBrasil" series. Lyra, *Carlos Reichenbach*.
4. Feng, *Identities in Motion*, 4. A similar idea is found in Linger, *No One Home*. For broad examinations of the relationship between film and history, see Rosenstone, *Visions of the Past*; Ferro, *Cinema and History*; and Sorlin, *Film in History*. See also White, *Content of the Form*; and Fiske, "British Cultural Studies."
5. Tange also had roles in *O Espantalho* (1977), *Cara a Cara* (1979), and *Os Imigrantes* (1981). A study of the scriptwriter of *Os Imigrantes* is Souza, *Telenovela*. General information about telenovelas can be found at www.teledramaturgia.com.br/.
6. As the military sought to create a consumerism that would consolidate a "cultural products market," this position of the Nikkei leadership legitimized this space and this ethnic group as fields for identity negotiation. Ortiz, *Cultura brasileira*, 80; Ortiz, *Moderna tradição*, 113–14. Ortiz wrote about Japan in *Próximo e distante*.
7. Fung, "Looking for My Penis," 147.
8. Heine, "Sayonara Can Mean 'Hello,' " 32.
9. See, e.g., "O que é mulher bonita?" *Realidade*, October 1967, 92–101; "Mulher nua é boa leitura?" *Realidade*, June 1968, 15.
10. Tajima, "Lotus Blossoms Don't Bleed." For those interested in teaching issues related to filmic portrayals, see Alquizola and Hirabayashi, "Confronting Gender Stereotypes."
11. "Com a casa e as discriminações—Em busca de um papel," *Arigato* 2.16 (1978): 10.
12. Misaki Tanaka, interview by Jeffrey Lesser, São Paulo, 5 February 2002. The Japanese-Brazilian community struggled to maintain the idea of "geisha" as a legitimate tradition while rejecting the notion that geishas were simply prostitutes. See the cover story of *Página Um* of the *Diário Nippak*, 25 June 1983, 3–4.
13. Hosokawa, "Japanese Cinema." Used by permission of the author. See also Kobori, "Cinema japonês," 142–46.
14. Decree Law 406 (4 May 1938); Decree Law 479 (8 June 1938), art 2, no. 1a. Decree Law 1,377 (27 June 1938); Decree Law 1.545 (25 August 1939), arts. 1, 4, 7, 8, 13,

15, 16. Miyao and Yamashiro, "Comunidade nipônica no período da guerra," 248–49, 255.

15. Cytrynowicz, *Guerra sem guerra*.

16. Shuhei Hosokawa generously shared with me his list of every film shown in Brazil from 1957 to 1987. Many of these films are still held, in 35 mm form, in various Brazilian archives. See Abe Oi, *Cultura japonesa*. *Paulista Shimbun*, 22 January 1966; *O Estado de S. Paulo*, 23 March 1968; Watanabe and Abe Oi, "Cinema japonês no Brasil."

17. Futema, "Salas japonesas." "Embrafilme contra cinema japonês," *Cinema em Close-Up* 4.18 (1979): 51–55; *Folha de S. Paulo*, 11 March 1986. Most of the cinemas closed in the 1980s. The Cine Tóquio is today the Nipo-Brazilian Evangelical Church (Igreja Evangélica Nipo-Brasileira) and sits next to a recently built Buddhist temple. Most worshippers in both places are not of Japanese descent.

18. Ferreira, "Samurais."

19. A collection of his Ferreira's reviews can be found in Gamo, *Jairo Ferreira*.

20. Kobori, "Cinema japonês," 145.

21. Alfredo Sternheim, interview by Jeffrey Lesser, São Paulo, 10 April 2002.

22. Memo of Alvaro Teixeira Soares (Brazilian Embassy in Tokyo) to Itamaraty, 19 February 1968, EM 19/2/1968 (2342), Tokyo, Cartas Telegramas, 1968; Memo of Faust Cardona, Brazilian Consul in Kobe to Itamaraty, 26 July 1968, Consulado Geral Cobe/206/1968/2, Kobe Ofícios, July–September 1968; Faust Cardona, Brazilian consul in Kobe to Yonezo Kobayashi, president of Toho Co. Ltd, 24 September 1965, Consulado Geral Cobe/206/26/7/1968, Kobe Ofícios, July–September 1968, AHI.

23. *Mainichi Daily News*, 7 May 1968. Akiko Wakabayashi was familiar to Brazilian audiences from her roles in the Japanese films *Samurai Pirate* (1963, shown in Brazil in 1965) and *Interpol Code 8* (1963 and shown in Brazil that same year) and to U.S. audiences for her role as Suki Yaki in Woody Allen's *What's Up, Tiger Lily?* (1966). Probably the best-known film located in part in Rio de Janeiro was Philippe de Broca's French New Wave comedy, *L'homme de Rio* (*That Man from Rio*, 1964), starring Jean-Paul Belmondo.

24. Domenig, "Anticipation of Freedom." This is the English translation of the introductory essay originally published in German in Domenig, *Art Theatre Guild*.

25. *Japan Times*, 30 May 1968.

26. *Diário de São Paulo*, 9 December 1964. A similar review, noting the film's "extraordinary artistic dimension" can be found in *O Estado de S. Paulo*, 26 September 1964. Twenty years later Fernão Ramos called *Noite Vazia* "a Brazilian film that should be seen again" when a retrospective showing took place in São Paulo; *Folha de S. Paulo*, 23 July 1986.

27. Ely Azevedo, interview by Walter Hugo Khouri, *Filme Cultura*, May 1969; cited in

Silva Neto, *Dicionário de filmes brasileiros*, 585; "Os 10 mais importantes filmes brasileiros," *Filme Cultura*, March 1968.

28. Portaria 020/64-SCDP, Departamento Federal de Segurança Pública, Serviço de Censura e Diversões Públicas, 21 September 1964, D450/15, Fundação Cinemateca Brasileira (hereafter FCB). The film was released less than two weeks later; *Diário da Noite*, 30 September 1964.

29. Moreno, *Cinema brasileiro*, 178.

30. One of these films, *Kokusai himitsu keisatsu: Shirei dai hachigo* (Interpol Code 8, 1963), was directed by Toshio Sugie, an assistant director to Akira Kurasawa.

31. Stam, Vieira, and Xavier, "Shape of Brazilian Cinema," 412. Two other Khouri films that include strong images of Nikkei women are *O Prisioneiro do Sexo* (The Prisoner of Sex, 1979) and *Eros: O Deus do Amor* (Eros: God of Love, 1981), where the roles were played by Misaki Tanaka and Sueli Aoki.

32. Director's synopsis, ficha técnica, *Noite Vazia* (1964), Fundação Cinemateca Brasileira, São Paulo.

33. *Folha de S. Paulo*, 11 March 1986.

34. Khouri, "Influência do cinema japonês."

35. "Noite vazia," lista de diálogos, "Noite vazia" folder, roll 3, 1–4, FCB. Alfredo Sternheim, interview by Jeffrey Lesser, São Paulo, 10 April 2002.

36. More than one million Italians immigrated to São Paulo prior to 1934 and almost 75,000 more entered between 1950 and 1957; Trento, *Do outro lado do Atlântico*, 107; Holloway, *Immigrants on the Land*, 42; La Cava, *Italians in Brazil*, 59.

37. Mori, "Por que os brasileiros começaram a apreciar a culinária japonesa?" unpublished ms. used by permission of the author. I would like to thank my colleague Valerie Loichot for suggesting to me the deeper reading of pizza.

38. Misaki Tanaka, interview by Jeffrey Lesser, São Paulo, 5 February 2002; Alfred Sternheim, interview by Jeffrey Lesser, São Paulo 10 April 2002.

39. Alfredo Sternheim, interview by Jeffrey Lesser, São Paulo, 10 April 2002.

40. Alfredo Sternheim, interview by Jeffrey Lesser, São Paulo, 10 April 2002.

41. One might also look to the scenes with Misaki Tanaka in *Paixão e Sombras* (1977) and Sueli Aoki, Kenichi Kaneko, and Akemi Aoki in *Eros: O Deus do Amor* (1981). This is in sharp distinction with the United States, where academic analysis of Asian sexuality in film has developed notably since the eighties. See, e.g., Hamamoto, "Joy Fuck Club"; Feng, *Screening Asian Americans*; Xing, *Asian America through the Lens*; Marchetti, *Romance and the "Yellow Peril"*; Lee, *Orientals*.

42. *Última Hora*, 6 February 1964. See also *Diário da Noite*, 28 September 1964.

43. Paulo Perdigão, *Diário de Notícias*, 1 April 1965; *ABB-Bandeirante*, 16 December 1964. The same disjunction between image and text can be found in reviews of *O Prisioneiro do Sexo*. See, e.g., *Jornal da Tarde*, 20 April 1979.

44. Barbosa, "Amigos recordam o talento de Walter Hugo Khouri." Benguel was kidnapped in 1968 by a right-wing group opposed to her political positions. This kidnapping, and other incidents of artistic repression, are discussed in Deckes, *Radiografia do terrorismo*. For a broader view of the role of artists during the period of the dictatorship, see Ridenti, *Em busca do povo brasileiro*.

45. Memo of Faust Cardona, Brazilian consul in Kobe to Itamaraty, 13 May 1968. 133/5h0.612, Kobe Ofícios, May–June 1968, AHI.

46. Misaki Tanaka, interview by Jeffrey Lesser, São Paulo, 5 February 2002.

47. This kind of "ethnic adventurism" was not unique to São Paulo. In the United States, Euro-American visitors packed the Forbidden City Chinese nightclub in San Francisco's Chinatown because of its location and the chance to see some imaginary "Chinese" culture that was heavily Americanized and thus familiar; *Forbidden City USA* (1989), dir. Arthur Dong.

48. Alfredo Sternheim, interview by Jeffrey Lesser, São Paulo, 10 April 2002.

49. Klinger, *Melodrama and Meaning*, 75.

50. *O Estado de S. Paulo*, 26 September 1964; Desser, *Eros plus Massacre*.

51. *Jornal do Comércio*, 3 April 1965. *Samurai Pirate* (1963), dir. Senkichi Taniguchi, was also known as *The Lost World of Sinbad*.

52. *Última Hora*, 4 March 1964.

53. *Diário de São Paulo*, 2 October 1964.

54. *Última Hora*, 29 January 1964.

55. Ferreira, review of *As Cariocas*. *As Cariocas* (1966), dir. Fernando de Barros, Walter Hugo Khouri, and Roberto Santos.

56. *Isei, Nisei, Sansei* (1970), dir. Alfredo David Sternheim, 35 mm, documentary, 10 mins., produced with support from Comissão Estadual de Cinema da Secretaria da Cultura, Esportes e Turismo. Viewed at Museu de Imagem e Som, São Paulo, 27 March 2002. Sternheim, *David Cardoso*.

57. Alfredo Sternheim, interview by Jeffrey Lesser, São Paulo, 10 April 2002.

58. On the idea of the rural in Mazzaropi films, see Tolentino, *Rural no cinema*, 95–131.

59. Barsalini, *Mazzaropi*; Piper, *Filmusical e chanchada*.

60. Empresa Brasileira de Filmes, *Cinejornal/Embrafilme* 6, 52.

61. From the original trailer in *Meu Japão Brasileiro*, Coleção Mazzaropi, vol. 3:10. Cinemagia DVD-Video.

62. McCann, *Hello, Hello Brazil*, 70.

63. Dennison and Shaw, *Popular Cinema in Brazil*, 151, 153. Other Mazzaropi movies that took place "abroad" are *Um Caipira em Bariloche*, 1973 (about Argentina), and *Portugal . . . Minha Saudade*, 1973 (about Portugal).

64. Glauco Barsalini focuses on the "message of the organization of civil society

against the demands of antidemocratic power" that rose to the fore during the 1965 release, less than a year after the military coup; Barsalini, *Mazzaropi*, 113.

65. This anti-rural oligarchic position explains why a "revolutionary" film like Glauber Rocha's *Deus e o Diabo na Terra do Sol* (*White God, Black Evil*, 1964) was permitted to be released.

66. Recent interpretations of an antiracism component of the Brazilian Constitution suggest that the difference between racism (*racismo*) and prejudice (*preconceito*) is the consciousness of the behavior; Brazilian Constitution of 1988, article 5, paragraph 42.

67. Original trailer contained in *Meu Japão Brasileiro*, Coleção Mazzaropi, vol. 3:10. Cinemagia DVD-Video.

68. Duarte, "Dia cheio."

69. Gray, *A Tribuna* (Santos), 4 April 1965.

70. *O Estado de S. Paulo*, 28 January 1965.

71. Ibid.

72. . . . *E a Vaca Foi Para o Brejo* (1981), directed by José Adalto Cardoso. *Diário Nippak*, 2 December 1981.

2. CONTESTING IMAGES OF ETHNICITY

1. Dennison and Shaw, *Popular Cinema in Brazil*, 158. While the Boca do Lixo neighborhood was the location of many new alternative cinema production companies in the 1950s and 1960s, it was known as a marginal area filled with crime and prostitution. See Joanides, *Boca do Lixo*; and Ferreira, "Imaginário da Boca." Images of Japanese-Brazilians were virtually nonexistent in the films of the renowned *Cinema Novo* School. While this invisibility has not been studied, it is likely related to the idea that as members of the middle and upper classes, Nikkei could not be victims of class oppression.

2. A complete collection of *Cinema em Close-Up* can be found at the Biblioteca Jenny Klabin Segall of the Museu Lasar Segall in São Paulo. Many of São Paulo's cinemas showed martial arts/pornochanchada double features.

3. Moretti et al., *Hentai*.

4. Keizi, *Reflection* 46.

5. Hartog, "Interview with Carlos Reichenbach," 51. This interview was conducted for an edition of the Channel 4 (U.K.) television show *Visions* titled "Brazil: Cinema, Sex and the Generals" (February 1985), dir. Simon Hartog. This program was censored by the British Independent Broadcasting Authority and was seen for the first time some 20 years later in a series of Channel 4 shows on previously banned programs.

6. Ferreira, "Onibaba"; Serper, "Shindô Kaneto's films *Kuroneko* and *Onibaba*.

7. Simões, *Imaginário da Boca*, 10, 21.

8. Bernardet, "Chanchada, erotismo e cinema empresa," 21. Depoimento of Jean-Claude Bernardet, unmarked ms. 20656, Pornochanchada file, Museu de Arte Moderna (Rio de Janeiro), 3-I. My thanks to Stephanie Dennison for sharing this material with me. An analysis of the history of Brazilian censorship of cinema is Simões, *Roteiro da intolerância*. For a wide-ranging discussion of pornochanchada, see the special issue on the topic of the on-line journal *Contracampo: Revista de Cinema* 36: "A pornochanchada e suas fronteiras," www.contracampo.com.br/36/frames.htm.

9. Dennison and Shaw, *Popular Cinema in Brazil*, 23. Chauí, *Conformismo*. On the short propaganda films see Fico, *Reinventando o otimismo*; and Avellar, "Teoria da relatividade."

10. All four of the *O Estado de S. Paulo*'s film critics rated the film "ruim" (terrible). *O Estado de S. Paulo*, "Cotação dos filmes em cartaz," 8 October 1978. A dubbed version of *O Bem Dotado*, with the English title *Cocky*, was called "an execrable comedy" by Mark Lefanu in *Monthly Film Bulletin*, February 1982, 24.

11. See, e.g., review of *A Dança Final* by Ana Carolina Soares, *O Estado de S. Paulo*, 25 April 2002. A recent interview with Aldine Müller, who was in both films, is Alexandre Santos, " 'Os intelectuais esgotaram o Cinema Novo; a pornochanchada fez o cinema se levantar,' diz Aldine Müller," in *Revista Brasil de Cultura*, www.revistabrasil.com.br/mateporb021125.htm.

12. Kottak, *Prime Time Society*, 49.

13. Dennison and Shaw, *Popular Cinema in Brazil*, 157–64. Inimá Ferreira Simões contrasts the "Brazilian" way of the "Man from Itu" with the American way of the "Man of Steel"; Simões, *Imaginário da Boca*, 54–56. See also Simões, "Sou . . . mas quem não é?" 85–96.

14. *Asian Pride Porno* can be seen on line at www.gregpak.com/app/index.html. My thanks to my colleague Catherine Nickerson for directing me to this short film. Darrell Y. Hamamoto has pointed to the absence of Asian-American men in pornography as an example of the gendered nature of sexual stereotypes. His attempts to respond to this, by making the "first ever Asian American pornmovie (Skin on Skin)," are explored in James Hou's documentary *Masters of the Pillow* (2004). See also Hoang, "Resurrection of Brandon Lee."

15. Dennison and Shaw, *Popular Cinema in Brazil*, 97.

16. All quotes from "Com a casa e as discriminações: Em busca de um papel," *Arigato* 2.16 (1978): 9.

17. *Cinema em Close-Up* 2.5 (1976): 17.

18. All quotes from "Com a casa e as discriminações: Em busca de um papel," *Arigato* 2.16 (1978): 9.
19. Silva, "Bem dotado" (2002).
20. Some of these posters and promotional stills can be seen in the photographs in Simões, *Imaginário da Boca*, 31.
21. See, e.g., the captions of the still for Ody Fraga's *Macho e Fêmea* (1974), which uses Vera Fischer's name but shows Misaki Tanaka, or the still for Rajá de Aragão's *O Dia Das Profissionais* (1976), which uses Arlete Moreira's name but shows Niki Fuchita; Cinema em Close-Up 1.3 (1976): 6, and 2.6 (1976): 23.
22. *Macho e Fêmea* (*Male and Female*, 1973), dir. Ody Fraga; *Escola Penal das Meninas Violentadas* (*Prison School for Violated Girls*, 1977), dir. Antônio Meliande; *Pensionato de Vigaristas* (*Bilker's Hostel*, 1977), dir. Oswaldo de Oliveira; *As Fugitivas Insaciáveis* (*The Insatiable Female Fugitives*, 1978), dir. Oswaldo de Oliveira; *O Bom Marido* (*The Good Husband*, 1978), dir. Antônio Calmon; *Terapia do Sexo* (*Sex Therapy*, 1978), dir. Ody Fraga; *Damas do Prazer* (*Pleasure Dames*, 1978), dir. Antônio Meliande; *Os Depravados* (*The Depraved*, 1978), dir. Tony Vieira; *A Força dos Sentidos* (*The Force of the Senses*, 1980), dir. Jean Garret.
23. "Yoko Tani: Superstar," *Arigato*, January 1977, 50–51; "Luzes, câmera: Midori em ação," *Arigato*, March–April 1977, 36–37. It appears that film and television producers scouted the many Nikkei beauty contests held in São Paulo for actresses. Midori Tange had been the Miss Simpatia do Concurso Miss Colônia (Miss Congeniality of the Miss "Colony" Competition [i.e., the Japanese-Brazilian colony]) and also had starred in a number of television soap operas as well as in two erotic films, *Desejo Violento* (*Violent Desire*, 1978), dir. Roberto Mauro, and *Belinda dos Orixás na Praia dos Desejos* (*Belinda dos Orixás on Desire Beach*, 1979), dir. Antônio Bonacin Thome. Henrique Maximiliano's essay "Satoshi, Satoshi" is a contemporary example of how gay sexuality operates vis-à-vis Nikkei/majority Brazilian relations.
24. Images of the covers of both magazines can be found in "Com a casa e as discriminações: Em busca de um papel," *Arigato* 2.16 (1978): 6–17.
25. *Diário Nippak*, 10 September 1980 and 13 November 1981.
26. Misaki Tanaka, interview by Jeffrey Lesser, São Paulo, 5 February 2002. Ferreira, "Estripador está solto"; Biáfora, review of *Estripador de Mulheres*. Juliano Tosi calls Doo "uma das mais proeminentes e prolíficas vozes da Boca [do Lixo]"; Tosi, "Todos os filmes."
27. "Diabolismo erótico em novo filme," *Folha da Tarde*, 16 August 1978; "Erotismo e bruxaria no filme de estréia de Doo," *Diário Popular*, 13 August 1978; "Ninfas Diabólicas: Erotismo feito por um sino-brasileiro," *Fiesta: Cinema*, 14 August 1978, 22–23.

28. Rubem Biáfora, review in *O Estado de S. Paulo*, 20 August 1978, 29. Later Doo films were not so well received by critics, although audiences lined up to see them. One, *A Noite das Taras* (1980), stunned the critic Jairo Ferreira with its huge box office grosses in spite of being "Nothing like a pornochanchada. Only porno"; *Folha de S. Paulo*, 19 July 1980.

29. Bernardet and Biáfora, quoted in "Com a casa e as discriminações," 8.

30. Aoki quoted in "Com a casa e as discriminações," 12. For a brief discussion of the question of plastic surgery in Brazil, see Gilman, *Making the Body Beautiful*, 215–27.

31. Misaki Tanaka, interview by Jeffrey Lesser, São Paulo, 5 February 2002.

32. Rubem Biáfora, *O Estado de S. Paulo*, 11 June 1978.

33. Misaki Tanaka, interview by Jeffrey Lesser, São Paulo, 5 February 2002.

34. Carmen Angélica, interview by Minami Keizi, *Cinema em Close-Up* 1.3 (1975): 49.

35. André, "Pornochanchada." Ferreira, "Império do desejo." Another mainstream magazine, *Istoé*, called the film a "beautiful pornochanchada," 11 March 1981.

36. Reichenbach, "Segunda parte," 94–95. Borges, *Cinema à margem*, esp. 43–50.

37. Moreino, *Cinema brasileiro*, 204–17.

38. Hartog, "Interview with Carlos Reichenbach," 51.

39. Khouri, "Influência do cinema japonês." On Cinema Novo see Johnson, *Cinema Novo*; Burton, *Cinema and Social Change*; Johnson and Stam, *Brazilian Cinema*; Dunn, *Brutality Garden*, 74–77; Nagib, *New Brazilian Cinema*; and Ridenti, *Em busca do povo brasileiro*, 89–103. On the Japanese New Wave, see Desser, *Eros plus Massacre*.

40. Hartog, "Interview with Carlos Reichenbach," 53. Trevisan, "Entrevista com A. P. Galante," 71–75. Galante also produced three Khouri films, including *O Prisioneiro do Sexo*. An excellent documentary on Galante is Gamo and Melo, *O Galante Rei da Boca*. See also Lyra, *Carlos Reichenbach*, 53; and Melo, "Galante."

41. Tanaka had previously performed in a Reichenbach short film, *Sonhos de Vida* (1979).

42. For viewers, an actor's image can be a kind of persona constructed from the roles, advertisements, and publicity of a body of films; Dyer, *Stars*.

43. Publicity poster and official synopsis of *Império do Desejo*, D567/8, FCB.

44. Scenes 100–106, shooting script of *Império do Desejo*, R494, 63–67, FCB.

45. Hartog, "Interview with Carlos Reichenbach," 51.

46. Misaki Tanaka, interview by Jeffrey Lesser, São Paulo, 5 February 2002.

47. *Página Um* of the *Diário Nippak*, 1 September and 1 October 1984.

48. Carlos Reichenbach in response to a question asked by Jeffrey Lesser, roundtable with Carlos Reichenbach, 31 March 2002, Fundação Cinemateca Brasileira, São Paulo.

49. Misaki Tanaka, interview by Jeffrey Lesser, São Paulo, 5 February 2002. A similar position is taken by the many Chinese, Japanese, and Filipino Americans interviewed about their participation in modern dancing and singing at San Francisco Chinatown's Forbidden City nightclub; *Forbidden City USA* (1989), dir. Arthur Dong. See also Fong-Torres, "Pioneer Performers."

50. Misaki Tanaka, interview by Jeffrey Lesser, São Paulo, 5 February 2002. Melo, "Ody Fraga"; Rodrigues, "Pornografia é o erotismo dos outros." See also Fraga, "Quilombo de Ody."

51. Ramos and Miranda, *Enciclopédia do cinema brasileiro*, 531.

52. *O Bom Marido* also starred Nuno Leal Maia and received a script translation into English (although I found no mention of it being dubbed and released outside of Brazil). Calmon was honored in 2003 with a retrospective by the Centro Cultural Banco do Brasil de São Paulo that included *O Bom Marido*. English script at R843/1, FCB.

53. Others include the feature films *Aleluia Gretchen* (Sylvio Back, 1976) and *Jakobine* (also known as *Os Mucker*) (Jorge Bodanzky, 1978) and the documentaries *Vida e Sangue do Polaco* (Sylvio Back, 1983), as well as three by Olga Futema, *Retratos do Hideko* (1980), *Hia Sá Sá—Hai Yah!* (1986), and *Chá Verde Sobre Arroz* (1998). For more on Futema, see Aliança Cultural Brasil-Japão and The Fact, *Universo em segredo*, 50, 69. *Gaijin* has many scenes in Japanese, with Brazilian subtitles, and thus can be linked to *Como era Gostoso o Meu Francês* (*How Tasty Was My Little Frenchman*, 1971), a film by Nelson Pereira dos Santos, one of Yamasaki's mentors, which is largely in Tupi.

54. Cinema students filmed the military takeover of the Universidade de Brasília. Much of the footage became available with the release of Vladimir Carvalho's documentary *Barra 68: Sem Perder a Ternura* (2001).

55. The definitive discussion of Yamasaki's work is Shuhei Hosokawa's careful study of Brazilian cinema and Nikkei identity, *Shinema-ya, Burajiru o iku* [*Japanese Film Goes to Brazil*] (Tokyo: Shinchosha, 1999). A short English-language study of some of Yamasaki's films can be found in Moniz, "Race, Gender, Ethnicity." A fascinating comparison of Cinema Novo and Argentina's Cine de Liberación is Tal, *Pantallas y revolución*.

56. "Apesar de falta de apoio, *Gaijin* está pronto," *Diário Nippak*, 27 June 1979.

57. Interview of Tizuka Yamasaki in *Página Um* of the *Diário Nippak*, 14 June 1980.

58. Stam, *Tropical Multiculturalism*, 368n12.

59. Lesser, *Negotiating National Identity*, 82–112.

60. This proposition is supported by the oral histories that Shuhei Hosokawa conducted with immigrants, who "often talked about how the birth of a child was decisive in their determination to live permanently in Brazil, their 'second

home' "; Hosokawa, text for lecture on *Gaijin* at Emory University, 29 March 2000. Used with permission of the author.

61. Hosokawa, text for lecture on *Gaijin* at Emory University, 29 March 2000. Used with permission of the author. Interview of Tizuka Yamasaki in *Página Um* of the *Diário Nippak*, 14 June 1980.

62. The film was based on a play by Gianfrancesco Guarnieri, who played Enrico in *Gaijin*.

63. *Folha de S. Paulo*, 4 November 1980.

64. "Japão propõe imigração em massa para o Brasil," *Folha de S. Paulo*, 10 August 1980. "Oposição reage à vinda maciça de imigrantes," *Folha de S. Paulo*, 11 August 1980. See also San Martín and Pelegrini, *Cerrados*.

65. *Folha de S. Paulo*, 15 September 1980.

66. From *Folha de S. Paulo*, 13 April and 15 September 1980.

67. "Renasce o grande cinema japonês," *Folha de S. Paulo—Ilustrada*, 11 January 1980.

68. *Folha de S. Paulo*, 12 September 1980.

69. *Jornal do Brasil—Caderno B*, 31 May 1980.

70. "Os velhos imigrantes e o Gaijin," *Diário Nippak*, 26 March 1980.

71. Hosokawa, text for lecture on *Gaijin* at Emory University, 29 March 2000.

72. Centro de Estudos Nipo-Brasileiros, *Pesquisa*; Koichi Mori, "Mundo dos brasileiros mestiços," unpublished ms. used by permission of the author.

73. Henri Kobata, interview by Jeffrey Lesser, São Paulo, 2 February 2002. *Retratos de Hideko* is now available on *O Brasil em curtas 12*, Festival Internacional de Curtas Metragems de São Paulo (Rio de Janeiro: Ministério da Cultura, 2001). A discussion of some of Futema's documentaries on the worker's movement in São Paulo can be found in Bernardet, *Cineastas e imagens do povo*, 221–40. "Tizuka Yamazaki, pela liberdade, sempre," *Página Um* of the *Diário Nippak*, 9 July 1983.

74. Misaki Tanaka, interview by Jeffrey Lesser, São Paulo, 5 February 2002.

75. "Gaijin: A estréia e as repercussões," *Diário Nippak*, 13 February 1980.

76. Prado, "*Gaijin: Os caminhos da liberdade.*"

77. Stam, *Tropical Multiculturalism*, 368n12.

78. *Embrafilme apresenta "Gaijin: Caminhos da Liberdade,"* in Fundação Cinemateca Brasileira (São Paulo), "Gaijin" folder, unnumbered pages. Misaki Tanaka, interview by Jeffrey Lesser, São Paulo, 5 February 2002. In a book about Guarnieri's career, largely told by the actor himself, there is no mention of *Gaijin* at all, not even in the filmography; Roveri, *Gianfrancesco Guarnieri*.

79. Yamasaki, quoted in *O Estado de S. Paulo*, 27 May 1979.

80. *Visão*, 24 March 1980.

81. "Gaijin, a aventura dos japoneses em nossa terra," *Folha de S. Paulo*, 5 February 1979; "A imigração vista por olhos puxados," *Istoé*, 2 April 1980. Other headlines

were "Gaisin [*sic*] tem tema da imigração japonesa," *O Estado de S. Paulo*, 27 May 1979; "Filme mostrará problemas de imigrantes japoneses," *Folha de S. Paulo*, 8 June 1979; "A imigração japonesa, no primeiro filme de Tizuka Yamasaki," *Jornal da Tarde*, 13 February 1979; "*Gaijin*, a saga do imigrante japonês no Brasil," *O Estado de S. Paulo*, 18 February 1980; "Saga: O lancinante caminho," *Jornal do Brasil: Revista do Domingo*, 11 May 1980.

82. See, e.g., the articles in *Jornal do Brasil: Caderno B*, 31 May 1980; *Folha de S. Paulo*, 18 June 1981; and *Jornal da Tarde*, 24 June 1981.

83. *Jornal do Brasil: Caderno B*, 31 May 1980. *O Estado de S. Paulo*, 1 June 1980.

84. *Folha de S. Paulo—Ilustrada*, 28 May 1980. The same article was also published in *Jornal do Brasil—Caderno B*, 31 May 1980.

85. Gerardo Mello Morão, "A galáxia chinesa," and (n.a.), "Gaijin, expectativa no festival," *Folha de S. Paulo—Ilustrada*, 22 February 1980.

86. "Cannes escolhe Fosse e Kurosawa," *Folha de S. Paulo—Ilustrada*, 24 May 1980.

87. Marcos Vinício, "Gaijin, O melhor 'mestiço,'" *Folha da Tarde*, 7 April 1980.

88. A sampling of some of the major scholarship on *dekasegui* can be found in Lesser, *Searching for Home Abroad*.

89. See www.tizukayamasaki.com.br/index—port.htm.

3. ETHNICITY AND ARMED STRUGGLE

1. Comissão de Recenseamento da Colônia Japonesa, *Japanese Immigrant*, table 337, "Urban-Rural Distribution by Every 5 Years, Period-Region" (630–33), Table 339, "Inflow to the City of São Paulo in Each Five Year Period, Former Resident–Region" (634–35). "Participação de descendentes no novo governo," *Diário Nippak*, 28 March 1979.

2. Ridenti, *Fantasma da revolução*, 122. For a fascinating discussion of learning in universities in this period, see Gusmão, "Memória, identidade e relações de trabalho," esp. chap. 3. In the United States, Laura Pulido notes the importance of university attendance to Japanese-American antiwar politicization; Pulido, *Black, Brown, Yellow and Left*, 77.

3. The average age of those tortured in the early years of the regime was 22; Catholic Church, Archdiocese of São Paulo, *Brasil, nunca mais*, 85–88; published in English as Archdiocese of São Paulo, *Torture in Brazil*; della Cava, "Torture in Brazil."

4. This agency was established in 1924.

5. Fernandes Júnior, *Baú do guerrilheiro*, 77.

6. Miranda and Tibúrcio, *Dos filhos deste solo*, 643–50.

7. The classic historical overview of the different militant groups and their broad

political positions, as well as the state's repressive tactics, is Gorender, *Combate nas trevas*. For the many different Brazilian opposition groups, their ideological positions, and the policies and workings of the military dictatorship, see also Archdiocese of São Paulo, *Torture in Brazil*; Alves, *State and Opposition*; Valle, 1968; Couto, *Memória viva*; Aquino, *Censura, imprensa, Estado autoritário*; D'Araujo, Soares, and Castro, *Visões do golpe*; D'Araujo, Soares, and Castro, *Anos de chumbo*; Ridenti, *Fantasma da revolução*; Reis, Ridenti, and Sá Motta, *Golpe e a ditadura militar*; Pereira, *Political (In)justice*. Studies of gender issues are an excellent model of how militancy can be analyzed in a nontraditional manner. See Costa et al., *Memórias das mulheres*; Patarra, *Iara*; Carvalho, *Mulheres que foram à luta armada*; Ferreira, *Mulheres, militância e memória*; and Cunha, "Face feminina."

8. Skidmore, *Politics of Military Rule*; 84–89, 117–25; Skidmore, *Brazil*, 164. A wide-ranging and careful analysis of the dictatorship can be found in Elio Gaspari's 4-volume examination of the period: *A ditadura envergonhada* (2002); *A ditadura escancarada* (2002); *A ditadura derrotada* (2003), and *A ditadura encurralada* (2004). Some of the regional variations in how the dictatorship operated can be found in the chapters on the state of Rio Grande do Sul in Wasserman and Guazelli, *Ditaduras militares*.

9. Vanguarda Popular Revolucionária (hereafter VPR), *Um balanço ideológico da revolução brasileira: 10 passos para a construção da vanguarda*, mimeograph, n.d., CX 69.03.196.8/n, Centro de Documentação e Memória (hereafter CEDEM); Truskier, "Politics of Violence"; Marighella, *Manual of the Urban Guerrilla*. Statement of the Central Committee of the Communist Party of Brasil (PC do B) of December 1969, "Responder ao banditismo da ditadura com a intensificação das lutas do povo," in Wladimir Pomar, org., *Araguaia, o partido e a guerrilha*, 119–34.

10. Pulido, *Black, Brown, Yellow and Left*, 105–13. Two studies that suggest the need for much more careful research on ethnicity and the left in Brazil are Pinsky, *Pássaros da liberdade*; and Iokoi, *Intolerância e resistência*.

11. Using subversive lists prepared by the DEOPS, I was able to extract Japanese-Brazilian names and then find information on birthplaces as listed on identity cards. Using this method I was able to identify the birthplaces of hundreds of Nikkei accused of leftist activity. See, e.g., the Japanese-Brazilian birthplaces listed in "Inquérito Policial: Infrações a dispositivos da Lei da Segurança Nacional," 31 March 1970, 30Z/160/5420–543, DEOPS Papers—Arquivo do Estado de São Paulo [hereafter AESP] and the untitled document in DEOPS Setor: Secreto, folder 129, 6, Arquivo Público do Estado do Rio de Janeiro (hereafter APERJ).

12. Yoshimura, "G.I.'s and Asian Women," 1. Also see the comments of an anonymous East Wind activist quoted in Pulido, *Black, Brown, Yellow and Left*, 79–80.

13. Centro de Estudos Nipo-Brasileiros, *Pesquisa*; Butsugan, "Participação social"; Vieira, "Sistema de casamento." For a fascinating autobiographical account of an intermarried couple, see Takeshita, *Grito de liberdade*.

14. Rioco Kaiano, interview by Jeffrey Lesser, São Paulo, 14 and 18 June 2002.

15. Marta Tanisaki, interview by Jeffrey Lesser, São Paulo, 11 June 2002; Rioco Kaiano, interview by Jeffrey Lesser, São Paulo, 14 and 18 June 2002; Shizuo Osawa, interview by Jeffrey Lesser, Rio de Janeiro, 25 January 2002; Carlos Takaoka, interview by Jeffrey Lesser, São Paulo, 3 July 2002. On the dekasegui movement, see Linger, *No One Home*; and Roth, *Brokered Homeland*.

16. Beozzo, "Padres conciliares brasileiros." My thanks to Kenneth Serbin for pointing this out to me. Information on the Diocese of Lins is at www.catholic-hierarchy.org/diocese/dlins.html#info.

17. Lesser, *Negotiating National Identity*, 61–66.

18. Secretaria de Estado das Relações Exteriores to Embaixada do Japão in Brasília, "Bens japoneses confiscados na Segunda Guerra Mundial," 13 April 1965, DAO 9443(56) (42). Japão Notas Expedidas, Secretaria de Estado das Relações Exteriores to Embaixada do Japão in Brasília, "Repatriação de cidadãos japoneses ligados a Shindo Renmei," 13 September 1967, DIM 551.4(56)/7 (56)/42 (02), Japão Notas Expedidas, AHI.

19. Rioco Kaiano, interview by Jeffrey Lesser, São Paulo, 14 and 18 June 2002.

20. See, e.g., "Auto de qualificação e de interrogatório de Manuel de Lima," 26 May 1970, 30Z/160/ 7694, DEOPS Papers, AESP. See also "Conferência pronunciada por Sua Excelência o Senhor Ministro de Estado das Relações Exteriores, Embaixador Antônio F. Azeredo da Silveira, por ocasião da abertura do Simpósio sobre os 70 Anos da Imigração Japonesa," Brasília, Câmara dos Deputados, 16 May 1978, Série Ministro das Relações Exteriores, Conferências 1974/75, AAS MRE ag 1974.05.27, Centro de Pesquisa e Documentação de História Contemporânea do Brasil, Rio de Janeiro [hereafter CPDOC-Rio]. My thanks to Jerry Dávila for sharing this document with me.

21. In 1964 12 ITA students, including João Yutaka Kitahara, also were expelled. While not all were imprisoned, they were prohibited from matriculating at other universities because of the political nature of the charges against them. The story of the expulsions, and of an attempt in 2004 to grant diplomas to some of those students, including Tokoro, is told in Athayde, "Justiça ainda que tardia." The diplomas were finally granted in 2005; *Correio Braziliense*, 20 May 2005. The head of the Brazilian Air Force's Aerospace Technical Center (Centro Técnico Aeroespacial) was so incensed by the decision that he fired the president of the Instituto Tecnológico de Aeronáutica, Michal Gartenkraut, announcing it on the Air Force Web site before informing Gartenkraut; *Folha de S. Paulo*, 26 July 2005.

22. Sumizawa, "Ex-presos políticos." Ito and Albino Wakahara were two Nikkei indemnified by the Brazilian government for their torture during the dictatorship; www.justica.sp.gov.br/sessoes/sessa027.htm.

23. *Jornal do Brasil*, 6 September 1969.

24. Pulido, *Black, Brown, Yellow and Left*, 59.

25. This was confirmed to me by a number of Jewish former militants who asked to remain anonymous. The relationship between Jewish ethnicity and militant activity in Brazil is much more tenuous than it is for the Nikkei. These weak connections are made clear by Kushnir, "Nem bandidos, nem heróis." Carlos Heitor Cony's novel *Pessach: A travessia* includes a Jewish-Brazilian character who joins a guerrilla organization.

26. Superior Tribunal Militar no. 40577, André Tsutomu Ota, 24 October 1974, Coleção Brasil Nunca Mais 068 (1), vol. 1, 33–34. In Arquivo Edgard Leuenroth, Instituto de Filosofia e Ciências Humanas da Unicamp (hereafter AEL); DEOPS Relatório and Inquérito Policial, 29 April 1970, 30Z/160/14088–13979, DEOPS Papers, AESP.

27. "Declarações que presta Mari Kamada (Isa, Mina, Shiruka) a turma de interrogatório preliminar 'c' das 1000 as 1800 horas do dia 12–13 março 1972," 50Z-9–33003, DEOPS Papers, AESP.

28. *O Estado de S. Paulo*, 7 December 1969.

29. Nair Yumiko Kobashi, interview by Jeffrey Lesser, São Paulo, 3 May 2002.

30. Polari, *Em busca do tesouro*, 75. Known today by his full name, Alex Polari de Alverga, he is an active member of the Ayahuasca or Santo Daime sect, which supports a journal, *Humanas*, that a number of critics have accused of anti-Semitism. See Lesser, "Brazil," 339. Polari's discussion of his spiritual journey can be found in his *Forest of Visions*.

31. Olga Yoshiko Futema, interview by Jeffrey Lesser, São Paulo, 24 April 2002.

32. Kaiano, "Estação Tiradentes." Morais and Silva, *Operação Araguaia*, 246–48. The nearest population center to Guaimbê is the town of Lavinha, relatively near the city of Lins.

33. Rioco Kaiano, interview by Jeffrey Lesser, São Paulo, 14 and 18 June 2002.

34. See handwritten declaration of Dowbor, "De próprio punho declaro o seguinte," 14 May 1970, 50z/9/13994, 1–18, DEOPS Papers, AESP. Dowbor had been born in France of Polish refugee parents who immigrated to Brazil in 1951 when he was 10 years old.

35. These names included Leila, Norma, Rita, Leda, Cláudia, Célia, Márcia, and Mara. I did find one oblique reference that someone, perhaps in the PCB and perhaps a professor of philosophy at the University of São Paulo, may have had

the code name "Israelita"; "Declarações que presta Eva Tereza Skazufka Bergel," 6 June 1970, 50Z-9–14235, DEOPS Papers, AESP.

36. The DEOPS files do suggest rare exceptions to the rule. Hans Rudolph Manz, a Swiss national and member of the ALN, was nicknamed "Alemão"; "Resumo das declarações prestadas por Otávio Angelo," 21 December 1969 30-Z-160 3696, DEOPS Papers, AESP. Student leader Marcelo Chueiri was called "O turco"; Costa, *Cale-se*. Monir Tahan Sab, accused of being a member of the MOLIPO/ALN, was said to have been called "Shariff," 50Z-9–3300, DEOPS Papers, AESP.

37. Seixas, "Nome, nome de guerra e nomes legendários," 10.

38. Fernandes Júnior, *Baú do guerrilheiro*, 193.

39. "Auto de reconhecimento de Virgílio Nunes Gomes," 26 December 1969, in Supremo Tribunal Federal no. 1396–4, Coleção Brasil Nunca Mais, 119(2), vol. 8, AEL.

40. Nova and Nóvoa, "Genealogias, transversidalidades e rupturas."

41. Marighella, "Canto para Atabaque."

42. For example, Marighella's background is only mentioned twice in a collection devoted to an analysis of his life, once by his wife Clara Charf (herself a member of an ethnic minority group) and once in the introduction in reference to Charf's comment; Nova and Nóvoa, *Carlos Marighella*.

43. See, e.g., Kehl and Venceslau, "Clara Charf."

44. *Marighella: Retrato Falado do Guerrilheiro* (2001), dir. Sílvio Tendler.

45. "Auto de qualificação e de interrogatório de Darci Toshiko Miyaki," 3 May 1972, in microfilm reel no. 250, 108, Brasil—Nunca Mais Project, University of Chicago, Joseph Regenstein Library [hereafter BNM]. "Declarações que presta José Edson Mesquita Fabia ('Zé')," 8–9 May 1972, 50 Z 9 31080, DEOPS Papers, AESP, Estado de Guanabara, Secretaria de Segurança Pública, Departamento de Ordem Política e Social, Divisão de Informações, Pedido de Busca Sp/SAS, no. 0578 Rio, 6 June 1969, Assunto: VPR, DOPS Setor: Terrorismo, folder 2, 106, APERJ. (In Rio, the organization was called Departamento de Ordem Política e Social; in São Paulo it was called DEOPS.)

46. On Tujiwara, see "Declarações que presta Lúcia Maria Lopes de Miranda Leão ('Júlia' ou 'Vera')," 9–10 May 1972, 50 z 9 31044; on Fujimori (also spelled *Fugimori* and *Fujimore*), see "Auto de qualificação e de interrogatório de Tercina Dias de Oliveira," 25 May 1970, 30Z/160/7702, and "Auto de qualificação e de interrogatório de Joaquim dos Santos," 1 June 1970, 30Z/160/7677; on Okabayashi, see "Declarações que presta Lúcia Maria Lopes de Miranda Leão ('Júlia' ou 'Vera')," 13–14 May 1972, 50 z 9 31026, DEOPS Papers, AESP.

47. On Kobashi see "Declarações que presta José Edson Mesquita Fabia ('Zé')," 8–9

May 1972, 50Z/9/31080–31044, DEOPS Papers, AESP. Nair Yukio Kobashi, interview by Jeffrey Lesser, São Paulo, 3 May 2002. For a careful discussion of the methodological issues involved in work with the DEOPS materials, see Aquino, Mattos, and Swensson, *No coração das trevas*; and Pereira, *Political (In)justice*.

48. "Auto de qualificação e interrogatório de Paulo de Tarso Vannuchi," 22 December 1971, o68 (2), vol. 7, 2023–24, BNM. See also "Auto de qualificação e de interrogatório de Tercina Dias de Oliveira," 25 May 1970, 30Z/160/7702; "Interrogatório de Manuel de Lima," 26 May 1970, 30Z/60/7692–94, 443–53, esp. 447; "Auto de qualificação e de interrogatório de Ladislas Dowbor," 5 June 1970, 30Z/160/7651; "Interrogatório de Ladislas Dowbor," 14 July 1970, 30Z/60/7642, 337–54, DEOPS Papers, AESP.

49. See, e.g., "Interrogatório de Ladislas Dowbor," 14 July 1970, 30Z/60/7642, 337–54; "Primeiras declarações que presta Anisio Costa Toledo," 7–8 October 1971, in Ministério do Exército–II Exército, CODI, 2nd Sec., Doi, 30Z/160/10453, 127. DEOPS Papers, AESP; Estado de Guanabara, Secretaria de Segurança Pública, Departamento de Ordem Política e Social, Divisão de Informações, Pedido de Busca Sp/SAS, no. 0578, Rio de Janeiro, 6 June 1969, Assunto: VPR, DOPS Setor: Terrorismo, folder 2, 106, APERJ; "Auto de qualificação e interrogatório of Pedro Lobo de Oliveira," 27 January 1969, in Fundo DOPS/MG, roll 2, folder 0025–2, Arquivo Público Mineiro, Minas Gerais.

50. Confidential report: Ministério do Exército, 1 Exército, 2nd Seção, Rio de Janeiro, 13 November 1970, Assunto: Curso de Guerrilha Rural e Urbana em Cuba, Origem: CIE, DOPS Setor: Secreto, folder 78, 208–02, APERJ.

51. Nair Yumiko Kobashi, interview by Jeffrey Lesser, São Paulo, 3 May 2002; Rioco Kaiano, interview by Jeffrey Lesser, São Paulo, 14 and 18 June 2002.

52. Central Committee of the Communist Party of Brasil (PC do B), "Mais audácia."

53. "Passeata só inova na bandeira: A do Vietcong," *O Estado de S. Paulo*, 9 April 1968.

54. Gorender, *Combate nas trevas*, 122–29; Lima and Arantes, *História da Ação Popular*; Projeto Brasil: Nunca Mais, *Brasil, nunca mais*, 100–102; in English as Archdiocese of São Paulo, *Torture in Brazil*, 90–93; Miranda and Tibúrcio, *Dos filhos deste solo*, 486–88.

55. Marta Tanisaki, interview by Jeffrey Lesser, São Paulo, 11 June 2002.

56. For a careful examination of the DEOPS São Paulo archive and the *mentalité* behind its organization and function, see Aquino, Mattos, and Swensson, *No coração das trevas*.

57. "Declarações que presta Paulo de Tarso Vannuchi à equipe interrogatório Preliminar 'C' das 14:00 as 16:30 do dia 15 de março de 1971 pertence a organização ALN," 50 Z 9 34260 to 34246, DEOPS Papers, AESP. See also "Auto de qualifi-

cação e interrogatório of Paulo de Tarso Vannuchi," 22 December 1971, 068(2), vol. 7, 2023–24, BNM.

58. This story was told by Army General Carlos Alberto Brilhante Ustra, a São Paulo regional DOI–CODI commander who was accused in 1985 by federal deputy Bete Mendes of torturing her in what became a highly public case. His version of the story, whether accurate or not, indicates exactly how ethnicity worked in militant/police relations; Ustra, *Rompendo o silêncio*, 198–99.

59. "Declarações que presta Mari Kamada (Isa, Mina, Shiruka) a turma de interrogatório preliminar 'C' das 1000 as 1800 horas do dia 12–13 março 1972," 50Z-9-33003, DEOPS Papers, AESP.

60. Jun Nakabayaski, interview by Jeffrey Lesser, São Paulo, 3 January 2002.

61. "Auto de reconhecimento de Almir Barros Cavalcante, soldado da Força Pública do Estado de São Paulo," 19 December 1969, in Supremo Tribunal Federal no. 1396–4, Coleção Brasil Nunca Mais, 119(2), vol. 7. "Auto de reconhecimento de Virgílio Nunes Gomes," 26 December 1969; "Auto de reconhecimento de Nivaldo Silva Bar," 7 January 1970, in Supremo Tribunal Federal no. 1396–4, Coleção Brasil Nunca Mais, 119(2), vol. 8. AEL. See also, e.g., "Interrogatório de Maria Barreto Leite Valdes," 25 May 1970, 30Z/160/7696–7967, DEOPS Papers, AESP.

62. Jun Nakabayaski, interview by Jeffrey Lesser, São Paulo, 3 January 2002.

63. Costa, *Cale-se*, 105. Okano's disappearance is discussed in Miranda and Tibúrcio, *Dos filhos deste solo*, 123.

64. *O Estado de S. Paulo*, 3 July 1970. Celso Lungaretti remarked on this confusion in his memoirs, *Náufrago da Utopia*, 123.

65. Lesser, *Negotiating National Identity*, 99–100.

66. "Não era brincadeira, era assalto," *O Estado de S. Paulo*, 16 October 1968, 11.

67. Assentada de 8 July 1969 na Delegação de Polícia de Santo André, Delegado Roberto Giovanetti Dordenale, in Supremo Tribunal Federal 1396–4, 10 April 1979, Coleção Brasil Nunca Mais 110(1), vol. 2, AEL.

68. Fernandes Júnior, *Baú do guerrilheiro*, 77.

69. Testimony of Edson Morini in Inquirição Sumária, 10th Batalhão Polícia Militar–Força Pública do Estado de SP, 9 August 1971, and Auto de reconhecimento (Fotográfico), 6 June 1972, Coleção Brasil Nunca Mais, 068 (2), vol. 5, 1141–42, 1157, 1193, AEL.

70. "Termo de Declarações de Isidor Leon Nahoum," in Supremo Tribunal Federal 1396–94, 10 April 1979, Coleção Brasil Nunca Mais, 110(1), vol. 3, AEL.

71. "Terroristas japoneses," *Diário Popular*, 12 February 1966.

72. "Os japoneses do terror," *Jornal da Tarde*, 14 March 1970. The relationship be-

tween the *Jornal da Tarde* and state repressive forces is explored in Perosa, *Cidadania proibida*, 53–92; and Kushnir, *Cães de guarda*.

73. See, e.g., the confidential report on "Terroristas/assaltantes" prepared by the Departamento Estadual de Investigações Criminais of the Secretário de Estado dos Negócios da Segurança Pública, 16 July 1969, Fundo DOPS/MG, roll 2, folder 0025–1, Arquivo Público Mineiro, Minas Gerais.

74. *O Estado de S. Paulo/Jornal da Tarde*, 13 January 1970.

75. "Aqui estão 19 faces do terror," *O Estado de S. Paulo/Jornal da Tarde*, 15 May 1969.

76. "Dez bilhões em meia hora," *Veja*, 4 February 1970.

77. Villaméa, "Verdadeira história do cofre do Dr. Rui." One U.S. government report argued that all of the 189 bank robberies in São Paulo between 1968 and 1970 (more than in the rest of Brazil combined) were political in nature; U.S. Department of State Airgram, from American Embassy, Brasília, to Department of State, Washington, "Robberies Committed by Terrorists," 9 November 1970, RG 59, General Records of the Department of State, subject files 1970–73, Political and Defense, POL 17–5 BRAZ–POL 23–8 BRAZ, box 2132, NWDPH-1997, NARC.

78. "Auto de reconhecimento de 19 dezembro 1969 de Almir Barros Cavalcante," and "Assentada de 19 dezembro 1969 de Tércio Antônio Provenza," in Supremo Tribunal Federal no. 1396–4, Coleção Brasil Nunca Mais, 119(2), vol. 7, AEL.

79. "Primeiras declarações de Francisco Antônio Coutinho e Silva," 8–9 October 1971, 30Z/160/10452, DEOPS Papers—Arquivo do Estado de São Paulo (hereafter AESP). The language in these kinds of reports is very similar. See, e.g., a report on the kidnapping of a physician who was taken to a safe house to care for an injured militant; "Primeiras declarações de Anisio Costa Toledo," 7–8 October 1971, 30Z/160/10453; "Seqüestro de médico," Secretaria da Segurança Pública, Coordenação de Informações e Operações, 5 November 1971, 30Z/160/10454, DEOPS Papers, AESP.

80. *O Estado de S. Paulo*, 1 August 1969.

81. "Panfletos causam prisões," *O Estado de S. Paulo*, 8 July 1976.

82. "Subversão: O absurdo," *Veja*, 26 January 1972, 22.

83. *Paulista Shimbun*, 19 January 1966, 8. Similar articles can be found in "Mendigos e bêbados japoneses em São Paulo," *São Paulo Shimbun*, 25 June 1959, 5; "Furtos prende nissei assaltante de carros," *Paulista Shimbun*, 10 February 1967, 8. My thanks to Ryan Lynch for sending these articles to me.

84. *Jornal da Tarde*, 14 March 1970; *Mainichi Daily News*, 16 March 1970. The word *Japanese* here was understood to mean Japanese-Brazilian.

85. On-line interview with Celso Lungaretti, 11 May 2006, www.geracaobooks.com .br/releases/entrevista—celso—lungaretti.php.

86. Langland, "Birth Control Pills and Molotov Cocktails," ms. p. 31. In our oral

history, Japanese-Brazilian militant Shizuo Osawa linked essentialist ideas among the police about Nikkei and blonde women; Shizuo Osawa, interview by Jeffrey Lesser, Rio de Janeiro, 25 January 2002.

87. See, e.g., untitled and unsigned document of 31 May 1979, 21z, 14, 7004–6996, DEOPS Papers, AESP.

88. Paz, Nas trilhas da ALN, 82, 105. See also Paz, Viagem à luta armada.

89. "Tipificação da atividade delituosa dos denunciados," in the "Denúncia" of the Justiça Militar, 9 August 1971, 100 1–1, 59, BNM, Arquivo Edgard Leuenroth, Campinas. See also Secretaria de Estado dos Negócios da Segurança Pública, Serviço de Informações, "Takao Amano," 18 November 1970, 52Z/0/2308, DEOPS Papers, AESP. Amano discussed some of his political positions, without any reference to ethnicity, in Nunes, "Dia na vida de um comunista," 70–74.

90. Jun Nakabayaski, interview by Jeffrey Lesser, São Paulo, 3 January 2002; Shizuo Osawa, interview by Jeffrey Lesser, Rio de Janeiro, 25 January 2002.

91. Tendai Educational Foundation, Japanese Eyes, American Heart; Tanaka, Go for Broke.

92. O Estado de S. Paulo, 19 September 1932. Yamashiro, Trajetória de duas vidas, 111–17; Sakai, "Return to the West/East," 187.

93. The most famous case was that of journalist Vladimir Herzog, who was arrested and tortured to death in October 1975. Shibata signed the autopsy report as a suicide although he later claimed that he had never examined the body.

94. Sirkis, Carbonários, 191, 237.

95. "Depoimento prestado pelo embaixador da Alemanha no Brasil, Sr. Ehrenfried von Holleben, em sua residência, as 0100 do dia 17 de junho de 1970," DEOPS Setor: Terrorismo, folder 5, 115L to 115A Secreto, APERJ.

96. "Eles não conseguiram morrer," Realidade, June 1968, 101–15; "Prontos para matar e morrer," Jornal Nippo-Brasil, 3–9 August 2005 (main headline).

97. "Dez bilhões em meia hora," Veja, 4 February 1970; Folha de S. Paulo, 16 May 1969.

98. See, e.g., Jornal do Brasil, 2 August 1972; Veja, 22 March 1972; O globo, 12 August 1972; and O Estado de S. Paulo, 25 June 1972.

99. "Terrorismo japonês no Brasil e na América Latina: Revelações e previsões— Internacionalização do terror," 26 August 1972, 30Z/160/12257, emphasis in original; Krauss, Japanese Radicals Revisited. "Campanha contra o Brasil: Amnesty International" noted a German Amnesty International report that was cited in German-language newspapers in the south of Brazil, 9 October 1973, 50Z/9/ 35415–35407, DEOPS Papers, AESP. For general information on the Japanese Red Army, see Steinhoff, "Hijackers, Bombers, and Bank Robbers"; Box and McCormack, "Terror in Japan"; and Farrell, Blood and Rage. See also Dower, War without Mercy.

100. Departamento Estadual de Ordem Política e Social, Serviço de Informações,

Carta mensal 4 (1975), 30 z 16, 351–45, DEOPS Papers, AESP. In the mid-1980s novelist Karen Yamashita translated a series of articles on Nikkei activists from São Paulo's *Página Um* for the U.S. Japanese-American newspaper *Hokubei Mainichi*; e-mail from Karen Yamashita to Jeffrey Lesser, 28 October 2004.

101. Miranda and Tibúrcio, *Dos filhos deste solo*, 257–58. An excellent analysis of how OBAN fit into a broader pattern of repression under the military is Fico, *Como eles agiam*. Examinations of the history of Brazil's intelligence agencies include Wasserman, "Império da Segurança Nacional," 27–44; Antunes, *SNI e ABIN*; and Lagôa, *SNI*.

102. Jun Nakabayaski, interview by Jeffrey Lesser, São Paulo, 3 January 2002; Shizuo Osawa, interview by Jeffrey Lesser, Rio de Janeiro, 25 January 2002.

103. U.S. Department of State Airgram, from American Consulate, São Paulo, to Department of State, Washington, "São Paulo 490, São Paulo 632 (NOTAL)," 14 July 1970, RG 59, General Records of the Department of State, subject files 1970–73, Political and Defense, POL 17–5 BRAZ–POL 23–8 BRAZ, box 2132, NWDPH-1997, NARC.

104. Gorender, *Combate nas trevas*, 219.

105. Mir, *Revolução impossível*, 307.

106. "Estanslau Ignácio Corrêa, vítima do 'inevitável,' " *O Estado de S. Paulo*, 10 April 1980; *O Estado de S. Paulo*, 3 July 1970.

107. "Messagio della opposizione rivoluzionaria e democratica brasiliana ai nemici del fascismo," n.a., n.d., CX 3.92.310/n, CEDEM. Gaspari, *Ditadura escancarada*, 197, 344.

108. Darci Rodrigues, quoted in "Estanslau Ignácio Corrêa, vítima do 'inevitável,' " *O Estado de S. Paulo*, 10 April 1980.

109. Deposition of Leonidas Pires Gonçalves in D'Araujo, Gláucio Soares, and Castro, *Anos de chumbo*, 240.

110. *Miami Herald*, 21 May 1970.

111. *O Estado de S. Paulo*, 3 July 1970.

112. *Manifesto da Vanguarda Popular Revolucionária (VPR) sobre a experiência guerrilheira no Vale do Ribeira*, setembro 1970, www.resgateHistórico.com.br/doc—22.htm; "SubverSão: A morte do tenente," *Veja*, 16 September 1970.

113. Sirkis, *Carbonários*, 333–35. An article in the *São Paulo Shimbun* suggests that it was Fujimori who killed the soldier; "O terrorista Fujimori morto em tiroteio contra agentes," *São Paulo Shimbun*, 9 December 1970, 8; Jacob Gorender, without mentioning who killed the lieutenant, tells the general story in the same way; Gorender, *Combate nas trevas*, 272–73. The *Folha de S. Paulo* published an unnamed militant's account of the events, which does not implicate Fujimori specifically, on 27 August 1979, 4–5. A similar version can be found in "A guerrilha pauli-

sta," *Veja*, 6 September 1978. Lieutenant Colonel Leonidas Pires Gonçalves, commander of one of the units in the Vale do Ribeira, blamed both Fujimori and Lamarca; Deposition of Leonidas Pires Gonçalves in D'Araujo, Soares, and Castro, *Anos de chumbo*, 240.

114. José and Miranda, *Lamarca*. A film based on the biography makes a similar point in a brief scene in the Vale do Ribeira, in which a Japanese-Brazilian guerrilla appears, stone faced and toting a machine gun; *Lamarca* (n.d. [1994?]), dir. Sérgio Rezende. An analysis of *Lamarca* can be found in Foster, *Gender and Society*, 28–37.

115. Note to judge of the 1ª Vara Exec. Crim., 31 July 1970, case no. 67, microfilm reel no. 250, 106, BNM. I would like to thank Anthony Pereira for first alerting me to this case.

116. Statement of Prosecutor Durval A. Moura de Araujo to the judge of the 2nd Auditoria of the 2nd Circumscripção Judiciária Militar, 27 July 1970, case no. 67, microfilm reel no. 250, 124–27, BNM.

117. "Assentada and auto de interrogatório de Kogi Kondo," 27 August 1970, case no. 67, microfilm reel no. 250, 130–32, BNM.

118. Ibid.

119. Apelação 38.692 of Kogi Kondo, 1971, microfilm reel 250, 310, BNM.

120. Letter of Victoria Langland to Jeffrey Lesser, 14 March 2005.

121. "Terrorista viu a foto e falou: Ele estava sendo traído," *Última Hora*, 29 January 1970. A similar version of this story, along with a photograph, can be found in "As rachas do terror," *Veja*, 4 February 1970. "Some of Sergio Fleury's Victims," in American Friends of Brazil, *Brazilian Information Bulletin* 5 (August–September 1971), 11. The torture suffered by Amano and Susuki are listed in Alarcón, *Brasil*, 65–66.

122. Huggins, Haritos-Fatouros, and Zimbardo, *Violence Workers*.

123. Tavares, *Memórias do esquecimento*, 91. In his own memoirs, Samuel Wainer comments on issues of anti-Semitism beginning in the thirties; Wainer, *Minha razão de viver*. The MAR eventually united members of POLOP and the VPR.

124. Della Cava, "Torture in Brazil," 137; "The Tragic Death of Chael Charles Schreier," *Terror in Brazil: A Dossier*, April 1970, 7. This material was generously shared with me by Joseph Love. Lungaretti, *Náufrágo da Utopia*, 130.

125. Gramont, "How One Pleasant, Scholarly Young Man."

126. Braylan et al., *Report on the Situation of the Jewish Detainees-Disappeared*; Kaufman, "Jewish Victims of Repression"; Timerman, *Prisoner without a Name*; Feitlowitz, *Lexicon of Terror*.

127. *O Estado de S. Paulo*, 22 October 1968, 13.

128. Jun Nakabayaski, interview by Jeffrey Lesser, São Paulo, 3 January 2002; Carlos

Takaoka, interview by Jeffrey Lesser, São Paulo, 3 July 2002; Shizuo Osawa, interview by Jeffrey Lesser, Rio de Janeiro, 25 January 2002.

129. Rioco Kaiano, interview by Jeffrey Lesser, São Paulo, 14 and 18 June 2002.

130. "O primeiro nissei da Acadêmia," *Arigato* 1.8 (1977): 10–11. I was unable to convince Nikkei police officers involved in the repressive apparatus to speak with me.

131. Miranda and Tibúrcio, *Dos filhos deste solo*, 92–93.

132. Rioco Kaiano, interview by Jeffrey Lesser, São Paulo, 14 and 18 June 2002.

133. Nair Yumiko Kobashi, interview by Jeffrey Lesser, São Paulo, 3 May 2002.

134. Rioco Kaiano, interview by Jeffrey Lesser, São Paulo, 14 and 18 June 2002.

4. TWO DEATHS REMEMBERED

1. Rioco Kaiano, interview by Jeffrey Lesser, São Paulo, 14 June 2002. See also Maia, Dantas, and Savignano, *Guerrilheiras do Araguaia*, 40.

2. Neide Richopo, e-mail to Kenneth Serbin, 11 July 2002; used by permission. Maia, Dantas, and Savignano, *Guerrilheiras do Araguaia*, 44.

3. On the ideological background to this movement, see Richopo, "Esquerda no Brasil." For an overview see Gaspari, *Ditadura escancarada*, 399–464. Some recent publications on the topic are Morais and Silva, *Operação Araguaia*; and Campos Filho, *Guerrilha do Araguaia*.

4. See, e.g., *Brazilian Information Bulletin*, January 1973, 12–14.

5. "Governo desiste de recorrer a documentos para achar corpos no Araguaia," *Folha de S. Paulo*, 11 March 2004.

6. An account written in 1975 but published some years later (1979) appeared in *Diário da guerrilha do Araguaia*. Another account, in which Kamayana is mentioned only a few times, under one of her code names (Chica), is Arroyo, "Relatório sobre a luta no Araguaia." For other brief mentions see Morais and Silva, *Operação Araguaia*, 246–48.

7. See www.vermelho.org.br/pcdob/80anos/martires/martires29.asp.

8. Richopo, "Esquerda no Brasil," 68.

9. Portela, *Guerra de guerrilhas*, 82. Elio Gaspari notes that a local resident claimed that Kamayana had been captured alive; Gaspari, *Ditadura escancarada*, 456–57.

10. Spínola, "Guerrilha do Araguaia."

11. For examples of how the myths are circulated, see www.desaparecidospoliticos .org.br/araguaia/10.html and www.torturanuncamais.org.br/mtnm—mor/mor—desaparecidos/mor—suely—kanayama.htm. On death practices see Paxton, *Christianizing Death*.

12. Cabral, *Xambioá*, 248. "O fim da guerra no fim do mundo," *Veja*, 13 October 1993.

Two years after the publication of *Xambioá*, a former Brazilian Air Force mechanic claimed he overheard soldiers discussing the cremation of a "Japanese nurse" in Araguaia; Luiz, "Porões da ditadura."

13. Cabral, *Xambioá*, 220.

14. In the interests of full disclosure, readers should know that Rioco Kaiano, the Nikkei militant quoted throughout this book, is married to José Genoino.

15. Henri George Kobata, interview by Jeffrey Lesser, São Paulo, 24 January 2002. Kobata, "Yumiko."

16. Kobata is a social marketing consultant and a former editorial director at Editora Abril, Brazil's largest publishing company.

17. Maia, Dantas, and Savignano, *Guerrilheiras do Araguaia*, 138.

18. "A nisei guerrilheira: No Araguaia, a vida pelo sonho maior," *Página Um* of the *Diário Nippak*, 1 November 1984.

19. Célia Abe Oi, interview by Jeffrey Lesser, São Paulo, 1 April 2002.

20. *Veja*, 8 July 1970.

21. This information comes from the "Termo de declarações" filled out by Massafumi Yoshinaga's parents when they visited him in prison. I found copies of these DEOPS documents, dated 1 July 1970, in the Departamento de Documentação da Editora Abril (DEDOC), in the file "Presidio–presos politicos–BR."

22. Nair Yumiko Kobashi, interview by Jeffrey Lesser, São Paulo, 3 May 2002. On a Rio de Janeiro school known for producing militants, see Abreu, *Intelectuais e guerreiros*.

23. Nair Yumiko Kobashi, interview by Jeffrey Lesser, São Paulo, 3 May 2002.

24. On-line interview with Celso Lungaretti, 11 May 2006, www.geracaobooks.com .br/releases/entrevista—celso—lungaretti.php. See also Lungaretti, *Náufrágo da Utopia*, 181.

25. "Terror sem saídas," *Veja*, 29 October 1969.

26. "As lições dos últimos tempos," *Política operária: Orgão mensal do Partido Operário Comunista*, July 1970.

27. Confidential Telegram from American Consulate, São Paulo, to Department of State, Washington, "Political Prisoners Recant," 22 May 1970, RG 59, General Records of the Department of State, subject files 1970–73, Political and Defense, POL 17–5 BRAZ–POL 23–8 BRAZ, box 2132, NWDPH-1997, NARC.

28. "Serviço de Informações," 29 June 1970, 52Z/0/1026, DEOPS Papers, AESP.

29. U.S. Department of State Airgram, from Embassy, Rio de Janeiro, to Department of State, Washington. "Publicity Concerning Terrorist Defections," 21 January 1971, RG 59, General Records of the Department of State, subject files 1970–73, Political and Defense, POL 23–8 BRAZ–POL 33–4 BRAZ, box 2133, NWDPH-2, NARC.

30. *O Estado de S. Paulo*, 3 July 1970; *Folha de S. Paulo*, 3 July 1970.

31. *Jornal da Tarde*, 3 July 1970. The military's use of the World Cup is recounted in the film *Pra frente, Brasil* (1982), dir. Roberto Farias.

32. *O Estado de S. Paulo* and *Jornal da Tarde*, 3 July 1970, *Folha de S. Paulo*, 3 July 1970.

33. U.S. Department of State Airgram, from American Consulate, São Paulo, to Department of State, Washington, "São Paulo 490, São Paulo 632 (NOTAL)," 14 July 1970, RG 59, General Records of the Department of State, subject files 1970–73, Political and Defense, POL 17–5 BRAZ–POL 23–8 BRAZ. Box 2132, NWDPH-1997, NARC.

34. NOZ-16mm-NE 15244.01A, Telejornalismo-TUPI, FCB.

35. *Veja*, 16 June 1976.

36. *O Estado de S. Paulo*, 16 July 1970.

37. *Folha de S. Paulo*, 3 July 1970; *O Estado de S. Paulo*, 3 July 1970.

38. *Jornal da Tarde*, 18 July 1970.

39. *Diário Nippak*, 9 July 1970; *Paulista Shimbun*, 8 July 1970. See also *Correio do Povo*, 11 July 1970.

40. E.g., Rioco Kaiano, interview by Jeffrey Lesser, São Paulo, 14 June 2002; Marta Tanisaki, interview by Jeffrey Lesser, São Paulo, 11 June 2002; Judge Kazuo Watanabe, interview by Jeffrey Lesser, São Paulo, 4 June 2002.

41. "Massafumi, este bom rapaz," *Jornal da Tarde*, 9 July 1970. Similar ideas are found in "Um entre tantos outros," *O Estado de S. Paulo*, 4 July 1970; and "Ameaça à sociedade mas não à segurança nacional," *Jornal da Tarde*, 6 July 1970.

42. *Jornal da Tarde*, 25 July 1970.

43. *Veja*, 15 July 1970.

44. *Veja*, "O terror renegado," 15 July 1970, front cover. Wider shots, from which the cover was taken, can be found in *Veja*, 22 September 1971 and 17 June 1976.

45. E-mail of Shizuo Osawa to Jeffrey Lesser, 15 April 2002. See also Centro Azione e Documentazione Sull'America Latina, "Ciò che Massafumi non disse."

46. Olga Yoshiko Futema, interview by Jeffrey Lesser, São Paulo, 24 April 2002.

47. Celso Lungaretti wrote his public confession in order to end 75 days of torture in "Um caso brasileiro," *Veja*, 30 January 1991, 38. An on-line interview with Lungaretti can be found at www.geracaobooks.com.br/releases/entrevista—celso—lungaretti.php.

48. "Morte em surdina," *Veja*, 16 June 1976.

49. Sei-cho-no-iê was introduced in Brazil in 1934, just a few years after it was founded. When Masaharu Taniguchi, the founder of the religion, visited Brazil in 1963, tens of thousands of people came to hear his lectures; *Panorama*, November 1963, 48–50. My thanks to Evan Ross for sharing this with me. See also Mullins, Susumu, and Swanson, *Religion and Society*; and Clarke, *Japanese New Religions*.

50. "Morte em surdina," *Veja*, 16 June 1976.
51. *O Estado de S. Paulo*, 9 June 1976.
52. Campinas Law no. 9497, 20 November 1997.

5. "MÁRIO THE JAP"

1. E.g., "Interrogatório de Ladislas Dowbor," 14 July 1970, 30Z/60/7642, 337–54, DEOPS Papers, AESP.
2. Gorender, *Combate nas trevas*, 210, 219; Patarra, *Iara*, 366–74; Gaspari, *Ditadura escancarada*, 179.
3. A slightly different narrative of Shizuo Osawa's childhood is recounted by Japanese diplomat Nobou Okuchi, who met Osawa's father after the son had been exiled to Brazil; Okuchi, *Seqüestro do diplomata*, 203–06.
4. Shizuo Osawa, interview by Jeffrey Lesser, Rio de Janeiro, 25 January 2002. All quotes in this chapter are from this interview unless otherwise noted.
5. Osava [Osawa], "Eles querem ser brasileiros."
6. DEOPS, Carlos Lamarca File, 30-Z-160 4150/4149/4163/4255/4253/4355/4789, DEOPS Papers, AESP.
7. Examples of the Nikkei guerrilla as supersoldier can be found in Miranda and Tibúrcio, *Dos filhos deste solo*; and Patarra, *Iara*, 363–77; as well as in the fictionalized accounts of Paz, *Viagem à luta armada* and *Nas trilhas da* ALN.
8. Maia, Dantas, and Savignano, *Guerrilheiras do Araguaia*, 38.
9. "Interrogatório de Manuel de Lima," 26 May 1970, 30Z/60/7692–7694, 443–53, esp. 446, DEOPS Papers–AESP.
10. Vianna, *Tempestade como a sua memória*, 66.
11. Reis Filho and Ferreira de Sá, *Imagens da revolução*, 222–76.
12. VPR, *Brésil: Documents sur le développement et la situation actuelle de la lutte armée*, March 1971, CX 21.03.68.8/039, CEDEM; Rodrigues [Dowbor], "Vanguarda armada"; Gorender, *Combate nas trevas*, 151.
13. Dowbor narrates his experience in Israel in Dowbor, *Mosaico partido*, 13–18.
14. Ibid., 26–27: "Perigosamente juntos," *Istoé/Senhor*, 4 September 1991, 60–61.
15. Vianna, *Tempestade como a sua memória*, 67.
16. Edsel Magnotti, Delegado do Polícia Adjunto à Especializada de Ordem Social, 29 April 1970, "Relatório: Indiciados—Chizuo Osava," 30Z/160/14088–89, DEOPS Papers, AESP. The Estrada das Lágrimas is in São João Clímaco, part of the city of São Caetano do Sul.
17. See handwritten declaration of Dowbor, "De próprio punho declaro o seguinte," 14 May 1970, 50Z/9/13994, 1–18, esp. 14, DEOPS Papers, AESP.
18. "Continuação do resumo das declarações prestadas por Heleny Telles Guarira

('Lucy') à Equipe da Interrogatório Preliminar 'B1' em 25 de abril de 1970 das 21:50 as 0300 horas," 30Z/160/6288; "Interrogatório de Ladislas Dowbor," 14 July 1970, 30Z/60/7642, 337–54, esp. 346; "Resumo das declarações prestadas por Ladislau Dowbor, 21 abril 1970 das 0930 as 0120 horas," 50Z/9/14060. DEOPS Papers, AESP.

19. DOPS–Divisão de Informações, 3 August 1970, SD/SAF 18202, Setor: Informações, folder 102, 2, APERJ.

20. Note of Secretaria de Estado de Relações Exteriores to Embaixada do México, Brasília, 14 March 1970, AHI Notas Expedidas, Mexico 1970, vol. 1, AHI.

21. Fon, Tortura, 52. Fon, brother of ALN member Aton Fon Filho, was one of the first journalists to publish materials on torture, initially in Veja and later in a book; Figueiredo, Ministério do silêncio, 294; Huggins, Haritos-Fatouros, and Zimbardo, Violence Workers, 180–81.

22. Carvalho, Mulheres que foram à luta armada, 132. This claim is supported in the DEOPS files, where notes of the interrogation of Osawa imply that his claim of never having been to the VPR training site, and thus not knowing exactly where it was, was accepted; 30-z-160 4150/4149/4163/4255/4253/4355/4789, AESP. "Torturado na ditadura, nikkei hoje é 'apolítico,' " interview with Shizuo Osawa in Jornal Nippo-Brasil, October 2001. For a very different memory of torture, see Gabeira, Carta sobre anistia, 26–33.

23. Vianna, Tempestade como a sua memória, 66.

24. Skidmore, Politics of Military Rule, 125.

25. VPR, "Considerações sobre os objetivos de uma operação de seqüestro." This undated document was supposedly found in the house of VPR member Juarez de Brito on 30 April 1970, Setor: Secreto, folder 62, 123–18, APERJ. See chapter 4 for a discussion of the reaction when Alfredo Sirkis, a Jewish-Brazilian VPR, argued against adding Israel's ambassador to the kidnapping list; Sirkis, Carbonários, 191.

26. Maria do Carmo Brito, quoted in Vianna, Tempestade como a sua memória, 67. Denise Peres Crispim, a VPR member involved in Okuchi's kidnapping, was reported by the Folha de S. Paulo to have said in court that "the objective was to liberate 'Mário Japanese' "; Folha de S. Paulo, 14 August 1970. Maria do Carmo Brito reports that the leader of the VPR, Carlos Lamarca, was "furious" that the consul was traded for so few militants; Vianna, Tempestade como a sua memória, 68. Augusto Boal, author of The Theatre of the Oppressed (for which he was imprisoned, tortured, and exiled), makes this point in his fictionalized account of the period in "Seqüestramos o embaixador ianque."

27. Mário Gibson Barbosa, interview by Jerry Dávila, Rio de Janeiro, 5 August 2003.

28. Veja, 18 March 1970.

29. Truskier, "Politics of Violence." The translated interview smuggled into Brazil can be found in Archivio Storico del Movimento Operaio Brasiliano, 03.136.8; 46.03.136.8/n, CEDEM.

30. Okuchi, Seqüestro do diplomata, 100, 66.

31. Dowbor's account of the first hours of the kidnapping can be found in Gramont, "How One Pleasant, Scholarly Young Man." Vianna, Tempestade como a sua memória, 67.

32. Okuchi, Seqüestro do diplomata, 98.

33. Chefe do SNI, "Seqüestro do cônsul geral do Japão no Brasil," 19 March 1970, in DSI, Nobou Okuchi, CX 587/05253, proc. 53052, 17, AN. On Brazil's National Intelligence Service, see Antunes, SNI e ABIN.

34. Telegram from U.S. Embassy to Secretary of State, Washington, D.C., 20 April 1970, RG 59, General Records of the Department of State, subject files 1970–73, Political and Defense, POL 17–5 BRAZ–POL 23–8 BRAZ, box 2132, NWDPH-1997, NARC.

35. Jornal da Tarde, 12 and 13 March 1970.

36. Kazuo Watanabe, the son of Japanese immigrants, received his law degree at USP in 1959. He was the first Nikkei to receive the title of desembargador (1962) and in 1979 was promoted to the position of juiz efetivo do egregio tribunal da alçada civil do Estado de São Paulo.

37. Veja, 18 March 1970. This Shindo Renmei connection was also reported in the Mainichi Shimbun, 16 March 1970. This story was confirmed to me by Damon Kanda; Damon Kanda, interview by Jeffrey Lesser, São Paulo, 28 September 2001. Watanabe was unable to remember the incident; Judge Kazuo Watanabe, interview by Jeffrey Lesser, São Paulo, 4 June 2002.

38. Folha de S. Paulo, 13 March 1970.

39. Damon Kanda, interview by Jeffrey Lesser, São Paulo, 28 September 2001.

40. VPR communiqué found in Barra Funda/SP on 12 March 1970, DOPS Assunto: Terrorismo, folder 2, 391, APERJ. The text can also be found in DSI, Nobou Okuchi, CX 587/05253, proc. 53052, 11, AN. I am grateful to James Green for pointing me toward this material and to William Martins for locating the files. A discussion of the texts of the demands in the other kidnapping cases can be found in Airgram from U.S. Embassy, Rio de Janeiro, 8 January 1972, RG 59, General Records of the Department of State, subject files 1970–73, Political and Defense, POL 23–8 BRAZ–POL 33–4 BRAZ, Box 2133, NWDPH-2, NARC.

41. Damon Kanda, interview by Jeffrey Lesser, São Paulo, 28 September 2001.

42. Paulista Shimbun, 17 March 1970. Translations from the Japanese by Koichi Mori.

43. Jornal da Tarde, 13 March 1970.

44. Diário Popular, 12 March 1970. See the similar reports in Última Hora, O Dia, and O Estado de S. Paulo, 12 and 13 March 1970.

45. *Folha de S. Paulo*, 14 March 1970.

46. "Resumo das declarações prestadas por Heleny Ferreira Telles Guarira ('Lucy') à Equipe da Interrogatório Preliminar 'BI' em 25 de Abril de 1970 das 21:50 as 0300 horas." 30Z/160/6289; see also "Informação" no. 307, Operação Bandeirantes, 30 April 1970, in 30Z/160/6290, DEOPS Papers, AESP.

47. "Interrogatório de Ladislas Dowbor," 14 July 1970, 30Z/60/7642, 337–54, esp. 346, DEOPS Papers–AESP.

48. Carlos Takaoka, interview by Jeffrey Lesser, São Paulo, 3 July 2002. "Interrogatório de Ladislas Dowbor," 14 July 1970, 30Z/60/7642, 337–54, esp. 346, DEOPS Papers, AESP.

49. *Mainichi Shimbun*, 13 March 1970, 1; *Diário Popular*, 14 March 1970.

50. *Notícias Populares*, 13 March 1970.

51. Telegram from U.S. Consulate, São Paulo to Secretary of State, Washington, D.C., 2 April 1970. RG 59, General Records of the Department of State, subject files 1970–73, Political and Defense, POL 17–5 BRAZ–POL 23–8 BRAZ, box 2132, NWDPH-1997, NARC.

52. Telegram from U.S. Consulate, São Paulo to Secretary of State, Washington, D.C., 2 April 1970, RG 59, General Records of the Department of State, subject files 1970–73, Political and Defense, POL 17–5 BRAZ–POL 23–8 BRAZ, box 2132, NWDPH-1997, NARC.

53. Barbosa, *Na diplomacia*, 230–34. The official decision can be found in Ministério da Justiça, Gabinete do Ministro, Memorando no. 411, 12 March 1970, DSI, Nobou Okuchi, CX 587/05253, proc. 53052, 1–2, AN.

54. Note of Alfredo Bruzaid (justice minister) and Mário Gibson Barbosa (foreign minister), Brasília, 13 March 1970, DSI, Nobou Okuchi, CX 587/05253, proc. 53052, 8, AN. See also Figueiredo, *Ministério do silêncio*, 212.

55. Djalma Pereira, Brazilian Federal Police, 14 March 1970, DEOPS 30-Z-160 5626, DEOPS Papers–AESP.

56. Note of Djalma Pereira, agent of the Departamento da Polícia Federal, that he had taken custody of the group from Benedite Nunes Dias, director of the DEOPS, 14 March 1970, 30Z/160/5626, DEOPS Papers, AESP. The communiqué from the VPR was published in all major Brazilian newspapers.

57. "Perigosamente juntos," *Istoé/Senhor*, 4 September 1991.

58. "Resumo das declarações prestadas por Ladislau Dowbor, 21 abril 1970 das 0930 as 0120 horas," 50Z/9/14060, DEOPS Papers, AESP. Diógenes José Carvalho de Oliveira, after his return to Brazil in the eighties, became Porto Alegre secretary of transportation (1989–92) and held a number of other posts linked to the Workers Party (PT) of Rio Grande do Sul.

59. *Jornal da Tarde*, 14 March 1970.

60. Quote from an interview with an unnamed Japanese-Brazilian in *Mainichi Shimbun*, 16 March 1970. Translation by Taku Yamamoto.

61. *Nihon Keizai Shimbun*, Tokyo, 16 March 1970; *Yomiuri Shimbun*, 16 March 1970. Translations by Taku Yamamoto.

62. Letter of Néstor Luiz Ottoni Fernandes Júnior Barros dos Santos Lima (embassy in Tokyo) to Itamaraty, 13 March 1970, 923.1 (56) (42), Tóquio Ofícios (03) 1970, AHI.

63. Okuchi, *Seqüestro do diplomata*, 120.

64. On Madre Maurina, see Gaspari, *Ditadura escancarada*, 265–66.

65. Medical report of 14 March 1970 by Mário Santalucia and José Henrique da Fonseca, DEOPS 30-z-160 5613, 16 March 1970, DEOPS Papers–AESP.

66. Confidential telegram from American Consulate, São Paulo to Secretary of State, Washington, D.C., 2 April 1970, RG 59, General Records of the Department of State, subject files 1970–73, Political and Defense, POL 23 Japan–POL Japan-UR, box 2406, NWDPH-1997, NARC.

67. Damon Kanda, interview by Jeffrey Lesser, São Paulo, 28 September 2001. Okuchi tells the story slightly differently, saying that as he approached his home the first person he recognized was Kanda; Okuchi, *Seqüestro do diplomata*, 137.

68. Okuchi, *Seqüestro do diplomata*, 163.

69. Mori's formal statement is reprinted in full as an appendix to Okuchi, *Seqüestro do diplomata*, 225–31. Mori's position was reported on the front page of the *Folha de S. Paulo*, 18 March 1970.

70. Okuchi, *Seqüestro do diplomata*, 183. Confidential telegram from U.S. Embassy to Secretary of State, Washington, D.C., 18 March 1970, RG 59, General Records of the Department of State, subject files 1970–73, Political and Defense, POL 23 Japan–POL Japan-UR, box 2406, NWDPH-1997, NARC.

71. Telegram from U.S. Consulate, São Paulo to Secretary of State, Washington, D.C., 15 April 1970, RG 59, General Records of the Department of State, subject files 1970–73, Political and Defense, POL 17–5 BRAZ–POL 23–8 BRAZ, box 2132, NWDPH-1997, NARC.

72. *O Estado de S. Paulo*, 12 and 13 March 1970; *Folha de S. Paulo*, 17 March 1970.

73. *Folha de S. Paulo*, 17 March 1970.

74. *Veja*, 18 March 1970.

75. *Mainichi Shimbun*, 16 March 1970, 14; *Asahi Shimbun*, 16 March 1970, 12; *Yomiuri Shimbun*, 16 March 1970, 13; *Japan Times*, 16 and 17 March 1970.

76. Editorial in *Japan Times*, 19 March 1970.

77. Editorial in *Daily Yomiuri*, 19 March 1970.

78. *Sankei Shimbun*, 16 March 1970. Translation by Taku Yamamoto.

79. *Asahi Shimbun*, 15 March 1970. Translation by Taku Yamamoto.

80. *Mainichi Shimbun*, 16 March 1970. Translation by Taku Yamamoto.

81. Japanese Ambassador to Brazil Koh Chiba to Brazilian Foreign Minister Mário Gibson Barbosa, 16 March 1970, 922.2 (56) (42), Japão Notas, January–June 1970, AHI.

82. Secretaria da Segurança Pública–DEOPS, "Relatório–Indiciados–Chizuo Osava," 29 April 1970, 30Z/160/15601, 30Z/160/15606, 30Z/160/15614, DEOPS Papers, AESP. Souza, Eu, *cabo Anselmo*, 135; Vianna, *Tempestade como a sua memória*, 126–28.

83. Okuchi, *Seqüestro do diplomata*, 206.

84. Ibid., 206.

85. *Veja*, 25 July 1979.

86. Osawa's naming story is similar to the one soccer player Edson Arantes do Nascimento tells of his anger at being given a nickname that "sounds like baby-talk in Portuguese." Like "Japa," Nascimento now has taken control of his nickname, "Pelé." See unsigned Reuters report, "Pele Says He Hated His Nickname" (Berlin, 1 January 2006), www.fifa.com/en/mens/index/0,2527,113065,00.html?articleid=113065.

EPILOGUE

1. See, e.g., *Veja*, 15 December 2004.

2. Schneider, *Futures Lost*. A different case of the same phenomenon is Munasinghe, *Callaloo or Tossed Salad?*

3. Non-Japanese sushi chefs can also be found in the United States, although not in as high proportions as in Brazil. *The Chicago Reporter*, for example, suggests that 30% of sushi chefs in Chicago are Latino; *Chicago Reporter*, June 2001, www.chicagoreporter.com/2001/6–2001/6–2001main.htm.

4. José Eduardo Belmonte (via e-mail), interview by Jeffrey Lesser, 31 October 2004.

5. *5 Filmes Estrangeiros* (1997), dir. José Eduardo Belmonte. The 13-minute film was awarded the Prêmio Especial do Júri at the Festival de Gramado 1998; *Pato Fu— Site oficial*, www.patofu.com.br/oldsite/home/home.html.

Glossary

colônia (colony): One of the terms used by Japanese immigrants and their descendants in Brazil to define the Nikkei community. This term was also used by other immigrant groups to represent a sense of Brazil as "home."

dekasegui (including the Portuguese variant *dekassegui* or the Japanese romanization *dekasegi*): In its original usage in Japan, this term was used for people who left their birthplace to work temporarily elsewhere. More recently it has come to mean foreign workers of Japanese descent living in Japan.

gaijin: A Japanese term for outsider or foreigner; a person who is not Japanese. In Brazil this term is often used by Nikkei for non-Nikkei Brazilians.

Issei, Nisei, Sansei, Yonsei: Japanese terms for succeeding generations of Japanese immigrants in another country: *Isei* refers to first-generation immigrants, *Nisei* to their children (the second generation), *Sansei* to their grandchildren (the third generation), and *Yonsei* to their great-grandchildren (the fourth generation).

japonês: While the term can refer to someone born in Japan, it is widely used in Brazil for anyone of Japanese descent.

manga: The Japanese word for comics and print cartoons, usually produced in black and white.

mestiçagem: Racial and cultural mixing.

mestiço: A person of mixed heritage.

nihonjin: Japanese.

nihonjin-kai: Japanese associations.

Nikkei (or *nikkeijin*): A person of Japanese descent born overseas.

nipo-brasileiro: Japanese-Brazilian.

Paulista: A resident of the state of São Paulo.

Paulistano/a: A resident of the city of São Paulo.

Bibliography

ARCHIVES AND LIBRARIES

Arquivo da Propaganda (São Paulo)
Arquivo do Centro de Estudos Nipo-brasileiros (São Paulo)
Arquivo do Estado de São Paulo (São Paulo)
Arquivo do Estado do Rio de Janeiro
Arquivo Edgard Leuenroth, Instituto de Filosofia e Ciências Humanas da Unicamp
  (Campinas)
Arquivo Histórico Itamarati (Brasília)
Arquivo Nacional (Rio de Janeiro)
Arquivo Público do Estado do Rio de Janeiro
Arquivo Público Mineiro (Belo Horizonte)
Biblioteca Jenny Klabin Segall of the Museu Lasar Segall (São Paulo)
Biblioteca Nacional (Rio de Janeiro)
Brasil, Nunca Mais Project, University of Chicago, Joseph Regenstein Library
Centro de Documentação e Memória (São Paulo)
Centro de Pesquisa e Documentação História Contemporânea do Brasil,
  Fundação Getúlio Vargas (Rio de Janeiro)
Departamento de Documentação da Editora Abril (São Paulo)
Fundação Cinemateca Brasileira (São Paulo)
Instituto Histórico e Geográfico Brasileiro (Rio de Janeiro)
Library of the Fundação Cinemateca Brasileira (São Paulo)
Museu de Imagem e Som (São Paulo)
National Archives and Record Center (Washington, D.C.)
Public Records Office (London)

Secretaria do Estado da Promoção Social—Centro Histórico do Imigrante (São Paulo)

INTERVIEWS

Barbosa, Mário Gibson. Interview by Jerry Dávila, Rio de Janeiro, 5 August 2003.
Belmonte, José Eduardo. Interview by Jeffrey Lesser (via e-mail), 31 October 2004.
Futema, Olga Yoshiko. Interview by Jeffrey Lesser, São Paulo, 24 April 2002.
Kaiano, Rioco. Interview by Jeffrey Lesser, São Paulo, 14 and 18 June 2002.
Kanda, Damon. Interview by Jeffrey Lesser, São Paulo, 28 September 2001 [Questions in Portuguese by Lesser, responses in Japanese translated by Koichi Mori].
Kobashi, Nair Yumiko. Interview by Jeffrey Lesser, São Paulo, 3 May 2002.
Kobata, Henri George. Interview by Jeffrey Lesser, São Paulo, 24 January and 2 February 2002.
Nakabayaski, Jun. Interview by Jeffrey Lesser, São Paulo, 3 January 2002.
Oi, Célia Abe. Interview by Jeffrey Lesser, São Paulo, 1 April 2002.
Osawa, Shizuo. Interview by Jeffrey Lesser, Rio de Janeiro, 25 January 2002.
Sternheim, Alfredo. Interview by Jeffrey Lesser, São Paulo, 10 April 2002.
Takaoka, Carlos. Interview by Jeffrey Lesser, São Paulo, 5 July 2002.
Tanaka, Misaki. Interview by Jeffrey Lesser, São Paulo, 5 February 2002.
Tanisaki, Marta. Interview by Jeffrey Lesser, São Paulo, 11 June 2002.
Watanabe, Judge Kazuo. Interview by Jeffrey Lesser, São Paulo, 4 June 2002.
Yoshi, Masako. Interview by Jeffrey Lesser, São Paulo, 1 July 2002.

NEWSPAPERS AND MAGAZINES

ABB-Bandeirante (São Paulo)
Arigato (São Paulo)
Asahi Shimbun (Tokyo)
Carta Capital (São Paulo)
Brazilian Information Bulletin (Berkeley)
Business Latin America (London)
Chicago Reporter
Cinejornal/Embrafilme (Rio de Janeiro)
Cinema em Close-Up (São Paulo)
Contracampo: Revista de Cinema (on-line)
Correio Braziliense (Brasília)
Daily Yomiuri (Tokyo)
O Dia (Rio de Janeiro)
Diário Catarinense (Florianópolis)

Diário da Noite (São Paulo)

Diário de Notícias (São Paulo)

Diário de São Paulo (São Paulo)

Diário Nippak (São Paulo)

Diário Popular (São Paulo)

O Estado de S. Paulo (São Paulo)

Fairplay: A Revista do Homem (São Paulo)

Fiesta—Cinema (São Paulo)

Filme Cultura (São Paulo)

Folha da Tarde (São Paulo)

Folha de S. Paulo (São Paulo)

Framework: The Journal of Cinema and Media (Detroit)

Gazeta do Paraná (Cascavel)

Hokubei Mainichi (San Francisco)

Istoé (São Paulo)

Istoé/Senhor (São Paulo)

Japan Times (Tokyo)

Jornal da Tarde (São Paulo)

Jornal do Brasil (Rio de Janeiro)

Jornal do Comércio (Rio de Janeiro)

Jornal Nippo-Brasil (São Paulo)

Los Angeles Times

Mainichi Daily News (Tokyo)

Mainichi Shimbun (Tokyo)

Miami Herald

Monthly Film Bulletin (London)

New York Times Magazine

Nihon Keizai Shimbun (Tokyo)

Notícias Populares (São Paulo)

Página Um (São Paulo)

Paulista Shimbun (São Paulo)

Realidade (São Paulo)

Revista Brasil de Cultura, www.revistabrasil.com.br/mateporb021125.htm

Revista Manchete (Rio de Janeiro)

Revista Panorama (Curitiba)

Sankei Shimbun (Tokyo)

São Paulo Shimbun (São Paulo)

Scene: The Pictorial Magazine (Los Angeles)

Scientific American (New York)

A Tribuna (Santos)
Última Hora (Rio de Janeiro)
Veja (São Paulo)
Visão (São Paulo)
Yomiuri Shimbun (Tokyo)

BOOKS AND ARTICLES

Abe Oi, Célia. Cultura japonesa: São Paulo, Rio de Janeiro, Curitiba. São Paulo: Aliança
Cultural Brasil-Japão, 1995.
Abreu, Alzira de. Intelectuais e guerreiros: O Colégio de Aplicação da UFRJ de 1948 a 1968.
Rio de Janeiro: Editora UFRJ, 1992.
Alarcón, Rodrigo. Brasil: Represión y tortura. Santiago de Chile: Orbe, 1971.
Aliança Cultural Brasil-Japão and The Fact, eds. Universo em segredo: A mulher nikkei no
Brasil. São Paulo: Círculo do Livro, n.d.
Alquizola, Marilyn C., and Lane Ryo Hirabayashi. "Confronting Gender Stereotypes
of Asian American Women: Slaying the Dragon." In Reversing the Lens: Ethnicity,
Race, Gender, and Sexuality through Film, ed. Jun Xing and Lane Ryo Hirabayashi,
155–68. Boulder: University Press of Colorado, 2003.
Alves, Maria Helena Moreira. State and Opposition in Military Brazil. Austin: University
of Texas Press, 1985.
Ando, Zempati. Estudos socio-históricos da imigração japonesa. São Paulo: Centro de Es-
tudos Nipo-Brasileiros, 1976.
Andrade, Mário de. Cartas a Anita Malfatti. Org. Marta Rossetti Batista. Rio de Ja-
neiro: Forense Universitária, 1989.
André, Bruno de. "Pornochanchada: Rir e brincar com um diretor udigrúdi." Veja,
23 March 1981.
Antunes, Priscila Carlos Brandão. SNI e ABIN: Uma leitura da atuação dos serviços se-
cretos brasileiros ao longo do século XX. Rio de Janeiro: Editora FGV, 2001.
Appelbaum, Nancy P., Anne S. Macpherson, and Karin Alejandra Rosemblatt, eds.
Race and Nation in Modern Latin American. Chapel Hill: University of North Carolina
Press, 2003.
Aquino, Maria Aparecida. Censura, imprensa, estado autoritário, 1968–1978: O exercício
cotidiano da dominação e da resistência, "O Estado de São Paulo" e Movimento. Bauru:
EDUSC, 1999.
Aquino, Maria Aparecida, Marco Aurélio Vannucchi Mattos, and Walter Cruz
Swensson Jr., eds.; Lucimar Almeida de Araújo and Orion Barreto da Rocha
Klautau Neto, co-orgs. No coração das trevas: O DEOPS/SP visto por dentro. São Paulo:
Arquivo do Estado, 2001.

Arbix, Glauco, and Mauro Zilbovicius, eds. *De JK a FHC: A reinvenção dos carros*. São Paulo: Scritta, 1997.

Archdiocese of São Paulo. *Torture in Brazil: A Report*, ed. Joan Dassin, trans. Jaime Wright. New York: Vintage, 1986.

———. *Brasil, nunca mais*. Preface by Paulo Evaristo Arns. 20th ed. Petrópolis: Vozes, 1987.

Arroyo, Angelo. "Relatório sobre a luta no Araguaia." In *Araguaia, o partido e a guerrilha*, ed. Wladimir Pomar, 249–73. São Paulo: Brasil Debates, 1980.

Athayde, Phydia de. "Justiça ainda que tardia." *Carta capital*, 18 February 2004.

Avellar, José Carlos. "A teoria da relatividade." In *Anos 70: Cinema*, 71–77. Rio de Janeiro: Europa, 1970.

Bad Objects-Choices, ed. *How Do I Look: Queer Film and Video*. Seattle: Bay, 1991.

Bal, Mieke, Jonathan Crewe, and Leo Spitzer, eds. *Acts of Memory: Cultural Recall in the Present*. Hanover, N.H.: University Press of New England, 1998.

Banco do Brasil. *Brasil: Comércio exterior, exportação*. Vol. 1. Rio de Janeiro: Banco do Brasil, CACEX, 1974.

Barbosa, Mário Gibson. *Na diplomacia, o traço todo da vida*. Rio de Janeiro: Record, 1992.

Barbosa, Neusa. "Amigos recordam o talento de Walter Hugo Khouri." *Cineweb*, 27 June 2003. www.cineweb.com.br/claquete/?idclaquete=289.

Barsalini, Glauco. *Mazzaropi: O Jeca do Brasil*. Campinas: Atomo, 2002.

Batista, Marta Rossetti. *Anita Malfatti no tempo e no espaço*. São Paulo: IBM Brasil, 1985.

Beozzo, José Oscar. "Os padres conciliares brasileiros no Vaticano II: Participação e prosopografia, 1959–1965." Ph.D. diss., Universidade de São Paulo, 2001.

Bernardet, Jean-Claude. "Chanchada, erotismo e cinema empresa." *Opinião*, 25 April 1973, 21.

———. *Cineastas e imagens do povo*. São Paulo: Companhia das Letras, 2003.

Bhabha, Homi. *The Location of Culture*. London: Routledge, 1994.

Biáfora, Rubem. Review of *O estripador de mulheres*. *O Estado de S. Paulo*, 10 December 1978.

Boal, Augusto. *Milagre no Brasil*. Rio de Janeiro: Civilização Brasileira. 1979.

Borges, Luiz Carlos R. *O cinema à margem, 1960–1980*. Campinas: Papirus, 1983.

Borrie, W. D., ed. *The Cultural Integration of Immigrants: A Survey Based upon the Papers and Proceedings of the UNESCO Conference Held in Havana, April 1956*. New York: UNESCO, 1957.

Borstelmann, Thomas. *The Cold War and the Color Line: American Race Relations in the Global Arena*. Cambridge: Harvard University Press, 2001.

Box, Meredith, and Gavan McCormack. "Terror in Japan: The Red Army (1969–

2001) and Aum Supreme Truth (1987–2000)." *Critical Asian Studies* 36.1 (2002): 91–112.

Braylan, Marisa, Daniel Feirstein, Miguel Galante, and Adrián Jmelnizky. *Report on the Situation of the Jewish Detainees-Disappeared during the Genocide Perpetrated in Argentina*. Buenos Aires: DAIA-Argentinean Jewish Community Centers Association, 2000.

Brubaker, Rogers, and Frederick Cooper. "Beyond Identity." *Theory and Society* 29 (2000): 1–47.

Burton, Julianne, ed. *Cinema and Social Change in Latin America: Conversations with Filmmakers*. Austin: University of Texas Press, 1986.

Butler, Kim D. *Freedoms Given, Freedoms Won: Afro-Brazilians in Post-abolition São Paulo and Salvador*. New Brunswick, N.J.: Rutgers University Press, 1998.

Butsugan, Sumi. "Participação social e tendência de casamentos interétnicos." In *A presença japonesa no Brasil*, ed. Hiroshi Saito, 101–12. São Paulo: Editora da Universidade de São Paulo, 1980.

Cabral, Pedro Corrêa. *Xambioá: Guerrilha no Araguaia*. Rio de Janeiro: Record, 1993.

Campos Filho, Romualdo Pessoa. *Guerrilha do Araguaia: A esquerda em armas*. Goiânia: Editora da UFG, 1997.

Cardoso, Ruth Correia Leite. *Estrutura familiar e mobilidade social: Estudos japoneses no Estado de São Paulo*. São Paulo: Primus Comunicação Integrada, 1995. (1st ed.; São Paulo: FELCH/USP, 1972.)

———. "O papel das associações juvenis na aculturação dos japoneses." *Revista de antropologia* 7.1–2 (1959): 101–22.

Carneiro, J. Fernando. *Imigração e colonização no Brasil*. Rio de Janeiro: Faculdade Nacional de Filosofia, 1950.

Carvalho, Luiz Maklouf. *Mulheres que foram à luta armada*. São Paulo: Globo, 1998.

Central Committee of the Communist Party of Brazil (PC do B). "Mais audácia na luta contra a ditadura" (July 1970). In *Araguaia, o partido e a guerrilha*, ed. Wladimir Pomar, 135–43. São Paulo: Brasil Debates, 1980.

Centro Azione e Documentazione Sull'America Latina. "Ciò che Massafumi non disse né mai potrà dire" (24 September 1970). In *Dossier sul Brasile*, 147–51. Milan: Sapere, 1970.

Centro de Estudos Nipo-Brasileiros. *Pesquisa da população de descendentes de japoneses residentes no Brasil, 1987–1988*. São Paulo: Centro de Estudos Nipo-Brasileiros, 1990.

Chauí, Marilena. *Conformismo e resistência: Cultura popular no Brasil*. São Paulo: Brasiliense, 1986.

Chu, Henry. "When Revolt Hit Rio: Leftists Who Abducted a U.S. Ambassador in '69 Now Are Part of Brazil's Mainstream." *Los Angeles Times*, 23 September 2004.

Clarke, Peter B., ed. *Japanese New Religions in Global Perspective.* Richmond, U.K.: Curzon, 2000.

Comissão de Elaboração da História dos 80 Anos da Imigração Japonesa no Brasil. *Uma epopéia moderna: 80 anos da imigração japonesa no Brasil.* São Paulo: Hucitec, 1992.

Comissão de Recenseamento da Colônia Japonesa. *The Japanese Immigrant in Brazil.* 2 vols. Tokyo: University of Tokyo Press, 1964.

Cony, Carlos Heitor. *Pessach: A travessia.* Rio de Janeiro: Civilização Brasileira, 1967.

Costa, Albertina de Oliveira, et al. *Memórias das mulheres do exílio (depoimentos).* Rio de Janeiro: Paz e Terra, 1980.

Costa, Caio Túlio. *Cale-se: A saga de Vannucchi Leme, a USP como aldeia gaulesa, o show proibido de Gilberto Gil.* São Paulo: Girafa, 2003.

Couto, Ronaldo Costa. *Memória viva do regime militar: Brasil, 1964–1985.* Rio de Janeiro: Record, 1999.

Cunha, Maria de Fátima da. "A face feminina da militância clandestina de esquerda: Brasil, anos 60–70." Thesis proposal, Universidade Estadual de Campinas, 2001.

Cyrelli de Souza, Hélder. "Selos postais e a ditadura militar no Brasil." In *Ditaduras militares na América Latina,* ed. Claudia Wasserman and Cesar Augusto Barcellos Guazelli, 123–36. Porto Alegre: Editora da UFRGS, 2004.

Cytrynowicz, Roney. *Guerra sem guerra: A mobilização e o cotidiano em São Paulo durante a Segunda Guerra Mundial.* São Paulo: Geração, Edusp, 2000.

D'Araújo, Maria Celina, Gláucio Ary Dillon Soares, and Celso Castro, eds. *Os anos de chumbo: A memória militar sobre a repressão.* Rio de Janeiro: Relume Dumará, 1994.

———, orgs. *Visões do golpe: A memória militar sobre 1964.* Rio de Janeiro: Relume Dumará, 1994.

Dávila, Jerry. *Diploma of Whiteness: Race and Social Policy in Brazil, 1917–1945.* Durham, N.C.: Duke University Press, 2003.

Deckes, Flávio. *Radiografia do terrorismo no Brasil, 1966/1980.* São Paulo: Icone, 1985.

Deleuze, Gilles, and Félix Guattari. *A Thousand Plateaus: Capitalism and Schizophrenia.* Trans. Brian Massumi. Minneapolis: University of Minnesota Press, 1987.

della Cava, Ralph. "Torture in Brazil." *Commonweal,* 24 April 1970, 135–41.

Dennison, Stephanie, and Lisa Shaw. *Popular Cinema in Brazil, 1930–2001.* Manchester, U.K.: Manchester University Press, 2004.

Desser, David. *Eros plus Massacre: An Introduction to the Japanese New Wave Cinema.* Bloomington: Indiana University Press, 1988.

Diário da Guerrilha do Araguaia. São Paulo: Alfa-Omega, 1979.

Diégues, Manuel, Jr. *Imigração, urbanização e industrialização: Estudo sobre alguns aspectos da contribuição cultural do imigrante no Brasil.* Rio de Janeiro: Ministério da Educação, 1964.

Dirlik, Arif, ed. *What Is in a Rim? Critical Perspectives on the Pacific Region Idea.* 2nd ed. Lanham, Md.: Rowman and Littlefield, 1998.

Domenig, Roland. *Art Theatre Guild: Unabhängiges Japanisches Kino, 1962–1984.* Vienna: VIENNALE, 2003.

——. "The Anticipation of Freedom: Art Theatre Guild and Japanese Independent Cinema." www.midnighteye.com/features/art-theatre-guild.shtml.

Dowbor, Ladislau. *O mosaico partido: A economia além das equações.* Petrópolis: Vozes, 2000.

Dower, John W. *War without Mercy: Race and Power in the Pacific War.* New York: Pantheon, 1986.

Duarte, B. J. "Dia cheio." *Folha de S. Paulo,* 27 January 1965.

Dunn, Christopher. *Brutality Garden: Tropicália and the Emergence of a Brazilian Counterculture.* Chapel Hill: University of North Carolina Press, 2001.

Dyer, Richard. *Stars.* London: BFI, 1998.

Dzidzienyo, Anani. *The Position of Blacks in Brazilian Society.* London: Minority Rights Group, 1971.

Empresa Brasileira de Filmes (Embrafilme). *Cinejornal/Embrafilme 6.* Rio de Janeiro: Embrafilme, 1986.

Farrell, William R. *Blood and Rage: The Story of the Japanese Red Army.* Lexington, Mass.: Lexington, 1990.

Fausto, Boris, Oswaldo Truzzi, Roberto Grün, and Célia Sakurai. *Imigração e política em São Paulo.* São Paulo: IDESP/Sumaré; São Carlos: Editora da UFSCAR, 1995.

Feitlowitz, Marguerite. *A Lexicon of Terror: Argentina and the Legacies of Torture.* New York: Oxford University Press, 1998.

Feng, Peter X. *Identities in Motion: Asian American Film and Video.* Durham, N.C.: Duke University Press, 2003.

——, ed. *Screening Asian Americans.* New Brunswick, N.J.: Rutgers University Press, 2002.

Fernandes Júnior, Ottoni. *O baú do guerrilheiro: Memórias da luta armada urbana no Brasil.* Rio de Janeiro: Record, 2004.

Ferreira, Elizabeth F. Xavier. *Mulheres, militância e memória.* Rio de Janeiro: Fundação Getúlio Vargas, 1996.

Ferreira, Jairo. Review of *As cariocas* in *São Paulo Shimbun,* 27 October 1966.

——. "Samurais, 008, Fatalismo." *São Paulo Shimbun,* 17 August 1967.

——. "Onibaba, a mulher abutre." *São Paulo Shimbun,* 16 February 1970.

——. "Um estripador está solto nas ruas." *Folha de S. Paulo,* 11 December 1979.

——. "O Império do Desejo." *Framework* 28 (1985): unpag.

——. "O imaginário da Boca: Pequenas omissões de uma obra fundamental." *Filme Cultura* 15:40 (August–November 1982): 76–77.

Ferro, Marc. *Cinema and History*. Trans. Naomi Greene. Detroit: Wayne State University Press, 1988.

Fico, Carlos. *Reinventando o otimismo: Ditadura, propaganda e imaginário social no Brasil*. Rio de Janeiro: Fundação Getulio Vargas, 1997.

———. *Como eles agiam: Os subterrâneos da ditadura militar—Espionagem e polícia política*. Rio de Janeiro: Record, 2001.

Figueiredo, Lucas. *Ministério do silêncio: A história do serviço secreto brasileiro de Washington Luís a Lula, 1927–2005*. Rio de Janeiro: Record, 2005.

Fiske, John. "British Cultural Studies and Television." In *Channels of Discourse: Television and Contemporary Criticism*, ed. Robert C. Allen, 254–89. Chapel Hill: University of North Carolina Press, 1987.

Flores, Moacyr. "Japoneses no Rio Grande do Sul." *Veritas* (Porto Alegre) 77 (1975): 65–98.

Fon, Antônio Carlos. *Tortura: A história da repressão política no Brasil*. São Paulo: Global, 1979.

Fong-Torres, Ben. "The Pioneer Performers of the Forbidden City." asianconnections.com/entertainment/columns/ben.fong.torres/2002/11/.

Foster, David William. *Gender and Society in Contemporary Brazilian Cinema*. Austin: University of Texas Press, 1999.

Fraga, Ody. "O Quilombo de Ody." *Filme Cultura*, April–August 1984, 110–12.

Freire, Alipio, Izías Almada, and J. A. de Granville Ponce, eds. *Tiradentes, um presídio da ditadura: Memórias de presos políticos*. São Paulo: Scipione, 1997.

Fung, Richard. "Looking for My Penis: The Eroticized Asian in Gay Porn Video." In *How Do I Look: Queer Film and Video*, ed. Bad Objects-Choices, 145–68. Seattle: Bay, 1991.

Futema, Olga. "As salas japonesas no bairro da Liberdade." *Filme Cultura*, August 1986, 79–82.

Gabeira, Fernando. *Carta sobre anistia: A entrevista do Pasquim: Conversação sobre 1968*. 3rd ed. Rio de Janeiro: CODECRI, 1980.

Gamo, Alessandro. *Jairo Ferreira e convidados especiais: Crítica de invenção—Os anos do São Paulo Shimbum*. São Paulo: Imprensa Oficial do Estado de São Paulo, 2006.

Gaspari, Elio. *A ditadura envergonhada*. São Paulo: Companhia das Letras, 2002.

———. *A ditadura escancarada*. São Paulo: Companhia das Letras, 2002.

———. *A ditadura derrotada*. São Paulo: Companhia das Letras, 2003.

———. *A ditadura encurralada*. São Paulo: Companhia das Letras, 2004.

Gibson, Pamela Church, and Roma Gibson, eds. *Dirty Looks: Women, Pornography and Power*. London: BFI, 1993.

Gilman, Sander. *Making the Body Beautiful: A Cultural History of Aesthetic Surgery*. Princeton: Princeton University Press, 1999.

Gorender, Jacob. *Combate nas trevas.* 6th ed. São Paulo: Útica, 1999.

Gramont, Sanche de. "How One Pleasant, Scholarly Young Man from Brazil Became a Kidnapping, Gun-Toting, Bombing Revolutionary." *New York Times Magazine,* 15 November 1970, 43–45 and 136–53.

Gusmão, Emery Marques. *Memória, identidade e relações de trabalho: A carreira docente sob o olhar de professores de história.* Ph.D. diss., Universidade Estadual Paulista Júlio de Mesquita Filho, Campus de Marília, 2002.

Hamamoto, Darrel Y. "The Joy Fuck Club: Prolegomenon to an Asian American Porno Practice." In *Countervisions: Asian American Film Criticism,* ed. Darrel Y. Hamamoto and Sandra Liu, 59–89. Philadelphia: Temple University Press, 2000.

——, and Sandra Liu, eds. *Countervisions: Asian American Film Criticism.* Philadelphia: Temple University Press, 2000.

Hanchard, Michael George. *Orpheus and Power: The Movimento Negro of Rio de Janeiro and São Paulo, Brazil, 1945–1988.* Princeton: Princeton University Press, 1994.

Handa, Tomoo. *O imigrante japonês: História de sua vida no Brasil.* São Paulo: T. A. Queiroz, Centro de Estudos Nipo-Brasileiros, 1987.

Hartog, Simon. "Interview with Carlos Reichenbach for the Television Program Visions." *Framework: The Journal of Cinema and Media* 28 (1985): 50–55.

Heine, Steven. "Sayonara Can Mean 'Hello': Ambiguity and the Orientalist Butterfly Syndrome in Postwar American Films." *Post Script* 16.3 (1997): 29–47.

Hellerman, Leon. *Japan's Economic Strategy in Brazil: Challenge for the United States.* Lexington, Mass.: Lexington, 1988.

Hirabayashi, Lane Ryo. "Pathways to Power: Comparative Perspectives on the Emergence of Nikkei Ethnic Political Traditions." In *New Worlds, New Lives: Globalization and People of Japanese Descent in the Americas and from Latin America in Japan,* ed. Lane Ryo Hirabayashi, Akemi Kikumura, and James A. Hirabayashi, 159–78. Stanford, Calif.: Stanford University Press, 2002.

Hoang, Nguyen Tan. "The Resurrection of Brandon Lee: The Making of a Gay Asian American Porn Star." In *Porn Studies,* ed. Linda Williams, 223–70. Durham, N.C.: Duke University Press, 2004.

Hoffman, Alice M., and Howard S. Hoffman. *Archives of Memory: A Soldier Recalls World War II.* Lexington: University Press of Kentucky, 1991.

Holloway, Thomas. *Immigrants on the Land.* Chapel Hill: University of North Carolina Press, 1980.

Hosokawa, Shuhei. *Shinema-ya Burajiru o iku: Nikkei imion no kyosho to aidentiti [Japanese Film Goes to Brazil].* Tokyo: Shinchosha, 1999.

——. "Japanese Cinema Goes to Brazil." Paper presented at the conference, "The Face of Another: Japanese Cinema/Global Images," Yale University, 21–24 February 2002.

Hu-DeHart, Evelyn. "Latin America in Asian-Pacific Perspective." In Dirlik, *What Is in a Rim?* 251–82.

Huggins, Martha K., Mika Haritos-Fatouros, and Philip G. Zimbardo. *Violence Workers: Police Torturers and Murderers Reconstruct Brazilian Atrocities.* Berkeley: University of California Press, 2002.

Iokoi, Zilda Márcia Grícoli. *Intolerância e resistência: A saga dos judeus comunistas entre a Polônia, a Palestina e o Brasil (1935–1975).* São Paulo: Humanitas, 2004.

James, Daniel. *Dona Maria's Story: Life History, Memory, and Political Identity.* Durham, N.C.: Duke University Press, 2001.

Joanides, Hiroito de Morais. *Boca do Lixo.* São Paulo: Labortexto, 2003 [1970].

Johnson, Randal. *Cinema Novo X 5: Masters of Contemporary Brazilian Film.* Austin: University of Texas Press, 1984.

———, and Robert Stam, eds. *Brazilian Cinema.* New York: Columbia University Press, 1995.

José, Emiliano, and Oldack Miranda. *Lamarca: O capitão da guerrilha.* São Paulo: Global, 1980.

Kaiano, Rioco. "Estação Tiradentes." In *Tiradentes, um presídio da ditadura: Memórias de presos políticos,* ed. Alipio Freire, Izías Almada, and J. A. de Granville Ponce, 335–41. São Paulo: Scipione, 1997.

Karam, John Taufik. *Another Arabesque: Syrian-Lebanese Ethnicity in Neoliberal Brazil.* Philadelphia: Temple University Press, 2007.

Kaufman, Edy. "Jewish Victims of Repression in Argentina under Military Rule (1976–1983)." *Holocaust and Genocide Studies* 4 (1989): 479–99.

Kehl, Maria Rita, and Paulo de Tarso Venceslau. "Clara Charf: Duas histórias de luta, uma história de amor." *Teoria e Debate* 8 (October–December 1989) at www.fpa.org.br/td/tdo8/tdo8—memoria.htm.

Keizi, Minami. *Reflection 46.* In "Milênio: Edição 320," special section of *Jornal Nippo-Brasil,* www.nippobrasil.com.br/zashi/2.milenio/320.shtml.

Khouri, Walter Hugo. "Influência do cinema japonês na concepção cinematográfica de diretores brasileiros." In Abe Oi, *Cultura japonesa,* 138–41.

King, Larry D., and Margarita Suñer. *Para a Frente! An Intermediate Course in Portuguese.* Los Angeles: Cabrillo, 1981.

Klinger, Barbara. *Melodrama and Meaning: History, Culture, and the Films of Douglas Sirk.* Bloomington: Indiana University Press, 1994.

Kobata, Henri George. "Yumiko, nissei guerilheira." *Página Um* of *Diário Nippak,* 28 July 1979.

Kobe Carnival 1968. Tokyo: Mainichi Daily News, 1968.

Kobori, Edna M. "O cinema japonês em São Paulo." In Abe Oi, *Cultura japonesa,* 142–46.

Kottak, Conrad Phillip. *Prime Time Society: An Anthropological Analysis of Television and Culture*. Belmont, Calif.: Wadsworth, 1990.

Krauss, Ellis S. *Japanese Radicals Revisited: Student Protest in Postwar Japan*. Berkeley: University of California Press, 1974.

Kushnir, Beatriz. "Nem bandidos, nem heróis: Os militantes judeus de esquerda mortos sob tortura (1969–1975)." In *Perfis cruzados: Trajetórias e militância política no Brasil*, ed. Beattiz Kushnir, 215–44. Rio de Janeiro: Imago, 2002.

——. *Cães de guarda: Jornalistas e censores, do AI-5 a Constituição de 1988*. São Paulo: FAPESP, Boitempo, 2004.

La Cava, Gloria. *Italians in Brazil: The Post–World War II Experience*. New York: Peter Lang, 1999.

Lagôa, Ana. *SNI: Como nasceu, como funciona*. São Paulo: Brasiliense, 1983.

Langland, Victoria. "Birth Control Pills and Molotov Cocktails: Reading Sex and Revolution in the 1968 Brazilian Student Movements." In *Gender, Sexuality and '68: Cultural Politics across Europe, Asia and the Americas*, ed. Jo Frazier and Deborah Cohen. Durham, N.C.: Duke University Press, forthcoming.

Lavie, Smadar, and Ted Swedenburg. Introduction to *Displacement, Diaspora, and Geographies of Identity*, ed. Smadar Lavie and Ted Swedenburg, 1–25. Durham, N.C.: Duke University Press, 1996.

Lee, Robert G. *Orientals: Asian Americans in Popular Culture*. Philadelphia: Temple University Press, 1999.

Lesser, Jeffrey. *Negotiating National Identity: Immigrants, Minorities and the Struggle for Ethnicity in Brazil*. Durham, N.C.: Duke University Press, 1999.

——. "Brazil." In *American Jewish Year Book 2003: The Annual Record of Jewish Civilization*, ed. David Singer and Lawrence Grossman, 335–43. New York: American Jewish Committee, 2004.

——, ed. *Searching for Home Abroad: Japanese-Brazilians and Transnationalism*. Durham, N.C.: Duke University Press, 2003.

Lima, Haroldo, and Aldo Arantes. *História da Ação Popular: Da JUC ao PC do B*. São Paulo: Alfa-Omega, 1984.

Linger, Daniel Touro. *No One Home: Brazilian Selves Remade in Japan*. Stanford, Calif.: Stanford University Press, 2001.

Lobo, Bruno. *De japonez a brasileiro—Adaptação e nacionalisação do imigrante*. Rio de Janeiro: Typ. do Dep. Nacional de Estatística, 1932.

Louie, Andrea. *Chinese across Borders: Renegotiating Chinese Identities in China and the United States*. Durham, N.C.: Duke University Press, 2004.

Luiz, Edson. "Porões da ditadura: Ex-sargento não esquece dias vividos no Araguaia." *Diário Catarinense* (Florianópolis), 30 July 1995.

Lungaretti, Celso. *Náufrago da Utopia: Vencer ou morrer na guerrilha aos 18 anos*. São Paulo: Geração, 2005.

Lye, Colleen. *America's Asia: Racial Form and American Literature, 1893–1945*. Princeton: Princeton University Press, 2005.

Lyra, Marcelo. *Carlos Reichenbach: O cinema como razão de viver*. São Paulo: Imprensa Oficial do Estado de São Paulo, 2004.

Maeyama, Takashi. "Ethnicity, Secret Societies, and Associations: The Japanese in Brazil." *Comparative Studies in Society and History* 21 (1979): 589–610.

Maia, Iano Flávio, Renata Dantas, and Verónica Savignano. "Guerrilheiras do Araguaia: Os caminhos de quatro jovens militantes." B.A. thesis, Unicamp, 2005.

Maio, Marcos Chor. "O Brasil no 'concerto' das nações: A luta contra o racismo nos primórdios da UNESCO." *História, ciências e saúde: Manguinhos* 5.2 (1998): 375–413.

———. "UNESCO and the Study of Race Relations in Brazil: Regional or National Issue?" *Latin American Research Review* 36 (2001): 118–36.

Mantega, Guido. *Sexo e poder*. São Paulo: Brasiliense, 1979.

Marchetti, Gina. *Romance and the "Yellow Peril": Race, Sex, and Discursive Strategies in Hollywood Fiction*. Berkeley: University of California Press, 1993.

Marighella, Carlos. *Escritos de Carlos Marighella*. São Paulo: Livramento, 1979.

———. *Manual of the Urban Guerrilla*, trans. Gene Hanrahan. Chapel Hill, N.C.: Documentary Publications, 1985.

———. "Canto para Atabaque." In *Poemas: Rondó da Liberdade*, 63–64. São Paulo: Brasiliense, 1994.

Maximiliano, Henrique. "Satoshi, Satoshi." In *Triunfo dos pelos e outros contos gls*. Preface by João Silvério Trevisan, 137–38. São Paulo: GLS, 2000.

McCann, Bryan. *Hello, Hello Brazil: Popular Music in the Making of Modern Brazil*. Durham, N.C.: Duke University Press, 2004.

Meihy, José Carlos Sebe Bom. "Oral History in Brazil: Development and Challenges." *Oral History Review* 26.2 (1999): 127–36.

Melo, Luís Alberto Rocha. "Ody Fraga, a dama e a filha." In "A pornochanchada e suas fronteiras," special issue of *Contracampo: Revista de Cinema* (36). www.contracampo.com.br/36/frames.htm.

———. "Galante, um produtor." In "A pornochanchada e suas fronteiras," special issue of *Contracampo: Revista de Cinema* (36). www.contracampo.com.br/36/frames.htm.

Miceli, Sérgio. *Nacional estrangeiro: História social e cultural do modernismo artístico em São Paulo*. São Paulo: Companhia das Letras, 2003.

Ministério das Relações Exteriores. *Resenha de política exterior do Brasil* 11 (July–September 1974).

Mir, Luís. *A revolução impossível*. São Paulo: Best Seller, 1994.

Miranda, Mário Botelho de. *Shindo Renmei: Terrorismo e extorsão*. São Paulo: Saraiva, 1948.

Miranda, Nilmário, and Carlos Tibúrcio. *Dos filhos deste solo: Mortos e desaparecidos políticos durante a ditadura militar—A responsabilidade do Estado*. São Paulo: Editora Fundação Perseu Abramo, Boitempo, 1999.

Mirsky, Steve. "The Big Dig: A Cross-Cultural Look at Cultural Crossings." *Scientific American*, July 2005, 94–95.

Miyao, Sussumu. "Posicionamento social da população de origem japonesa." In *A presença japonesa no Brasil*, ed. Hiroshi Saito, 91–112. São Paulo: Editora da Universidade de São Paulo, 1980.

——, and José Yamashiro. "A comunidade enfrenta um caos sem precedentes." In Comissão de Elaboração da História dos 80 Anos da Imigração Japonesa no Brasil, *Uma epopéia moderna: 80 anos da imigração japonesa no Brasil*, 265–360. São Paulo: Hucitec, 1992.

——. "A comunidade nipônica no período da guerra." In Comissão de Elaboração da História dos 80 anos da Imigração Japonesa no Brasil, *Uma epopéia moderna: 80 anos da imigração japonesa no Brasil*, 247–65. São Paulo: Hucitec, 1992.

Moniz, Naomi Hoki. "Race, Gender, Ethnicity and the Narrative of National Identity in the Films of Tizuka Yamazaki." In *New Worlds, New Lives: Globalization and People of Japanese Descent in the Americas and from Latin America in Japan*, ed. Lane Ryo Hirabayashi, Akemi Kikumura, and James A. Hirabayashi, 221–36. Stanford, Calif.: Stanford University Press, 2002.

Morais, Táis, and Eumano Silva. *Operação Araguaia: Os arquivos secretos da guerrilha*. São Paulo: Geração, 2005.

Morão, Gerardo Mello. "A galáxia chinesa." *Folha de S. Paulo—Ilustrada*, 22 February 1980.

Moreno, Antônio. *Cinema brasiliero: História e relações com o Estado*. Niterói: EDUFF; Goiânia: CEGRAF/UFG, 1974.

Moretti, Fernando, Rodrigo Guerrino, Nobuioshi Chinem, Minami Keizi, and Sérgio Peixoto. *Hentai: A sedução do mangá*. São Paulo: Opera Gráphica, 2005.

Mori, Koichi. "Mundo dos brasileiros mestiços descendentes de japoneses." Unpublished ms., 1994.

——. Por que os brasileiros começaram a apreciar a culinária japonesa? As condições de aceitação da culinária japonesa na cidade de São Paulo. Unpublished ms., 1997.

Moya, Jose. *Cousins and Strangers: Spanish Immigrants in Buenos Aires, 1850–1930*. Berkeley: University of California Press, 1998.

Müller, Antônio Rubbo, and Hiroshi Saito, eds. "Memórias do I Painel Nipo-Brasileiro." Special issue of *Estudos de antropologia teórica e prática* 3B (August 1956).

Mullins, Mark R., Shimazono Susumu, and Paul L. Swanson, eds. *Religion and Society in Modern Japan: Selected Readings.* Berkeley: Asian Humanities, 1993.

Munasinghe, Viranjini. *Callaloo or Tossed Salad? East Indians and the Cultural Politics of Identity in Trinidad.* Ithaca, N.Y.: Cornell University Press, 2001.

Nagib, Lúcia, ed. *The New Brazilian Cinema.* London: Palgrave Macmillan, 2003.

Nakasumi, Tetsuo, and José Yamashiro. "O fim da era de imigração e a consolidação da nova colônia nikkei." In Comissão de Elaboração da História dos 80 Anos da Imigração Japonesa no Brasil, *Uma epopéia moderna,* 417–58. São Paulo: Hucitec, 1992.

Nester, William R. *Japan and the Third World: Patterns, Power, Prospects.* London: Macmillan, 1992.

Neves, Herculano. *O processo da "Shindo-Renmei" e demais associações secretas japonesas.* São Paulo: n.p., 1960.

Nobles, Melissa. *Shades of Citizenship: Race and the Census in Modern Politics.* Stanford, Calif.: Stanford University Press, 2000.

Nova, Cristiane, and Jorge Nóvoa. "Genealogias, transversalidades e rupturas de Carlos Marighella." In Nova and Nóvoa, *Carlos Marighella,* 35–188.

——, orgs. *Carlos Marighella: O homem por trás do mito.* São Paulo: Editora UNESP, 1999.

Nunes, Edison. "Um dia na vida de um comunista: Takao Amano." *Lua nova: Cultura e política* 2.3 (1985): 70–74.

Okuchi, Nobou. *O seqüestro do diplomata: Memórias,* trans. Masato Ninomiya. São Paulo: Estação Liberdade, 1991.

Ortiz, Renato. *O próximo e o distante: Japão e modernidade-mundo.* São Paulo: Brasilense, 2000.

——. *A moderna tradição brasileira.* São Paulo: Brasiliense, 2001 [1988].

——. *Cultura brasileira e identidade nacional.* São Paulo: Brasiliense, 2003 [1985].

Osava, Chizuo [Osawa, Shizuo]. "Eles querem ser brasileiros." *Revista panorama* 16.164 (1966): 12–14.

Palumbo-Liu, David. *Asian/American: Historical Crossings of a Racial Frontier.* Stanford, Calif.: Stanford University Press, 1999.

Patai, Daphne. "Minority Status and the Stigma of 'Surplus Visibility.'" *Chronicle of Higher Education,* 30 October 1991.

Patarra, Judith Lieblich. *Iara: Reportagem biográfica.* 4th ed. Rio de Janeiro: Rosa dos Tempos, 1993.

Paxton, Frederick S. *Christianizing Death: The Creation of a Ritual Process in Early Medieval Europe.* Ithaca, N.Y.: Cornell University Press, 1990.

Paz, Carlos Eugênio. *Viagem à luta armada: Memórias romanceadas.* Rio de Janeiro: Civilização Brasileira, 1996.

———. *Nas trilhas da ALN: Memórias romanceadas*. Rio de Janeiro: Bertrand Brasil, 1997.

Pereira, Anthony W. "The Archive of the Brazilian Military Regime's Political Trials." Paper presented at 116th Annual Meeting of the American Historical Association, San Francisco, 4 January 2002.

———. *Political (In)justice: Authoritarianism and the Rule of Law in Brazil, Chile and Argentina*. Pittsburgh: University of Pittsburgh Press, 2005.

Perosa, Lilian Maria Faria de Lima. *Cidadania proibida: O caso Herzog através da imprensa*. São Paulo: Imprensa Oficial do Estado, Sindicato dos Jornalistas Profissionais no Estado de São Paulo, 2001.

Perrott, Roy. "Brazil's Reckless Dash for Tomorrow." *Observer*, 30 April 1972.

Petrone, Pasquale, ed. *Pinheiros: Estudo geográfico de um bairro paulistano*. São Paulo: Editora da Universidade de São Paulo, 1963.

Pinsky, Carla Bassanezi. *Pássaros da liberdade: Jovens, judeus e revolucionários no Brasil*. São Paulo: Contexto, 2000.

Piper, Rudolph. *Filmusical e chanchada*. 2nd ed. São Paulo: Global, 1977.

Polari, Alex. *Em busca do tesouro*. Rio de Janeiro: Codecri, 1982.

———. *Forest of Visions: Ayahuasca, Amazonian Spirituality, and the Santo Daime Tradition*. Rochester, Vt.: Park Street, 1999.

Portela, Fernando. *Guerra de guerrilhas no Brasil: Informações novas—Documentos inéditos e na íntegra*. São Paulo: Global, 1979.

Prado, Maria Lígia Coelho. "*Gaijin: Os Caminhos da Liberdade*—Tempo e história." In *A história vai ao cinema*, ed. Mariza de Carvalho Soares and Jorge Ferreira, 99–110. Rio de Janeiro: Record, 2001.

Pulido, Laura. "Race, Class, and Political Activism: Black, Chicano/a, and Japanese American Leftists in Southern California, 1968–1978."*Antipode* 34.4 (2002): 762–88.

———. *Black, Brown, Yellow and Left: Radical Activism in Los Angeles*. Berkeley: University of California Press, 2006.

Queiroz, Rachel de. "Nacionalidade." In Larry D. King and Margarita Suñer, *Para a Frente! An Intermediate Course in Portuguese*, 98 (Los Angeles: Cabrillo, 1981).

Radhakrisnnan, R. "Ethnicity in an Age of Diaspora." In *Theorizing Diaspora*, ed. Jana Evans Braziel and Anita Mannur, 119–31. Malden, Mass.: Blackwell, 2003.

Ramos, Fernão, and Luiz Felipe Miranda, eds. *Enciclopédia do cinema brasileiro*. São Paulo: Editora SENAC, 2000.

Reichenbach, Carlos. "Segunda parte: Com a palavra, Carlão." In Lyra, *Carlos Reichenbach*, 94–95.

Reis Filho, Daniel Aarão, and Jair Ferreira de Sá, eds. *Imagens da revolução: Documentos políticos das organizações clandestinas de esquerda dos anos 1961 a 1971*. Rio de Janeiro: Marco Zero, 1985.

Reis, Daniel Aarao, Marcelo Ridenti, and Rodrigo Patto Sá Motta, eds. *Golpe e a ditadura militar: Quarenta anos depois (1964–2004)*. Bauru: EDUSC, 2004.

Ribeiro, Darcy. *O povo brasileiro: A formação e o sentido do Brasil*. São Paulo: Companhia das Letras, 1995.

———. *The Brazilian People: The Formation and Meaning of Brazil*. Trans. Gregory Rabassa. Gainesville: University Press of Florida, 2000.

Richopo, Neide. "A esquerda no Brasil: Um estudo de caso." M.A. thesis, University of São Paulo, 1987.

Ridenti, Marcelo. *O fantasma da revolução brasileira*. São Paulo: Editora UNESP, 1993.

———. *Em busca do povo brasileiro: Artistas da revolução, do CPC à era da TV*. Rio de Janeiro: Record, 2000.

Rodrigues, Jamil [Ladislau Dowbor]. "A vanguarda armada e as massas na primeira fase da revolução" (June 1969). In Reis Filho and Ferreira de Sá, *Imagens da revolução*, 233–47.

Rodrigues, João Carlos. "A pornografia é o erotismo dos outros." *Filme Cultura* 15:40 (August–November 1982): 66–71.

Roett, Riordan. "Brazil and Japan: Potential versus Reality." In *Japan and Latin America in the New Global Order*, ed. Susan Kaufman Purcell and Robert M. Immerman, 101–20. Boulder: Lynne Rienner, 1992.

Ropp, Steven Massami. "The 'Nikkei' Negotiation of Minority/Majority Dynamics in Peru and the United States." In *New Worlds, New Lives: Globalization and People of Japanese Descent in the Americas and from Latin America in Japan*, ed. Lane Ryo Hirabayashi, Akemi Kikumura, and James A. Hirabayashi, 279–95. Stanford, Calif.: Stanford University Press, 2002.

Rosenstone, Robert A. *Visions of the Past: The Challenge of Film to Our Idea of History*. Cambridge: Harvard University Press, 1996.

Roth, Joshua Hotaka. *Brokered Homeland: Japanese Brazilian Migrants in Japan*. Ithaca, N.Y.: Cornell University Press, 2002.

———. "Urashima Taro's Ambiguating Practices: The Significance of Overseas Voting Rights for Elderly Japanese Migrants to Brazil." In *Searching for Home Abroad: Japanese Brazilians and Transnationalism*, ed. Jeffrey Lesser, 103–20. Durham, N.C.: Duke University Press, 2003.

Roveri, Sérgio. *Gianfrancesco Guarnieri: Um grito solto no ar*. São Paulo: Imprensa Oficial do Estado de São Paulo, 2004.

Saito, Hiroshi. "Alguns aspectos da mobilidade dos japoneses no Brasil." *Kobe Economic and Business Review* 6th Annual Report (1959): 49–59.

———. *O japonês no Brasil: Estudo de mobilidade e fixação*. São Paulo: Sociologia e Política, 1961.

———, and Takashi Maeyama, eds. *Assimilação e integração dos japoneses no Brasil*. São Paulo: Vozes/EDUSP, 1973.

Sakai, Naoki. "Return to the West/Return to the East: Watsuji Tetsuro's Anthropology and Discussions of Authenticity." *boundary 2* 18.3 (1991): 157–90.

Sakurai, Célia. *Romanceiro da imigração japonesa*. São Paulo: IDESP/Sumare, 1993.

——. "A fase romântica da política: Os primeiros deputados nikkeis no Brasil." In Boris Fausto, Oswaldo Truzzi, Roberto Grün, and Célia Sakurai, *Imigração e política em São Paulo*, 127–77. São Paulo: IDESP/Sumaré; São Carlos: Editora da UFSCAR, 1995.

San Martín, Paulo, and Bernardo Pelegrini. *Cerrados: Uma ocupação japonesa no campo*. Rio de Janeiro: CODECRI/Ibase, 1984.

Schneider, Arnd. *Futures Lost: Nostalgia and Identity among Italian Immigrants in Argentina*. Oxford: P. Lang, 2000.

Seixas, Ivan. "Nome, nome de guerra e nomes legendários." Preface to Carlos Eugênio Paz, *Nas trilhas da ALN*, 9–11. Rio de Janeiro: Bertrand Brasil, 1997.

Serper, Zvika. "Shindô Kaneto's films *Kuroneko* and *Onibaba*: Traditional and Innovative Manifestations of Demonic Embodiments." *Japan Forum* 17:2 (July 2005): 231–56.

Silva, Gilberto, Jr. "O Bem Dotado: O Homem de Itu, de José Miziara." In *Contracampo: Revista de Cinema* 36. "A pornochanchada e suas fronteiras." www.contracampo .com.br/36/frames.htm.

Silva Neto, Antônio Leão da. *Dicionário de filmes brasileiros: Longa-metragem*. São Paulo: Antônio Leão da Silva Neto, 2002.

Simões, Inimá. *Roteiro da intolerância: A censura cinematográfica no Brasil*. São Paulo: Editora SENAC São Paulo, 1999.

Simões, Inimá Ferreira. "Sou . . . mas quem não é? Pornochanchada: O bode expiatório do cinema brasileiro." In Guido Mantega, *Sexo e poder*, 85–96. São Paulo: Brasiliense, 1979.

——. *Imaginário da Boca*. São Paulo: Departamento de Informação Artística, Centro de Documentação e Informação sobre Arte Brasileira Contemporânea, 1981.

Sims, Harold D. "Japanese Postwar Migration to Brazil: An Analysis of the Data Presently Available." *International Migration Review* 6.3 (1972): 246–66.

Sirkis, Alfredo. *Os carbonários: Memórias da guerrilha perdida*. Rio de Janeiro: Record, 1998 [1980].

Siu, Lok C. D. *Memories of a Future Home: Diasporic Citizenship of Chinese in Panama*. Stanford, Calif.: Stanford University Press, 2005.

Skidmore, Thomas. *The Politics of Military Rule in Brazil, 1964–1985*. New York: Oxford University Press, 1988.

——. *Brazil: Five Centuries of Change*. New York: Oxford University Press, 1999.

Sorlin, Pierre. *The Film in History: Restaging the Past*. Totowa: Barnes and Noble, 1980.

Souza, Maria Carmo Jacob de. *Telenovela e representação social: Beneditor Ruy Barbosa e a representação do popular na telenovela "Renascer."* Rio de Janeiro: E-Papers Serviços Editorias, 2004.

Souza, Percival de. *Eu, cabo Anselmo: Depoimento a Percival de Souza.* São Paulo: Globo, 1999.

Spickard, Paul R. *Japanese Americans: The Formation and Transformations of an Ethnic Group.* New York: Twayne; London: Prentice Hall International, 1996.

Spínola, Rodolfo. "Guerrilha do Araguaia será contada em livro: Aqui e no Japão." *Gazeta do Paraná* (Curitiba), 23 February 1992.

Spitzer, Leo. *Hotel Bolivia: The Culture of Memory in a Refuge from Nazism.* New York: Hill and Wang, 1999.

Stallings, Barbara, and Gabriel Székely, eds. *Japan, the United States, and Latin America: Toward a Trilateral Relationship in the Western Hemisphere.* Houndmills, U.K.: Macmillan, in association with St. Antony's College, 1993.

Stam, Robert. *Tropical Multiculturalism: A Comparative History of Race in Brazilian Cinema.* Durham, N.C.: Duke University Press, 1998.

——, João Luiz Vieira, and Ismael Xavier. "The Shape of Brazilian Cinema in the Postmodern Age." In *Brazilian Cinema,* ed. Randal Johnson and Robert Stam. Expanded ed., 387–472. New York: Columbia University Press, 1995.

Steinhoff, Patricia G. "Hijackers, Bombers, and Bank Robbers: Managerial Style in the Japanese Red Army." *Journal of Asian Studies* 48 (1989): 724–40.

Sternheim, Alfredo. *David Cardoso: Persistência e paixão.* São Paulo: Imprensa Oficial do Estado de São Paulo, 2004.

Sumizawa, Shigueaki. "Ex-presos políticos da ditadura recebem indenização no Paraná." *Jornal Nippo-Brasil,* 3–9 August 2005.

Tajima, Renee. "Lotus Blossoms Don't Bleed: Images of Asian Women." In *Anthologies of Asian American Film and Video,* 28–33. New York: Third World Newsreel, 1984.

Takeshita, Hermengarda Leme Leite. *Um grito de liberdade: Uma família paulista no fim da belle-époque.* São Paulo: Alvorada, 1984.

Tal, Tzvi. *Pantallas y revolución: Una visión comparativa del Cine de Liberación y el Cinema Novo.* Buenos Aires: Lumiere; Israel: Universidad de Tel Aviv, 2005.

Tanaka, Chester. *Go for Broke: A Pictorial History of the Japanese American 100th Infantry Battalion and the 442d Regimental Combat Team.* Richmond, Calif.: Go For Broke; distributed by JACP, 1982.

Tavares, Flávio. *Memórias do esquecimento.* São Paulo: Globo, 1999.

Tendai Educational Foundation. *Japanese Eyes, American Heart: Personal Reflections of Hawaii's World War II Nisei Soldiers.* Honolulu: distributed by University of Hawai'i Press, 1998.

Tigner, James L. "Shindo Renmei: Japanese Nationalism in Brazil." *Hispanic American Historical Review* 41 (1961): 515–32.

Timerman, Jacobo. *Prisoner without a Name, Cell without a Number.* Trans. Toby Talbot. Madison: University of Wisconsin Press, 2002 [1981].

Tolentino, Célia Aparecida Ferreira. *O rural no cinema brasileiro.* São Paulo: Editora UNESP, 2001.

Torres, Ernani T. "Brazil-Japan Relations: From Fever to Chill." In *Japan, the United States, and Latin America: Toward a Trilateral Relationship in the Western Hemisphere,* ed. Barbara Stallings and Gabriel Székely, 125–48. Houndmills, U.K.: Macmillan, in association with St. Antony's College, 1993.

Tosi, Juliano. "Todos os filmes citados." *Contracampo: Revista de Cinema* 36. www.contracampo.he.com.br/27/todososfilmes.htm.

Trento, Angelo. *Do outro lado do Atlântico: Um século de imigração italiana no Brasil.* Trans. Mariarosaria Fabris and Luiz Eduardo de Lima Brandão. São Paulo: Nobel, 1989.

Trevisan, João Silvério. "Entrevista com A. P. Galante: o rei do cinema erótico." *Filme Cultura* 15:40 (August–November 1982): 71–75.

Truskier, Andy (interviewer). "The Politics of Violence: The Urban Guerilla in Brazil." *Ramparts* 9.4 (1970): 30–34, 39.

Turim, Maureen. "The Erotic in Asian Cinema." In *Dirty Looks: Women, Pornography and Power,* ed. Pamela Church Gibson and Roma Gibson, 81–89. London: BFI, 1993.

——. *The Films of Oshima Nagisa: Images of a Japanese Iconoclast.* Berkeley: University of California Press, 1998.

Ustra, Carlos Alberto Brilhante. *Rompendo o silêncio: OBAN DOI/CODI, 29 set. 70–23 jan. 74.* Brasília: Editerra, 1987.

Valle, Maria Ribeiro do. *1968: O diálogo é a violência—Movimento estudantil e ditadura militar no Brasil.* Campinas: Editora da Unicamp, 1999.

Vianna, Martha. *Uma tempestade como a sua memória: A história de Lia, Maria do Carmo Brito.* Rio de Janeiro: Record, 2003.

Vieira, Francisca Isabel S. "Sistema de casamento entre issei e nissei." In *Assimilação e integração dos japoneses no Brasil,* ed. Hiroshi Saito and Takashi Maeyama, 302–16. Petrópolis: Vozes; São Paulo: Editora Universidade de São Paulo, 1973.

Villaméa, Luiza. "A verdadeira história do cofre do Dr. Rui: Trinta anos depois, *Istoé* revela fatos inéditos da maior ação da guerrilha brasileira, que tomou US$2,596 milhões da amante de Adhemar de Barros." *Istoé,* 21 July 1999.

Vinício, Marcos. "Gaijin: O melhor 'mestiço.'" *Folha da Tarde,* 7 April 1980.

Wainer, Samuel. *Minha razão de viver: Memórias de um repórter.* Rio de Janeiro: Record, 1987.

Warren, Jonathan W. *Racial Revolutions: Antiracism and Indian Resurgence in Brazil.* Durham, N.C.: Duke University Press, 2001.

Wasserman, Claudia. "O império da segurança nacional: O golpe militar de 1964 no Brasil." In Wasserman and Guazelli, *Ditaduras militares*, 27–44. Porto Alegre: Editora da UFRGS, 2004.

——, and César Augusto Barcellos Guazelli, eds. *Ditaduras militares na América Latina*. Porto Alegre: Editora da UFRGS, 2004.

Watanabe, Nelson, and Célia Abe Oi. "Cinema japonês no Brasil: Câmara lenta." *Página Um* of *Diário Nippak*, 3 September 1983.

Weinstein, Barbara. "Racializing Regional Difference: São Paulo versus Brazil, 1932." In *Race and Nation in Modern Latin America*, ed. Nancy P. Appelbaum, Anne S. Macpherson, and Karin Alejandra Rosemblatt, 237–62. Chapel Hill: University of North Carolina Press, 2003.

White, Hayden. *The Content of the Form: Narrative Discourse and Historical Representation*. Baltimore: Johns Hopkins University Press, 1987.

Williams, Linda, ed. *Porn Studies*. Durham, N.C.: Duke University Press, 2004.

Willems, Emílio, and Hiroshi Saito. "Shindo Renmei: Um problema de aculturação," *Sociologia* 9 (1947): 133–52.

Xing, Jun. *Asian America through the Lens: History, Representations, and Identity*. Walnut Creek, Calif.: AltaMira, 1998.

Yamashiro, José. *Trajetória de duas vidas: Uma história de imigração e integração*. São Paulo: Aliança Cultural Brasil-Japão/Centro de Estudos Nipo-Brasileiros, 1996.

Yoshimura, Evelyn. "G.I.'s and Asian Women." *Gidra* 3 (1971): 1, 15.

Zilbovicius, Mauro. "Modelos de produção e produção de modelos." In *De JK a FHC: A reinvenção dos carros*, ed. Glauco Arbix and Mauro Zilbovicius, 285–326. São Paulo: Scritta, 1997.

WEB SITES

2000 U.S. Census—factfinder.census.gov/home/saff/main.html?—lang=en

Asian Connections—asianconnections.com/entertainment/columns/ben.fong .torres/2002/11/

Chicago Reporter—www.chicagoreporter.com/2001/6-2001/6-2001main.htm

Cineweb—www.cineweb.com.br

Contracampo Revista Cinema—www.contracampo.com.br

Desparecidos Políticos—www.desaparecidospoliticos.org.br/araguaia/10.html

Diocese of Lins—www.catholic-hierarchy.org/diocese/dlins.html#info

Governo Estado de São Paulo—www.justica.sp.gov.br/sessoes/sessao27.htm

Greg Pak/Asian Pride Porn—www.gregpak.com/app/index.html

Jovem Pan Radio—jovempan.uol.com.br/jpamnew/opiniao/consultores/consultores —all.php?id=14&last—id=5182&act=sim

Partido Comunista do Brasil—www.vermelho.org.br/pcdob/80anos/martires/mar tires29.asp

Patu Fu–Site Oficial—www.patofu.com.br/oldsite/home/home.html

Resgate Histórico—www.resgatehistorico.com.br/doc—22.htm

Revista Brasil—www.revistabrasil.com.br/mateporbo21125.htm

The Midnight Eye: The Latest and Best in Japanese Cinema— www.midnighteye.com/features/art-theatre-guild.shtml

Tizuka Yamazaki—www.tizukayamasaki.com.br/index—port.htm

Tortura Nunca Mais—www.torturanuncamais.org.br/

MOTION PICTURES

Back, Sylvio. *Aleluia Gretchen* (1976)

——. *Vida e Sangue do Polaco* (1983)

Barreto, Bruno. *Amor Bandido* (1979)

Belmonte, José Eduardo. *5 Filmes Estrangeiros* (1997)

Bodanzky, Jorge. *Jakobine* [also known as *Os Mucker*] (1978)

Broca, Philippe de. *L'Homme de Rio* (1964)

Calmon, Antônio. *O Bom Marido* (1978)

Cardoso, José Adalto. *E a Vaca foi para o Brejo* (1981)

Carvalho, Vladimir. *Barra 68—Sem Perder a Ternura* (2001)

Dong, Arthur. *Forbidden City USA* (1989)

Doo, John. *Ninfas Diabólicas* (1977)

——. *A Noite das Taras* (1980)

Farias, Roberto. *Pra Frente, Brasil* (1982)

Fraga, Ody. *Macho e Fêmea* (1973)

——. *Terapia do Sexo* (1978)

Futema, Olga. *Retratos de Hideko* (1980)

——. *Hia sá sá—Hai yah!* (1986)

——. *Chá Verde sobre Arroz* (1998)

Gamo, Alessandro, and Luis Rocha Melo. *O Galante Rei da Boca* (2003)

Garret, Jean. *A Força Dos Sentidos* (1980)

Hou, James. *Masters of the Pillow* (2004)

Khouri, Walter Hugo. *Noite Vazia* (1964)

——. *Paixão e Sombras* (1977)

——. *O Prisioneiro do Sexo* (1979)

——. *Eros: O Deus do Amor* (1981)

Laurelli, Marko. *Meu Japão Brasileiro* (1965)

Mauro, Roberto. *Desejo Violento* (1978)

Mazzaropi, Amácio. *Portugal . . . Minha Saudade* (1973)

———. *Um Caipira em Bariloche* (1973)

Meliande, Antonio. *Escola Penal das Meninas Violentadas* (1977)

———. *Damas do Prazer* (1978)

Oliveira, Oswaldo de. *Pensionato de Vigaristas* (1977)

———. *As Fugitivas Insaciáveis* (1978)

Pak, Greg. *Asian Pride Porno* (on-line) www.gregpak.com/app/index.html

Reichenbach, Carlos. *Sonhos de Vida* (1979) (short movie)

———. *O Império do Desejo* (1981)

Rezende, Sérgio. *Lamarca* (1994)

Rocha, Glauber. *Deus e o Diabo na Terra do Sol* (1964)

Santos, Nelson Pereira. *Como era Gostoso o meu Francês* (1971)

Sternheim, Alfredo David. *Isei, Nisei, Sansei* (1970)

———. *Borboletas e Garanhões* (1985)

Sugie, Toshio. *Kokusai himitsu keisatsu: Shirei dai hachigo* (1963)

Taniguchi, Senkichi. *Samurai Pirate*, a.k.a. *The Lost World of Sinbad (Daitozoku)* (1963)

Tendler, Sílvio. *Marighella: Retrato Falado do Guerrilheiro* (2001)

Thome, Antonio Bonacin. *Belinda dos Orixás na Praia dos Desejos* (1979)

Vieira, Tony. *Os Depravados* (1978)

———. *O Matador Sexual* (1979)

Yamazaki, Tizuka. *Gaijin: Os Caminhos da Liberdade* (1980)

Music

Premeditando o Breque. *Premeditando o Breque*. "Marcha da Kombi (Wandy)." (Spalla, 1981).

———. *Quase lindo*. "São Paulo, São Paulo" (Lira Paulistana/Continental), 1983.

Index

Militancy: Brazilian press and, 88, 93–94, 110, 115–16, 145; as imagined by majority, 108; Japanese press and, 142

Military: *abertura* (political opening) and, 26, 66; advertising by, 19; cinema and, 59; Coup of 1964 by, 1, 64, 74; dictatorship, 42, 47; generational change and, 26; identity and, 47; public relations and, 115; university students and, 76

Minority: in Brazil, 21; model minority, xxix, 2, 95

Miranda, Carmen, 14

Miscegenation, 14, 27, 42, 53, 62, 70, 73, 148

Miyake, Rosa, 16

Miziara, José, 49

Modernity, xxvii, 5, 38

Motorcycles, 14–15

Music and film, 33, 38

Nakabayashi, Jun, 80, 92, 99, 104

Naming patterns, 63, 82–90, 113, 125–26, 130, 133; code names and, 75, 84, 86, 123, 130; ethnic names, 84, 86; false names, 86; "foreign" names, xix, 90; gender and, 63, 70; Mário Japa and, 123–24; physical attributes and, xxiii; Tizuka Yamasaki and, 70, 83

National identity: anti-Japanese sentiment and, 6, 29; ethnicity and, 25, 151; memory and, 23; nation and, xxii, 21

Nikkei: bank robberies and, 92, 114, 117, 133; beauty and, 46, 58; as Bolivians, 92–93; as Chinese, 58–59; definition of, xix; educational patterns of, 2, 9, 11, 74–75, 125; as farmers, 38, 41–42, 141, 145; films about, 20; gender and, 43, 51, 104–5; as Indians, 110; in Latin America, 24; as northeastern Brazilians, 92–93; otherness and, 1; population of, 3; professional patterns of, 11, 38; questions of loyalty and, xxi; songs about; 9, 20; technology and, 14, 98; telenovelas and, 27, 50; as "Vietcong," 88–89

Osawa, Shizuo, 22, 24, 79, 81, 99, 105, 116–18; as Atomic Brain, 126, 145; banditry and, 127; as Fernando, 131; as Jesus, 126, 130; as journalist, 127–28; as Mário, 129–30; as Mário Japa, 122–47 *passim*; as student, 129

Oshima, Nagisa, 61–62, 67

Pato Fu, 152

Paz, Carlos Eugênio, 96, 111

Pereira dos Santos, Nelson, 64, 68

Physiognomy: xix, xxvii, 38, 87; body language and, 65; foreignness and, 70; militancy and, 93; sexual organs and, 52, 54, 77

Plastic surgery, 58

Pornochanchada, 47–63; posters and, 53–55

Portugal, xxii

Posters: for *O Bem Dotado*, 54; for *Gaijin*, 71; images in, 56; for *Meu Japào Brasileiro*, 40; wanted posters, 94, 99, 114, 122

Prosopography, 23

Race: "Brazilian" race, 73; color and, 39, 72, 87; ethnicity, 21; ethnic pluralism and, 27; foreignness and, xxvi, 70; ideas of, xxiii, 13, 21, 44, 69; "Japanese" race, 138; poverty and, 72; rac-

JEFFREY LESSER is the Winship Distinguished Research Professor of the Humanities, professor of history, and director of the Program in Latin American and Carib-
bean Studies at Emory University. He is the author of *Negotiating National Identity:
Immigrants, Minorities, and the Struggle for Ethnicity in Brazil* (Duke, 1999) and *Welcoming
the Undesirables: Brazil and the Jewish Question* (1995). He is also the editor of *Searching for
Home Abroad: Japanese Brazilians and Transnationalism* (Duke, 2003) and the coeditor of
Arab and Jewish Immigrants in Latin America: Images and Realities (1998).

Library of Congress Cataloging-in-Publication Data

Lesser, Jeff.

A discontented diaspora : Japanese-Brazilians and

the meanings of ethnic militancy, 1960–1980 / Jeffrey Lesser.

p. cm.   Includes bibliographical references and index.

ISBN 978-0-8223-4060-7 (cloth : alk. paper)

ISBN 978-0-8223-4081-2 (pbk. : alk. paper)

1. Japanese—Brazil—Ethnic identity.

2. National characteristics, Brazilian. I. Title. F2659.J3L47 2007

305.895'6081—dc22   2007015040